Feathering Custer

University of Nebraska Press : Lincoln & London

W. S. PENN 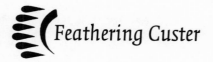 Feathering Custer

Publication of this volume was assisted by The
Virginia Faulkner Fund, established in memory of
Virginia Faulkner, editor-in-chief of the University
of Nebraska Press. Copyright © 2001 by W. S. Penn.
All rights reserved. Manufactured in the United
States of America ⊗

Library of Congress Cataloging-in-Publication Data
Penn, W. S., 1949 –
Feathering Custer/W. S. Penn. p. cm. Includes
bibliographical references.
ISBN 0-8032-3731-6 (cl.: alk. paper) 1. American
literature—20th century—History and criticism—
Theory, etc. 2. Indians in literature. 3. American
literature—Indian authors—History and criticism—
Theory, etc. 4. Custer, George Armstrong, 1839 –
1876—In literature. 5. Indians of North America—
Intellectual life. 6. Indians of North America—
Historiography. I. Title.
PS173.I6 P46 2001 810.9'897—dc21 2001017446

For Jennifer, Rachel, and Willy, without whom nothing.

With special thanks to Patrick O'Donnell

for his unstinting support and friendship

CONTENTS

ACKNOWLEDGMENTS   The following essays have appeared in slightly different forms:

"Feathering Custer," in *Power, Race, and Gender in Academe*, ed. Shirley Geok-Lin Lim and Maria Herrera Sobek (New York: Modern Language Association, 2000).

"Paving with Good Intentions," *Modern Fiction Studies* 45, no.1 (spring, 1999).

"Leaving the Parlor," *Cimarron Review* no.121 (October 1997).

"In the Garden of the Gods," *Here First: Autobiographical Essays by Native American Writers*, ed. Arnold Krupat and Brian Swann (New York: Random House, 2000).

Feathering Custer

Tonto Meets Chuang Tzu

I

Tonto, the Indian man whose modus vivendi was as the quintessential sidekick, was not afraid to be wrong. For his lack of fear, for his very real courage, he was denigrated by his very nickname, which means "stupid" or "idiot."

But the truth is, next to the Lone Ranger, Tonto did seem stupid or slow, and we have to wonder why Tonto did not hire a lawyer to force the studio to give him better lines and make him equal to the Lone Ranger. But we now know, given the charitable and generous activities of the man behind the role, Jay Silverheels was wise enough to realize that, while he could have played a second and equal Ranger, he would not have been happy. As much as he was alone both on and off the set, he knew that while he had always wanted to be one with the boys, he usually preferred the company of girls, who, in those days, seemed less likely to mark territory with barbed fences or pee—not unlike the reasons for which one might tend to like other outcasts like Jews, Chicanos, and often gay men—which is not to imply anything regarding Tonto's masked friend.

Imagine Tonto, a Fat Indian Boy, growing up in the late 1940s and 50s. No doubt he wears glasses, and between fourth and twelfth grades he will attend at least six different schools. Whether it's the fat, the Indian, the Dr. Pepper four eyes, or the fact that during the first week in every new school he has to defend himself from being picked on physically, he has to learn to ignore the name-calling.

"Hey, Four Eyes," Ranger calls.

"You spick-a da Ing-liss, or what?"

"Come on, Piggy, let's move it."

"Fucking Greasers."

"Hey, those glasses or Coke bottle bottoms?"

"Dr. Pepper," he answers, smiling. "Coke isn't thick enough."

His smile makes them vengeful. He has to learn to defuse their vengefulness by controlling his own sense that he is inferior and by standing up to them without fear—like dogs, the scent of fear or even caution makes them foam at the mouth. Otherwise, he would spend his halcyon school days fighting just for the sake of battle.

The whole time Tonto is trying to overcome his feelings of inferiority, he can't help but see some of the foolishness that accompanies the exhibitions of superiority. He learns to flip baseball cards farther on the playground. His cards rise in the hazy distance like deep fly balls, forcing the smaller kids to go back on the fly like Willie Mays. He feels warmed by streaks of boyish admiration of his prowess. His wrist and arm action balances force with method in such a way as to impart just the right pitch and yaw to let the card carry itself out over the asphalt playground. But when a tow-headed, hapless second grader with farsighted eyes and a butch haircut stumbles up to him at the end of recess empty-handed, having caught no cards at all, let alone one worth having, he shuffles through his pack of keepers and hands him a Willie McCovey.

The second grader's eyes grow wider, dark like plums glistening in the gratitude of rain. "Gee. Thanks."

"I have two," Tonto says. He doesn't. And he knows in the accidental fickle world of baseball card collecting, he will never see another. Because of the American love of sheer power over finesse, Willie McCoveys are more rare than Willie Mayses, the Say-Hey Kid who could go back on a fly ball or stroke a game-winning double to the gap in the opposite field.

When Tonto's friends, the other fifth graders who grudgingly admired his ability to flip cards farther, find out what he has done, there is hell to pay.

"You idiot!"

"Man, are you ever the stupidest, slowest four-eyed greaser that ever walked the face of Hollywood."

"Pendejo," his friend Arturo laughs. He tosses an arm across Tonto's shoulders as they walk off the playground—an acre of black asphalt painted with lines that mean nothing unless you are playing a game between them.

Fortunately, as the inheritors of a history of relocation, the fat Indian boy's family moves all the time. So around the time the other boys in his grade first hear of a Willie McCovey existing in someone's card collection, before they find out that it was actually given away and not traded for a red Corvette or the promise of someone's firstborn, Tonto's father, Sidekick Sr., will have moved him and his family far enough away that the reputation cannot follow him. He will move his baseball card collection, even though his father thinks it silly, and the reputation for stupidity will take time to blossom faintly anew like the perennial ground cover it resembles.

When he finally outgrows the collection, he will not store it away because someday it'll be worth something, meaning money and only money. He simply will forget it in a box on the top shelf of his closet. When his mother, in one of her divorced angers, gives the collection away while he's at college, he will mind the anger, the mean-spirited gesture, but not the loss itself—because he is no good at buying and selling, at maintaining what he feels is a false sense of monetary value for something so silly as an athlete's image and stats on cutout cardboard.

This bad attitude toward money—seeing its use but not its religious qualities—is part of a practical compromise with college. Agreeable sidekick that he is, when two of his friends apply to the most prestigious (by which he realizes later is meant "expensive," class distinctions being more important than intellectual abilities) private college in the West, he will let himself be convinced by the school's counselor that he too should apply. All three gain early acceptance.

His grades in high school are high because he has become what can be called nothing but agreeable, and an agreeable student, though maybe not wise, is diligent. And he has an interesting individuality to go with it (he "tans" well), which is why, when the captain of the football team runs for senior class president unopposed, he lets some of the girls talk him into becoming the opposition. As an Agreeable Contrary, our Tonto figures, What the heck, Why not? The worst he can do is lose. He expects to. But maybe he will make some new friends. What he doesn't figure on is demographics and the undercurrents of social change. That is, there are more girls than boys. And a few boys should feel obliged to vote for him—the Talmudic Jews, who do not value athletics; the homosexuals, who are, in the 1950s, mostly undeclared; the Chicanos, whose resentment over all those years of leading their classes in dancing La Cucaracha resembles an innate class hatred; and the hoodlums.

Normally, the hoodlums wouldn't even try to read the campaign posters, sounding them out one letter at a time. But Tonto, in his conciliatory fashion, promises them a "Smoking Area" out behind the school where they can go during each of their four or five study hall periods to smoke whatever they wish without being harassed by principals or police and without the innocent getting high by going into the small and almost ventless bathrooms. The hoodlums not only turn out in numbers, but they turn out in force; and the football team captain's posters vanish like morning dew—or, as the campaign reaches its pitch, the captain's campaign manager chooses not to bother putting them up and thus risking the disapproval of the Hoodlum Seven.

When he wins, Tonto has to make good on this promise, and he gets his first real-world lesson in the value of appearances over ethics. It is all too easily done. The principal thinks it's a great idea. It's a new, state-of-the-art high school, so the public and parental eyes are upon them—especially the eyes of parents of the kids stuck at the cross-town rival high school from which the new high school's students were drawn. With the hoods smoking way out behind a small burial mound beyond the football field, there will be no complaints or questions. The area can be viewed from the commuter train tracks, which are trafficked mainly before and after school hours, and the tinted windows of a Veteran's Administration Hospital, where quivering old men shout obscenities or piss on the shoes of missionaries—as Tonto, as a VA volunteer on weekends, has seen.

After instituting rules about policing the grounds, the principal grants the hoodlums some room of their own out in open space. Tonto sometimes visits the keeping of his promise to savor the surprise of it, but also because, in this middle-class high school where he has become popular as class president, the Hoodlum Seven makes him feel more comfortable, more welcome. Still, most of the time, he plays out his happy role of adopted mascot to the majority girls. He discovers that he likes girls. He really likes them, likes being around them, likes eating lunch with them. Except for the ones named Gigi or

Suzi, some of them seem to have brains—and even Suzi will one day abandon Gigi, cropping her hair and changing her name to "Suze."

Eventually, the boys get over the fact that they lost.

"Hey, it surprised me as much as you," Tonto consoles the football team's captain and (not very good) quarterback. "But we had a good race."

The captain receives this consolation in silence, either because he is unable to string together more than three words at once or because he ran no race at all, assuming he would win against this nobody, this Fat Indian Boy. He was beneath notice, let alone contempt.

But the other boys, once they get used to the idea of Tonto as class president, invite him to drink Canadian Club poured into paper cups of black cherry cola at the student council meetings at which they merrily (and one should say agreeably) govern—which means mainly allocating money to clubs and planning dances as well as Senior Cut Day. And to reward them, Tonto imagines two Senior Cut Days—the one sanctioned by the too-liberal principal, who provides busses to the seniors; and the authentic one, where they all cut school and go to Half Moon Bay to drink and throw up on the sides of cars as those like Tonto who could hold their liquor and sort of see to drive take them home.

Why a guy who enjoyed girls would agree to apply to—and, worse, attend—a private, expensive men's college, even one located across the street from two women's colleges, is a question. Perhaps hanging with the hoods and drinking with the alums renewed Tonto's wish that he could be one of the guys. Whatever his reasons, he continues to lack the slick self-deceptions of the suave. He is embarrassed by his complete inability to ask a girl out. He is inevitably awkward and clumsy and blurtive, in part because even though he was a popular mascot in high school, he has never figured out why a girl would want to go out with him. At the same time, he knows there are qualities in him that should make them all want to go out with him. He cultivates these qualities. Mainly, he tries to listen, to pay attention to the expressions of their character—at least until he discovers that the Pitzer girls have none—and then, instead of taking advantage of their willingness to be lied to, he will only take them back to their dormitories and drop them off.

He gets invited on overnight camping trips out to Lake Arrowhead. There is, he learns, something truly discouraging in having a girl invite him to share her sleeping bag and him replying that he's okay in his own. He is simply too shy to crawl out of his bag and into hers, too afraid that if he does, he will goof the whole thing up by farting in the middle of the night or accidentally dislocating her jaw with a clumsy elbow, so he turns her down. She is sweet about it. Perhaps she is even more attracted to him because of his timidity. But he could kick himself, kick himself, kick himself.

It doesn't take many of these experiences to turn him into a kind of voyeur, watching other boys and girls, smiling at other people's fun. He becomes the kind of boy a girl will try to include when she senses danger on a casual first or lunch or coffee date. To please them (the girls—he still doesn't like many boys, and he distrusts and envies the intentions and motives of most), to be good in this role of "my pal Tonto" ("You don't mind if he joins us, do you?"), he becomes brave, remembers and redevelops the courage of grammar schools, able to take the lowering looks of athletes the size of tanks and twice as explosive.

He also becomes a true connoisseur of the superficial, able to keep any conversation going with barely a yawn. To the Polyphemic jocks with their groping univision, he is an *outis*, a nobody, and they don't have to take anything he says or does as much more than a minor inconvenience that needs to be gotten rid of. To the girls, he becomes even more popular as a pal, a sidekick, and more often he finds himself having to defuse the rage of a girl's super-sized boyfriend because she's told him she has to wash her hair and then has gone for coffee or a movie with her sidekick Tonto. He understands and sympathizes with their wanting an evening out without the pressures of begging out of sex because of headaches, early classes, or being tired. For the single semester during which he manages to stay at this prestigiously expensive college, he relishes his role as dilettante and plays it to the extreme.

A sidekick must be someone who is interested in a lot of different subjects, as our Tonto is. If something is even modestly well-told, he'll happily listen to any telling, from engineers to plumbers to some scientist who studies The Life of Nickel. At other times daily life at the Malls of American Thinking impresses him as a tedious waste of time, if only because, like trips on drugs, trips to the mall of banal cannot be well-told enough to interest. And tedium begins to foment anger.

Before long other connections begin to work on his agreeability. Connections of class: cars are forbidden to freshmen, but his roommate, who has the brains of an arachnid but whose father is a state supreme court judge, gains special dispensation to have his car parked in a reserved space beside the dean of boys. Connections of contentment: except for the Jews, the kind of people he enjoyed in high school are now found trimming the lawns or dodging the pale green cars of the Border Patrol. Connections of meaning: forced to join ROTC by financial circumstances and encouraged to join by his continued desire to belong to America, he starts to question why anyone would want to protect or defend the connections of class and what gets sold in the Malls of American Thinking. Why would anyone die to kill Vietnamese instead of his privileged roommate, who has to plagiarize obscure library books to pass freshman English? The very assumptions on which his roommate bases what little thinking he does burn Tonto's skin like a naked skid on the basketball court.

It's these assumptions that, one late night in Ensenada, cause a huge Indio by the name of Ramon to offer to knock his roommate out in order to keep his big mouth from getting him beaten—or worse, killed. Tonto and three of his friends have used his roommate. By means of the very privilege Tonto objects to, they have driven down for the weekend. The first night, his roommate, used to drinking Cherry extract in glasses of Coke to get high, has gotten so drunk on Dos Equis that he has fallen in love with all things and people Mexican, even the almost unbelievable poverty. He talks a blue streak. He verily dribbles patronization, the friendly Norte Americano in a poor man's bar on the flip side of Ensenada.

Ramon's offer is not mean, and it is not meant to be angry or resentful. He only stiffens, his massive oil rig shoulders hunching round and hard against his self-restraint, when the slurpy Lone Ranger throws his arm around Ramon's shoulder and declares his love for "America's brown neighbors" to the south.

"The way you take things so easy and slow," his roommate says, if you can understand his words through the heavy molasses of liquor affecting his tongue.

Ramon speaks little or no English. But Tonto can tell that he doesn't need Ranger's words to understand what they mean.

"*Perdoneme*," Ramon says to Tonto. "*Pero su amigo es muy borracho*" Pardon me, your friend is pretty drunk. *Me quieres dejarlo sin conocimiento?* You can take him home, then.

Tonto knows some Spanish. He doesn't know the words for "knock out," but the way Ramon slams his fist into his open palm and then points his finger at his own jaw is plain enough. Ramon has a fist, Tonto notices, that you could bowl with.

The offer is meant in friendship to Tonto. As the Lone Ranger's sidekick, it is his job to take care of the Ranger. And without comment on his roommate's behavior, Ramon is offering to save the life of Tonto's sidekick and possibly the lives of the other boys who couldn't resist the ride. They hate his roommate. And they are keeping their distance from him now, making it plain by their looks that they want nothing to do with him, especially not in his current condition. But distance themselves as they would, there is no distance between white *Norte Americanos* in this bar, in this town. The border has erased any distance they might want to maintain, and they are as close as twins and triplets.

Ramon makes the offer blank-faced, without emotion, and in Spanish. Tonto refuses the offer, also in Spanish, and with a kind of emotion that doesn't show. It is a strange and deep gratitude. He takes the warning; however, he sees the resentful glares of the other men around them in the bar at this *guero Americano*. He makes the other boys help him get the Ranger out of the bar, carrying him, his two legs dragging like a rag doll's, badly scuffing the toes of his expensive brogues, back to the motel. He returns to drink quietly in desultory and broken conversation with Ramon. His Spanish is vestigial, like a language once spoken by his grandparents or like blood divided only by a black incision on a map.

"Your fren, *fue muy borracho*," Ramon says. "*Su amigo, lo duermo?*"

"Yeah. And thanks. *Gracias por . . . come se dice . . . ?*"

"*De nada*," Ramon says, a slight wave with the long-neck beer he holds in his hand.

"*Lo siento*," Tonto says, and for Ramon and his friends in the bar, it is sufficient.

★ ★ ★

But not for Tonto. Something in him snaps that night. Or else it's that something important is remembered. It's only an echo, undefined. Its origin is without location, but like standing in the shower beside a night-dark window raked by the wind, it is, if he lets it in, chilling enough to make him overreact.

And he lets it in. In fact, Tonto indulges it, nurtures it on the slow ride home the following day as though extreme reactions to his fear can make up for his sense of wasted nights—all the nights and days he did not spend with the lawn trimmers and dodging migrants, with the Ramons and their friends in dimly lit but almost familial comfort.

When he gets back to the privilege and expense of college, our imaginary Tonto finds that he resents the way girls (women, now, really) use him to keep the banalities of their boyfriends at bay, to provide interest in the form of tension—mostly the jocks'—with his own discomfort. He now minds very much being a buffer for them from the demands for sex as though he were a social prophylactic. He finds that when they call, he is busy; or when they drop by his dorm room, he hints broadly about his own sexual desires or needs, fuming to himself when the girls laugh as though of course he could be doing nothing but kidding.

Sex between friends?

Really.

It would spoil everything.

"Not everything," Tonto fumes.

He finds that inside he has always had a real hatred of America interwoven with his need to belong to it. After numerous infractions on the ROTC parade grounds, when the captain suggests that it would be a shame for him not to receive the waivers and stipends that ROTC can provide, he quits. Drops out, knowing that this means he can't stay at the expensive college. And when the dean of boys calls him in and tries to explain what a shame it would be for someone like Tonto to lose the potential in later life that the prestige and connections ("friendships," the boys' dean calls them) of this expensive college will give him de facto, he still fails to change his mind.

Tonto suspects then that it is only by a spectacular lack of success that he can remain a nobody, and that being a nobody is a truly happy position. Being nobody, he can duck Polyphemus's groping around the floor of their mutually shared cave and let the Cyclops devour his friends with significance. When the other Cyclopes call through the stone rolled across the door, "Who has blinded you?" his answer can remain—unlike Odysseus, whose Parthian shot at Polyphemus was the noise of his name—"No One."

The major problem with all this is that a nobody does not take part in the world. He is alone. The friends he has sneak off to a protective distance in the cave or they get eaten because he is powerless to help them. And in the end, Tonto knows, as did Jay Silverheels, who gave local habitation as well as a name to the role, that everyone gets eaten. That is why Mr. Silverheels did so much community work. Alone, one simply ends up hiding in a cave, fending off or dodging the blind gropes of a clumsy monster.

The problem with being a nobody isn't that people suffer you to have a kind of innocent anonymity. It's not that they do not recognize you as being someone. It's that they go out of their way to denigrate you, as Tonto learns when, out of school and out of work, he takes up landscaping to make some money—a rather formal way of saying that he mows lawns and trims hedges—for which most people balk at paying him more than the low wages of an untaxable boy. Tonto doesn't mind. He's outdoors, on his own, with almost no one to answer to, and he can think his own thoughts.

This contentment lasts until the Sunday morning he arrives early to a job. At the gate to the side fence, he overhears Mr. Beasley, who owns a cowboy theme bar a few blocks away and pockets hundreds of dollars a week in unreported quarters from his pool tables. Beasley is yelling at Bonni, his wife or mistress, who always puts a small heart over the i when she writes out checks for Tonto's payment, handing the checks to him with accidental friendly touches and looks that make the heart seem like a solicitation.

"Don't blame me," Beasley is shouting. "I didn't hurt your pe-onies."

Bonni says something Tonto can't understand except for its tone, which is plaintive and a little frightened.

"Why don't you blame that boy you hired? Maybe you should ask him who broke the stalks off your precious flowers. Huh? Maybe ask the boy. Sneaky bastard probably did it and then didn't have the guts to tell you."

He couldn't have spit that word *boy* at her with any more force if it were chewed tobacco. But it isn't being called a boy by cowboy Beasley that stops our Tonto—anyone paid what he is paid, no matter how old he gets, will always be a "boy" to people like them. (Bonni pays him half what he gets from everyone else.) He was about to quit when, last week when he was done mowing, she brought out a pitcher of lemonade and sat with him on the iron patio chairs. She began to talk. (Just talk, I'm sorry to say for those of you hoping otherwise.) Tonto was hot and thirsty, so he was glad for the lemonade. But the talk worried him. He could tell there was much more she wanted to say about her relationship with Beasley. It was information he didn't want. And he was afraid of where it might lead: he could envision ending up in her bed wondering how he could manage to be kind and gentle when the time came for him to stop trimming her lawn and leave. He cared about her as he would care about anyone who was kind to him, thinking that he might be hot and tired and want a cool drink or something. Her life with Beasley seemed, well, if not terrifying, then edged with a caged feeling; and it was a picture of marriage that made him feel sorry for her. But care as he might, he knew he was a sidekick only, and not a savior.

So when he hears Beasley spit the word *boy* in her face, he stops outside the fence. He lifts his hand to rattle the iron latch. He prepares to walk into the yard and defend himself. It makes him angry to be attacked and blamed unjustly. He'll walk in and surprise them and tell Beasley to go screw himself, tell him that he has taken great care not to injure Bonni's peonies or any other plants and flowers in her garden. He is prepared to tell Beasley that if he doesn't believe him, he can mow his own lawn. He takes a deep breath, steps forward, and then stops, dropping his hand to his side. He knows this is not the way to beat them, in anger. Tell Beasley off, he might, but win he won't, because men like Beasley are not smart enough to smart from unfairness. He turns, walks back to the mower waiting for him on the sidewalk, wheels it back onto his truck, and drives away.

Now, one reason we work is so that we can feel as though we belong to a group. We belong not just to our jobs but to the group of people who do the job with us. Recognizing the need for something to replace family, Hewlett-Packard Corporation gives employees the sense that everyone belongs to one big family. Even across divisions within the company, it promotes a democratic atmosphere in which even the lowliest, like Tonto, share in the decision making, attending semiannual lunches in which R&D reports are presented and the health of the company is projected, a health which is always in part attributed to the fellow feeling of its employees. In the summer, HP hires a hundred acres of a state park and throws a company picnic that requires truckloads of beer and barbecue, and everyone goes because they want to, not because they feel obliged to.

In the basement warehouse of Hewlett-Packard there are other people to lunch with, take breaks with, joke with in passing. Up and down aisles of high metal shelving Tonto pushes a cart, removing bins by their stock numbers, counting out the required numbers of each item, packaging it in clear plastic baggies stapled shut with the punch card that identifies its stock number. He arranges them in a wooden box, and, when the pieces are all collected, sets it on a conveyor belt that takes the box up to a sorting station where it is transferred to a conveyor that takes it to the appropriate assembly line. Mislabeling or pulling the wrong transistor or capacitor will use up someone else's time and energy by making her get up and come downstairs to get the correct part, a journey that will take nearly half an hour. Putting the stock in the conveyor box haphazardly causes less delay, but it still slows the process.

Tonto learns to staple the bags lightly shut so the staple releases the plastic easily when the assemblers pull it open. He takes pride in making few mistakes and in the neatness of his box. Without telling anyone, he figures out the stock coding system and learns to place the bags of parts in the exact order the assemblers will need to remove them as they assemble the sterling HP products.

His best friend, Michael, is close in age and exhibits what Tonto recognizes as a need to belong. Whereas Tonto attended a private men's college, Michael joined the U.S. Army, serving as a corporal during the Vietnam War. Michael's need to belong is greater than Tonto's, however. Serving two years on the Cambodian border, Michael enlisted for a second tour, a second two-year stint in hell from which he has returned to tell them all that war has changed, that the mold of honor and courage has been broken.

"The rules haven't changed," Michael tells Tonto. "There are no rules."

Tonto knows that there have never been rules, or that there have only been rules that changed to suit the needs of the memorials. He knows Sand Creek was a massacre. And he knows the sculptural image of Iwo Jima was staged while Sleeping Beauty was raped by her charming prince. He says nothing, however, preferring to be Michael's pal. He nods with apparent stoicism. And when Harvey laughs at Michael, Tonto leaves his half-drunk beer behind and walks out of the Old Pro with Michael, never to return after work with Harvey and the rest of the older guys, half of whom are veterans from World War II.

Something has snapped in Michael too—something that occurred between the day he shipped out for home and the day he began work at Hewlett-Packard. And it causes Michael to work with the fury of an Uzi, spraying parts into the baggies and tossing the bags into the conveyor box with the recklessness of a death wish.

When Harvey asks him not to toss the bags of parts into the box, but to be a little neater and even try to arrange the baggies full of parts upright, Michael says that this is not what he risked his life for. He takes a tone not unlike a parent who ignores his children to keep busy making money, or a young man raised on television and the vague notion of human rights who sees that this work is the sum of his future. He resents it. The flick of his wrist, the toss of the bag is the way in which he expresses what he feels about these prospects, past and future; and his boxes go up the line a pile of parts slung together, parts that have to be re-sorted upstairs or simply junked and replaced by an order made up by Michael's sidekick, Tonto, who does it without Michael even knowing.

Tonto, on the other hand, knows some things Michael does not: that money is only money, and it can be gotten. This need not be anyone's future, although it isn't such a bad one compared to what a child on a reservation might face. He does not resent this job, because this is an easier way to get it than mowing lawns. And it lacks the personal conflicts of belonging to ROTC at a college for the privileged with a few mascot-students thrown in so that the privileged will be able to learn to be comfortable with the people who mow their lawns and clean their houses. He tries to pass this knowledge on to Michael, and for a while it works, or seems to.

Until one night the pair of them are riding home in Michael's van, up El Monte Avenue, through the upper-middle-class neighborhoods to the apartment complex beside the expressway where Tonto lives. Tonto is the one who spots the police car, and knowing the Los Altos police have little to do but give out tickets, he warns Michael that the speed limit is thirty miles an hour along that section of road.

"Shit," Michael says. "God dammit." He mutters. He begins to watch the police in his side mirrors nervously.

"Mike," Tonto says, trying to keep Mike's attention on the road in front of him as the van weaves over the double line and back.

"God damn cops. I hate being followed," Michael says.

"It's okay," Tonto says.

"No it's not," Michael says. And though the turn to Tonto's apartment is just ahead, he swerves left into a dark side street. As luck would have it, the side street divides like a tuning fork into two dead-end roads that form a "U." Michael picks the right arm of the "U." The police car, its headlights off now, follows them, skulking along in the darkness like a night-patrol in black pajamas.

Michael slows in inverse proportion to the amount of cursing that spills from his mouth. "Now what do I do?" he asks, his voice high, almost shrill, as he realizes the road is a dead end.

"Turn around, I guess," Tonto says. He knows Michael, but this panic over a police car following them makes him wonder how well. He wonders what Michael may have in the back of the van. Any trouble the Lone Ranger gets into puts Tonto in equal danger.

"Sorry, officer, I didn't know he had an AK 47 hidden beneath the peonies."

Or: "Yep, it sure does look like ten pounds of hashish. You're right, there. And is that the ever-stylish white opium coat it's wearing?"

Michael pulls into a driveway. His head drops to the steering wheel, and he begins to moan.

"Mike," Tonto says. "Sit up." He's as surprised as Michael that he does. "Put it in reverse. Back up. Now put it in first. Second. Hold it there, at twenty-five." As they exit the stem of the tuning fork, he directs Michael left onto El Monte again, and then left onto his street, at which point—who can justify the ways of police to men?—the cops turn on their bubblegum lights. Tonto has to talk the Lone Ranger down. Calmly, he convinces him that a high-speed chase through the darkened jungle of suburban Los Altos would do as much good as lighting a campfire while on patrol in Cambodia. Michael reins in his van right in front of Tonto's apartment building.

How do you explain to policemen, whose biggest thrill that night has been to catch a carload of underage drinkers and pour out their case of beer can by can into the gutters, that the wild-eyed driver of an empty van and his exotic looking friend riding shotgun are not casing houses to rob? Tonto's job is twofold: to exude such a sense of quietude that it blankets the anxious wishes of the cops ("Run, mothereffer. Please. Give me an excuse to draw my weapon or to put all the hours of practice to use swinging my nightstick"), while at the same time it quells the anxious fear Michael retains from thirteen hundred nights of hunting and being hunted. He tries to convince the policemen that he is, indeed, gainfully employed and that thus he actually has money. And yes, he lives in the very apartment building in front of which the cops have Michael and him sprawled against the van's side.

Meanwhile, Michael's fuse is burning. Tonto can feel it. He's scared, and he resents the one cop holding out his thirty-eight, pointing it first at Michael and then at Tonto as his partner checks their papers. Michael has risked his life for freedom, he believes. But everywhere he turns, he sees only the loss of it. Being questioned this way is one more cap to his desperate disappointment at America, a desperation he expresses by telling Tonto that sometimes he'd rather be back in Vietnam. "But this time," he has said, "I think I'd fight for the Cong."

This is not a healthy attitude, Tonto thinks. And he can feel Michael's mind spinning and weaving with his palms against the van. He fears Michael's fatalism, his despair, his willingness to wish for death by suddenness instead of the slow descent toward death that most of us call life.

"This license says you live around here," one cop says.

"Right behind you."

The officer's body freezes with predetermined doubt.

"I've been trying to tell you that, officer." Tonto knows better than to play smart-ass with men with guns. Nonetheless, his politeness is so overwhelming that a sensitive person might detect a deep-seated sarcasm. "The key is in my pocket. I could give it to you. You could go check and see if it unlocks apartment three."

Slowly, Tonto defuses the situation. Although Michael's slamming his hand against the van's side and shouting, "God dammit! I didn't spend four years crawling around Cambodia so a couple of fucking dickhead pigs could get away with threatening me," seems to delay the process. At long last the other policeman returns, hands Tonto his house key, and takes him aside.

"I locked the door back up," he says.

"Thanks."

"I still don't get it. If you live here, why did you turn into that dead-end?"

"He got scared."

"Of what?"

"Of you guys tailing us."

"We weren't tailing you. We were behind you was all."

Tonto nods. "I know. But a police car behind you makes people nervous."

"Yeah. But they don't suddenly turn into a side street that goes nowhere."

"They do after four years in Vietnam," Tonto says.

The policeman shakes his head. "Okay, Tom," he calls to his partner. "Let 'em go."

Tonto stays with Michael, who paces up and down the sidewalk, cursing. He tries to calm him. Reason with him.

"I don't like being treated like a criminal," Michael says over and over.

That is Friday night. On Monday morning, Michael does not show up to work in the basement warehouses of Hewlett-Packard; and on Tuesday, Tonto begins to wonder to whom he is sidekick and friend if Michael doesn't answer his telephone. By Wednesday Michael's phone is disconnected, and when Tonto tries to find him, he finds that he is gone. Then he realizes how little he knew of Michael, at least of the Michael who reenlisted for a tour on the Cambodian border. Who are his people? Where is his family? Where would he go if he fled from the persecution of the Los Altos Police Department, and where would he find the freedom he thought he fought for?

Michael, for Tonto, remains completely masked, the person he once was and might one day have become again hidden behind four years of war in Southeast Asia and six months of work and side-kickery in a company that wanted you to feel like family. For years to come, Tonto will feel sorry that he lost touch with Michael. Imagining Michael running through the underbrush of Georgian forests, hiding out like the bomber of an abortion clinic, sheltered by others who are disaffected from the freedom they believe is lost to the federal and state governments and law enforcement agencies, Tonto will return to school, suspecting now that work is no way to belong to a group.

II

Years pass, and after one dead end or another, one wrong turn or another, he becomes an "academic." Once again he finds himself part of the group. More than once he finds himself sitting around the theoretical campfire listening to a job candidate maintain, against a barrage of questions, that his "position" is one of "de-positionality." To Tonto, all that means is that the candidate wants to be able to use a variety of theoretical approaches without being cornered in one, a respectable and understandable desire as far as Tonto is concerned, being not only without fixed position but not a little clueless as well. Evidently, to others of fixed "positions," such "de-positionality" smacks of opportunism; so a heated—or what passes for heated—discussion ensues as people seek the roots of "depositionality" in Derrida and Durkheim.

Asked to "position" himself once again, the candidate refuses.

Tonto considers speaking. He wants to say that this "depositionality" is an insistence on flexibility. "At worst," he thinks, "it's a kind of dilettantism in which the love of art is replaced by a love of turgid writing about art, or actually not about art at all but about other turgid writing, though in an Edenic sense, at the moment of original sin, the writing must originally have been about art."

While Tonto thinks about daring to speak up, tries to find in himself the boldness and effrontery to disagree however gently, the arguers fail to find professional roots for position's absence. A colleague reiterates everything that has been said since breakfast and insists once again that the candidate define his position. After five more mind-stuttering minutes, Tonto blurts, "Jeez-us. Now I know why I'm a dilettante."

A few people cough and smile wanly. Most lean away from Tonto as though he has just admitted to carrying an incurable and highly communicable disease. Some look shocked as though he's professed a love of extracting the eyes of frogs with needle-nosed pliers. Tonto feels like Jack in Wilde's *The Importance of Being Earnest*, who says, "I know nothing," to which Lady Bracknell replies,

> I am pleased to hear it. I do not approve of anything that tampers with natural ignorance. Ignorance is like a delicate exotic fruit; touch it and the bloom is gone. The whole theory of modern education is radically unsound. Fortunately in England, at any rate, education produces no effect whatsoever.[1]

Unfortunately, there are no Lady Bracknells in the room.

Nonetheless, Tonto has hit on something. He can insist on knowing nothing, but not for the fruit of ignorance so much as for the bloom of beginnings. For he remembers how, as a young fat Indian boy, his education tended to be training that limited the imagination while teaching minds to be expert without ever worrying if the expertise is worth having. This is, after all, why these days, when he leaves his daughter at her school, accepting a verbal IOU for the hug and kiss she used to give (and her brother still gives, but someday won't?) but is now too embarrassed to give for fear someone with a name like "Sting" or "Aire" (or the Star Formerly Known as "Aire") might see it, why on each of these days he feels his heart pulled slightly out of balance with fear that schooling will make her pay for having an imagination that is not manufactured by the self-negating contradiction labeled "popular" and "culture."

It is not that he doesn't trust his daughter's character. He does, as completely as he is coming to trust his son's, four years her junior. He and his daughter have always told stories (as he and his son are beginning to). Their original stories were often about "Stuart" the brown squirrel. And last year, when her friend Natalie demanded, "How do you know that one is Stuart?" his daughter replied, "How do you know it isn't?" And when the school counselor told them to make friends by asking each other questions, like who their favorite musicians were, his daughter came home and said with some distress,

18

"No one even knows who Vivaldi is." She said it without real pain, and though when he leaves her at the school building's corner he injects the moment with his own fear of pain, she seems to notice but not really to care. When he visits her class and says he prefers Puccini, she says in that exasperated way kids have, "Dad, I like Puccini too," not realizing that her classmates think Puccini is a tubular green vegetable with a slightly bitter taste. And when he threatens to tell her friends what he thinks of television, her mother says, "Don't worry, honey. He's just kidding."

Well, sort of, he is. His wife has just reminded him that he'd better be.

But after an hour with her class, telling stories and gently trying to say that no, he never has received an Academy Award for writing, but wasn't that more for movie acting than storytelling, his daughter leans over and whispers, "Tell them about TV." He smiles. But instead of saying what he really thinks, he says, "I know you'll think I'm nuts, but the best thing you can do is . . . ," giving the little future homogenes room to hear the faint sexless echoes of their parents deny the fact (parents who want their kids to read, even though there's not a book in the house and probably nothing worse for the mind than *Playboy* or *Vogue* on the one shelf free of bowling trophies).

As though, even with fourth graders, he is willing to know nothing, or happy to be wrong, if not know nothing.

III

So Tonto has become a dilettante. He still seems stupid and slow, but now it is his aspiration, his protection, and not his failing. Secretly, instinctively, he knows from past experience with the Lone Ranger, with maskedness and mobility, that dilettantism is complicated. Whereas the superficial think dilettantism is an easiness resulting from a flighty or superficial interest in many different subjects, deeper people know—though they often don't understand—that dilettante also means "a lover of art," and that "art" is not a product, but a process that involves perception and understanding.

Thus, as a lover of art, a dilettante is a dabbler in many things until he finds one thing he loves, and he dives diligently into it. When he does, he often resurfaces from his long dive to find himself put in the position of having to defend his interest. Worse, when he moves on to another interest, he does not discard. And this is the heaviest burden of a dilettante: he begins to seem something like a bag lady of satisfied curiosities, pushing a wire shopping cart around, full of what people see as old news and ideatic possessions that, unlike baseball card collections, will never have value. He collects, and he does not replace what he collected before with what he now is busily collecting. He considers it his good fortune to see that while things may, on the surface, appear disconnected and discretely separate, they are all connected — most of them at the root. And because he collects and does not replace, he is forced to forget some things in order to make room for other, newer things — and at his age, forgetting is not the same joy that flits across an old person's face as he loses himself in thought only to discover he has fewer of them. It makes him a little cranky.

And cranky, he begins to say things. In a truly American twist of fate, the more he insists that he knows nothing, the more people start to take him seriously. And in this atmosphere of seriousness, while not an expert, each time he unwisely shouts out his name, like Odysseus stupidly shouts his at Polyphemus, they take him even more as one of them — until a friend, given to thinking well of Tonto, tells him in all seriousness that he has become "Someone."

It makes him afraid.

"The world's a funny place, you know?" he says to his wife. "All those years wanting not to be no one, and just about the time I manage to find real peace in being no one, I find out that I may be someone after all."

"Don't get carried away," his wife says, with her usual admiration.

Just as it would be angering to grow up proud of your descent from the Mayflower crowd of Tea-Party colonials only to emerge into a world that deflowered your pride and made it something that should be hidden, it is frightening to grow up no one in a cave of otherness only to emerge into a world that finds Otherness its central wish and longing.

What then? Cleverness? Or cuteness?

Deep in his heart, hidden away from all who would know only a little of him, Tonto suspects that claiming to be a dilettante is merely cuteness. Nonetheless, it is what he is and what, as a Someone, he wants to go back to being, at least intellectually. If he finds a novel he loves—say, *One Hundred Years of Solitude* or *Midnight's Children*—he wants to love it. Or, perhaps a better example, though a lesser novel, if he wants to enjoy *Like Water for Chocolate*, he does not want to hear from a Chicano friend that it is politically incorrect to like Laura Esquivel's novel because she and her husband seem to support the encomienda systems of colonialism.

Or he doesn't want to hear it and have to pay any attention (and someone you don't have to pay attention to is also someone who need not pay you attention).

Or he doesn't mind hearing it, but he wants to remain free to say that he doesn't see how, in the novel, Ms. Esquivel supports anything other than the generational narratives of resistance to packaged perceptions. And a dilettante in his cave, who has no limited or clearly defined field, is, if nothing else, free. Certainly, a free person can say that Ms. Esquivel's novel expresses many of the elements of Latino oral traditions as they overlap with Native American oral traditions—augmentation (or the apparently digressive thematic organization of the narrative); circularity (or better, non-linearity, since the circle may really be a spiral, as in *One Hundred Years of Solitude*); cultural instruction (how to arm yourself in Homer, how to build a Sweat Lodge in Coeur d'Alene life, or how to store fresh-killed chickens in Esquivel); interconnectedness of spirit with life (Rosauria hates food, is a picky eater, and literally farts herself to death; Mama Elena's asperity causes her to overdose on ipecac); the importance of identity (Coyote is always going upstream, and Esperanza's niece needs to tell this history of the women in her family); and the emphasis on process over plot (recipes are instructions that may be interpreted and modified according to context).

He wants to be free to say those things, just as elsewhere he wants to assert that . . . *y no se lo tragó la tierra* is a great novel in a literary world of at best modestly tolerable novels, while reading Stephen Jay Gould or Michael Kammen. In other words, he wants the stack of books to be read—actually, there are two stacks, one by the bed and one on the corner of the bookshelf, along with a list of books to buy and read—to include the journals of Lewis and Clark, *The Song of Solomon*, *Border Matters*, *La Maravilla*, a collection of Dave Barry's or Calvin Trillin's essays, and always, now, Daniel Reveles and Bill Bryson. In other words, he does not want his reading to be systematic, and he simply does not believe in focus. He does believe in laughing.

Focus, in the sense of limiting the field of investigation, is what he has fought all his life. Though secretly he admires the Lone Rangers who are both focused and deep, like academic intellectuals who can talk about the "argument" of a book (which often is the way they talk about books they've skimmed, and for which skimming—having tried to read some of them himself—he doesn't blame them), he has always in his own mind poked fun at the way the focal valorization of logic has tended to disconnect the Lone Ranger from the messiness of life, and the smoke screen of analysis has banished most academics from the messiness of literature or storytelling or art. After all, only an academic can say that a novel "analyzes" a certain "problematics" with no indication that an author with rhetorical intentions was involved, thereby reducing the complexities of narrative to forlorn simplicities and outright lies that cannot be well told. In that case, the walls of Wonderland grow even narrower, and the nourishing rain that falls can be measured in inches or tears.

There is a price they pay, however, for this deepness: they not only have to stick to the same subject, but they are supposed to stick to the same methods of approaching the subject. Thus, they end up doing the same thing over and over again. Though writers do the same things over and over again—Faulkner kept writing because he never satisfied himself—they do it by asking questions. Critics or theorists, it seems, learn a method in graduate school that is a lot more difficult to abandon than leaving their firstborn in a basket on the steps of the nearest daycare center; and anyone who knows "method" knows that in method is a set of propositions that only fake questions that are already answered in their minds. Thus, you can write about an unreadable novel even though you yourself do not enjoy it. Simply by calling it "post-modern" or "post-colonial," you can teach it, get an article out of it. You can paint the white roses red or make hay at a cocktail party with it. But if you listen carefully to the critical posts—post-colonial and post-modern—you will suspect and eventually learn that there is no such thing as "post-colonial" (and for the "postcolonial" quibblers who remove the hyphen, it is still a leaky container of historical time). When did attempts at hegemony and dominance cease? All that has happened in the so-called post-colonial world is that the tools have changed—indeed, they have become more obvious, less subtle, and therefore less visible. You hardly notice MacDonalds or Nike. And it is not the golden arches that are the problem as much as it is the global wanting to have it all, as though "it" is a thing that may be purchased and not something that atrophies and dies in the greed of wanting.

Post-modern is similar: it is a quick stroll by a funambulist. That is, in order to have the "post-modern," one needs a foreshortened sense of time and importance. Only with a snubbed elision of the sense of time as a progressive line can one "see" modernism to have occurred, and only with "modernism" can there be anything after it to call "post"-modernism. But what was called "modernism" could be seen as an artistic extension of what in Euramerican terms occurred with industrial capitalism, in which storytelling (or painting?) began to lose its sense of meaning, substituting beauty for meaning and calling it art for art's sake. But art for art's sake demands a loss of breadth, a loss of connection to all things human in the dreamt-of past and remembered future, a limited temporality that at its extreme is purely momentary. Eventually, in the interplay of the senses of time and beauty, beauty itself comes under attack as people search for meaning in the increasingly abstracted beauties; and, unable to connect with broader senses of time and meaning where the "I" has little or none and where even the meaning of "We" is multigenerational in a way that makes Homer modern, the new meaning becomes not meaning but statement. Declaration. You declare something to be and declare it to be meaningful, and thus it is. You place a dildo on a gallery floor and call it "Time Out of Mind" or "The Ravages of Time," and it matters—though not much more than a urinal on a gallery wall. And to pee on another person's religious icon, such as Christ, makes or creates nothing but anger—even from those like me who are exceptionally non-Christian. It makes neither beauty nor meaning outside of simple (and simplistic) declaration.

Worse than the price of repetition and meaninglessness, the price for seeing this way, for aspiring to and even achieving this narrowed depth, is boredom. In this boredom, it's true, is another kind of freedom: when you teach, you teach the same things, and that leaves you free to enjoy your evenings; when you lecture or go to conferences, you do so with a tremendous sense of confidence and security in the feeling that other bored people will at least pretend to take you seriously.

People should not take dilettantes seriously. They need to be seen for what they are, disturbers of the linear peace and una-bombers of complacency.

Not being taken seriously is a cheap price to pay for freedom—the freedom to speak but also to listen, the freedom to change not only what one works on but how one does the work, the freedom to develop new courses when the old ones have staled.

IV

On the other hand, perhaps all this is just the studio effect: a painter cannot have a neat studio if for no other reason than it makes him worry about neatness and not the inspired mess of painting. And one thing Tonto's family remembers with joy is his father-in-law purposely and purposefully walking around with a paint-laden palette in hand, dripping color all over the brand new floor of his Soho loft thirty years ago. His greatness, from Tonto's perspective, was his ability to change: other painters were always checking in with him to see what new things he had come up with. And visiting New York to sit down in his studio and look at new work was always a surprise that was most often stimulating. The price he paid—gallery owners do not want artists who are going to change on them the minute they manage to create a market for work already done and on exhibit—was a lack of reputation. The difference between him and Tonto was that he lived in the world of New York and was an *outis* in that; Tonto lives in the world, but he also lives in a smaller world that no one outside of its academic members takes seriously, so he can be an *outis* who is not taken seriously by a community that is not taken seriously. Slow, stupid Tonto is lucky in that.

Painting aside, a writer almost by nature has to be a dilettante. He has to be curious, and nowhere is his curiosity better represented than in the place in which he works. As Mark Twain said, it's better to be creative than to have a neat desk. If a writer has a neat desk, we should be very suspicious if not of his writing, then certainly of his passionate curiosity. Lawyers have neat desks. The Owners and Colonists, who have people to clean up after them, have neat desks. Writers bring home papers to add to the scraps of papers they affectionately call "notes"; they have old coffee mugs, dictionaries, objets de superstition, and, as they age, bottles of ibuprofen, Celebrex, Viagra, and the like.

Of course you can imagine that believing such nonsense as that, Tonto's study has, in addition to five tables that are covered with all manner of things, three or four hundred square feet of floor space that is also covered with dictionaries, papers, notes, and other (apparently) "prioritized" matter (the closer to where he sits is usually more important, though close-in items run the risk of burial beneath the avalanche of new matter), most of which he can find when he needs it and the rest of which gets thrown out every six months because he hasn't needed it enough to try to find it. Only when—as has happened more since that friend said he was "Someone"—he has to make a methodical search of his study to find something he knows is somewhere in it, does he ever consider straightening it up.

A "methodologically sound" search in Tonto's study begins with a visit to the locations where he thinks it likely to find what he wants (an essay, a stapler, a floppy diskette, a pen that has taken evasive action). Then he pauses to search his visual memory of where he put the material and visits the same places over again (he might have missed it the first time), adding in the newly envisioned places. Then he tries to determine where he would have put the material if he had put it in a place that it could never be lost because, like keys in an auto's ignition, it's in its right and logical place. He visits those sites, revisiting the above two kinds of sites just in case. And then he goes from one pile of papers and books to another, one by one, including all sites of possibility, until he goes upstairs in frustration and forgets about the material—until it comes to him where it is, and he returns to his study to find it.

Or not.

Before becoming "Someone," the finding outscores the not finding eight to two, and the twenty things out of a hundred that he couldn't find didn't seem of great concern. When, much to his dismay, he finds himself "Someone," it seems to approach a five to five tie; and it is this more than anything that makes him want to retreat to less than someone-ness and not to face the possibility that finding materials, like holding on to freedom, could be inversely proportional to reputation.[2]

And that's the final reason Tonto remains a dilettante: a yellow post-it note above his desk that reads "OUTIS." Once you enter the pipeline of "someone," you cannot return to being "no one," as much as you might want to. It isn't like smoking, something you can give up, but rather is something like T. S. Eliot's "knowledge," after which there is no forgiveness. The only recourse is the other aspect of Odysseus's *outis*—*metis*, a cleverness that allows you to disguise your knowledge for which you should never be forgiven.

That is what it means to mean to be a dilettante; and even though Tonto can never quite achieve "no one" again, he can deflect someone-ness into unseriousness, or he can write essays that have in their augmentations a formless all-form of refusal. Though he may continue to have trouble finding things in his study, at least by this cleverness he may be able to find things in his imagination.

V

At a Modern Literature Conference at which there is little literature but a lot of modern, the last panel includes Reinhard Duessel from Tamkang University. Professor Duessel rises, sets aside his planned paper, draws the Chinese figure "Chuang Tzu" on the blackboard, and then explicates—at some length and with some sprightly energy—how that figure represents life partly as flowing water that by not being contained by fixed banks flows into places of which it is unaware, places that are eddies of change, surprise, creativity. Professor Duessel himself, to the stilted and over-refined, probably seems overly augmentative and sometimes wandering like the water of his Chinese character. But to someone like Tonto, he is charming, energetic, playful, and truly a delight. Coming last after three days of stuff and theory, he is an instance of simultaneity and perfection. What was wrong with the bad theory at the conference was not just that the half of Chuang Tzu that represents the vitality of life seemed absent, but that the other half, the watery half, the flowing half, was not free to eddy and swirl. It was not a river or a stream but a high viscosity contained in preformed viaducts.

At a reception following the end of the conference, Tonto stands *outis metis* in a corner enjoying a conversation with Anne Marie, who is married to one of his colleagues. (Tonto tends to prefer the husbands and wives, the slightly outis and often more metis people at receptions and parties.) A pompous critic—who has been going around telling everyone about the psychological travails of his divorce—interrupts to ask Tonto and Anne Marie, "How did we like our idiot savant with the Chinese characters?"

Tonto—in defense of himself as much as Reinhard Duessel, in defense of the nonpompous, and in defense of real imaginative freedom—opens his mouth to reply, curtly, "At least he had the savant."

Perhaps it is the pleasantness of his conversation with Anne Marie. Perhaps it is the sheer joyful relief that the conference is finally over. But what he thinks at that moment is that the Lone Ranger who allows his sidekick Tonto to agree with him no matter what he really thinks does not exist, has no real matter or power in the world's on-going imagination. Instead, there is only Tonto, *outis* and *metis*. Sometimes he falls out of balance and says stupid, or worse, cruel things, like an idiot. But at other times he is, like Chuang Tzu, the complicated character of an idiot savant, the generous Jay Silverheels in a costume-ball mask. At his worst, he is disagreeable; at his best, he is in between, and in disguise, and willing to be without theory.

So Tonto controls himself, smiles agreeably, and says with a laugh, "What do you mean, 'We,' kemosabe?"

Paving with Good Intentions

It seems odd that it's only been a year since the Tuesday—around eleven-thirty, on my way to class to lecture on historical images and attitudes of Native Americans—I walked out of my building and there he was, sitting on a cement bench as though he was one of the tobacco users outside in the frosty air, huddled against the truths of their times and their own solitude. It was a slab bench fit for a bus stop, alongside a road pitted by the respect that universities give to the humanities. With his short hair, hazel eyes, and nearly complete absence of turquoise—there were two small beads hidden on his leather belt—he didn't look like an Indian.

"Hey. What's up?" I said.

"Not much," he replied. He looked worried or as though he'd been trying not to cry.

"How's your work?"

"Crap," he replied.

Crap was good. These days, about all he could say about anything was expletives like "a bunch of shit," or "Who gives a good goddamn?" Crap seemed an improvement over a bunch of shit. Ask him if he wants to do lunch, and he'll say, "Ya gotta ★★★★ing eat." Ask him where, and he'll say, "Who gives a flying ★★★★?"

The week before, in the middle of a talk by a candidate for a job in our department, he leaned over and whispered, "See the moon? It ★★★★ing hates us. Donald Barthelme, page thirty-three." And he's been known to make fun of what he calls the royal purple of political correctness by muttering loud enough for the speaker to hear, "Who the ★★★★ does he/she think she/he is?"

He only messes around, in other words, with pretensions like slashes.

Too often I catch him hanging his curled middle and index fingers in the air the way my four year old son hangs dinosaur horns at his temples to form quotation marks: "Who gives a [fingers raised curled in the air] flying [fingers dropped] ★★★★?"

Well, obviously he does, for one. And it's pretty apparent that he does.

I guess I would too if every time I sat basking amongst my peers in an audience of academics I had to hear about my own uneulogized death from a bunch of critics who were theoretically trying to kill me like they are him.

Besides being Indian, he is an author.

The author has died.

We assume it.

Or so his friends like me, who are mostly critical theorists, sometimes say (and have been try to say since the year of his birth, 1949, with the publication of Wimsatt and Beardsley's essay on "The Intentional Fallacy"). According to him, they wrote that essay three days after they spotted a white rabbit diving into an apparently bottomless hole. He does a whole routine, mimicking critical voices:

"Look at that," Wimsatt says. "A hole."

"I should add," he says, "that Wimsatt, Old Wimsy as his friends called him with their piercing sense of irony, was the more descriptive of the two."

"At what?" Beardsley asks. "There's nothing there."

"Precisely," replies Wimsatt, "It's a hole."

"A hole," Beardsley replies, "with a rabbit in it."

"Goodness gwaacious," Wimsy says, running to the profane. "Whatever can that mean?"

"Can't tell," Beardsley concludes. "Is it a rabbit surrounded by holeness? Or is it a hole filled partially with rabbithood? To assert either would be to create a fallacy. After all, a hole is by its very nature empty, and the rabbit may be nothing more than an illusion. A delusion we two have, to put it plainly, shared."

"There's an article in that," Wimsy replies.

"*Certainement*," Beardsley answers in cocktail *Français*. "Even promotion."

"Tenure," Wimsatt says.

"Sinecure," says Beardsley.

"They have to assume it," he says. "They want to believe that they have killed him, too. Like they could kill anything other than an iguana limping across the four-lane expressway of their fantasies."

According to him, the fallacy of intention is a fear of being wrong, combined with a presumption that anyone can be analytically right: the critical theorist, often a writer whose failure is of imagination and not skill, of heart and not intellect, does not want a higher authority (he'll note the etymology of that word) who can come along and say, "Nope, you're full of shit there, my pal."

"So he ****ing murders me, the author, by murdering my ability to rhetorically structure my gee-dee work or my freakin' language not only to say what I mean . . ."

"But in fiction, isn't meaning often not saying what you mean in any other way but structure, or not saying in any other way but asking questions?" I ask.

He'll cast you a look like you're the last home fry, as if to say, "of course," and keep right on going, " . . . but also to evoke the appropriate emotions. He murders, in other words, my able right to give context to my story, provide the canvas of assumptions and techniques against which are painted the specific generalities of the guidelines of meaning—dialogue, description, scene, result (life, death, marriage with or without love, trial and punishment or recompense), a canvas which is not necessarily that of the normal historical and periodic assumptions, as the historicists would have it, but which may draw out assumptions from ancient Greece and dust them off and reuse them or provoke assumptions still lurking around the vague edges of the not-so-distant future. He wants my story 'cause he can't get his own. So he reinvents me to be as exacting or incapable as himself, either transfixed by Saussurean solipsism or ****ing dead from the neck down."

As a critic who happens to be his friend (and who actually made the mistake of continuing to care about him even as he fell over the edge of eccentricity), I understand that he thinks it's fear that we critics have about the author's intentions. But it isn't. It's logical analysis. "After all," I say, "who is able to intervene in a text with any certainty that his intervention is guided by the author?"

"After all," he says, "who wants to bend over in public and bare his(slash)her undies, which is your academic equivalent of plumber's butt?"

But is it so unreasonable that, uncertain of our own intentions as well as our ability to express them, we come along and say we can't discern the author's intention, a saying that eventually leads us to "problematize" and "thematize," while at the same time to "theorize" the death of the author and make the patterns and interpretations of literature a problem, not of intention, but of critical intervention, interrogation, and even sometimes interpretation?

He just does not seem able to understand the simple truth that all books in the public sphere belong, not to an author, but to the "public"—which doesn't really mean the general public, which rarely interrogates anything, but the theorist in public, who intervenes between the author and the general public to tell them what the text means in all its subtlety. He seems to think this is a trick of the light, sort of like the word Indian can be used to mean, not the general and diverse group of folks called Indian who are always in the process of being Indian, but the wannabe essentialist elitists who want to tell other Indians just how "indian" they are.

Oh. Did I mention he is an Indian author? I believe I did. Talk about dead.

Maybe it's because he's a minority who grew up rough on the streets of Los Angeles that he says things like "But what the ★★★★? I mean, who gives a shit? Should we take seriously anyone, including you, my only friend, who uses words like problematize? Aren't 'Z-words' just plain ugly? Uglier, even, than my expletives and equally inelegant, half as effective?"

"Problematize is shorthand is all. It means formulating the problem in such a way that you can thematize the elements of its discursive qualities."

"And you guys can make a problem out of anything," he says. "Look, I want to ask you one question—and yes, I realize it's not a very intelligent question and that it really is a calmer way of asking, Who gives a ★★★★, flying or otherwise? But after you Ravening critics spy the author's corpse and pick the mess off the bones of his skeleton, revealing a pattern to his ribcage and a logic to his legs, what do we have? Tolstoy's flawed human artist whose flaws we seek, not to prove him inadequate or wrong, but to feel the final messy human connection to him in his flawedness?

(You see? He meant "flawdicity" in the hermeneutics of thematized problematics. But I refrained from correcting him so as not to hurt his feelings. Even though I took exception to being called a Ravenizer.)

"Do we have a connection that recognizes the reader's or listener's common humanity with the 'author'—a term which, in the sense of his 'making,' includes writer as well as teller? Do we even have anything resembling life or vaguely interesting?"

"All very good interrogationalizations to formulaize, but . . ."

"But no. No, we do not have humanity."

"But that's the point, isn't it? We're trying to get closer to the science of literary discourse, to objectify our investigations."

"Come on. Even you know it's a flaw to see science as cold and without soul or humanity. What we get are bones, something similar to the Cliff's Notes of plot outline, something that, though it rattles, is dull and very likely dead. Although death is not necessarily dull. Indeed, I can imagine some dyings that would be very interesting, more interesting than Hamlet's, or even the death of Socrates." (Do you see how he goes off in all directions?) "The movement of those bones is the process of gesture in storytelling. The flesh of those bones is the process of language. The heart is the processional life of the dialogue, description, juxtaposition. The head of those bones is the structure and placement . . . get my drift?"

I laugh. "The knee bones connected to the thigh bones, the thigh bones connected to the (pause) hip bones, the hip bones connected to the . . . ?"

"Don't get it, huh?" he says. "Okay. I'll circle in on it."

"Of course, no real author would come along and say, 'Nope, you're all ★★★★ed up, pal. You got it all wrong.' "

Questions of his own realness aside, even expletivatorily he would not come along and say that. I am fully aware of that. Although he does engage in this sort of etiological problematization of the partially theorized positionality of the ontological framework.

"For one thing, if someone came along and killed me and stripped me down to my bones (so that for the first time in my life I might be thin enough to be popular) and then described each of those bones—because description is all that's left besides humming the song (the neck bone's connected to the breast—no chest, no unisex flatness just below the chin, so please stop staring—bone)—I would listen with great interest and curiosity. Because even someone who is a murderer sometimes has interesting reasons for the slash of his/her crimes. Jeffrey Dahmer horrifies us but still makes us curious, titillates the atrophy of our emotion or spirit by the way he sorted and separated, described and consumed. Jack the Ripper is legendary in the vesúgials of our pre-Rubber Souls. Though you critics will never determine just who killed Cock Robin, I want to offer some possibilities.

"I remember graduate school. That was the first time I was laid bare. It was by my own students who asked if they could 'teach' a short story of mine. Possibly, it was the most interesting experience of my early writing career. In fact, if I could have interested and modestly intelligent students 'teach' all my drafts I would learn what Athol Fugard learns by putting his plays through Rep and perhaps a good deal more. And the more that I would learn would come from the relative inexperience but interested participation of the students who, critically, lack a theoretical background. Yet, in terms of what a living author wants, their interest and their willing participation qualifies them as friend and part of the community for which and in which the author invents, writes, and revises. I would have the added advantage of imaginatively placing myself in the role of modestly but relatively inexperienced student and seeing my own production.

"It's an exception, perhaps, that I would use to prove the rule, but I learned more from listening to these kids talk about my story than I learned from several years of graduate students in creative writing workshops at Syracuse University where Margaret Robe punctiliously put toothpaste on her index and brushed her teeth in class and Michael What's-his-name compared the stuttering death of his mother by cancer to an automobile's engine dieseling; and Ed Goon angrily attacked me for the conceit and arrogance of submitting my stories to literary magazines; and Carolyn Wright borrowed brand new books and underlined them in red ink; and Greg Barron hit the **** out of a softball while writing the one novel I know that he later published—Greg, whose quite real emotional distress over a fallen fledgling sparrow remains a picture in my memory that I am unlikely to forget: two hundred and fifty pounds of compulsively exercised muscle bending, helpless, above a few ounces of chirping feather and motherless despair.

"By teaching my story, these students pointed to rhetorical uses of language of which I was only partly conscious and, by the time they were done, made me feel pretty pleased with the depth of the story, a result I have since felt should be the one main raison d'être of literary critics."

"Partly conscious. What about . . ."

"Partly conscious does not mean the same thing as unconscious. Like the muscle memories of sports like golf or basketball, it indicates years of practice, training, and preparation that allow the writer to seek and sometimes find that implied author who is better and deeper than the limited and sometimes solipsistic 'I' that he/she is. It is not a ready-made excuse for the literary critic to divorce the writer from the processes of invention and revision or, in a declaration of hyper-consciousness and systematization, to assert that his/her consciousness is equal to or better than the writer's."

"D. H. Lawrence says, 'Never trust the artist, trust the tale.' He says that my proper function as a critic is to save the tale from the artist who created it."[1]

"Save it from Lawrence, perhaps. After all, it's David Herbert who somehow manages not to choke himself with laughter over that low-life, ridiculous Mellors running around saying in a crude parody of Spinal Tap, "I want to fuck thee" and weaving Daisies into the pubic hairs of the Chatterley Lady. Only Lawrence would, of course—of course!—have the Lady just happen to be married to a sexual cripple. Besides, who will save the critic from himself? Are we to trust the intentions of a nonmaker over the questions of the maker? Some—not, by any means, all, though the numbers seem to be growing—critics are merely failed authors. They aren't the Greg Barrons but the Michael What's-his-names of the world. Failed literary authors, at least. Because in the perishing world of academics, they do author 'texts,' a notable difference from what I do, which is write books.

"I don't want to write texts. Though I understand that texts is a word you folks use to level the hierarchy by broadening the subject of so-called reading to include film, commercials, rock-and-roll songs, and squiggly piles of snow-bleached dog poo in spring that make my daughter go 'Yuck.' One 'reads' the world. The world is 'text' to you critical theorists who, by the by, when you examine your lives, prove notoriously poor in reading the world. Maybe you think it's specious or just plain immature, but I don't 'read' the world. Sometimes I try to not know it. Sometimes I just drift along trying to endure it, though I am willing, like Conrad, to try to make someone including myself 'see' it and understand it a little bit better; and I am all too willing to talk about it."

"As if I couldn't tell," I said. What was I doing sitting here on this cement bench? My backside was near frozen by the permafrost of the cement slab—even in the summertime, it is cold to the touch—and with the hard gray steel of Michigan skies bearing us down, one could hardly mistake the gloomy signs of impending endless winter. Though I'd left my office half an hour early—I like to get to class early and greet those students who will look at me (it is the Midwest, after all) with a restrained smile—I was going to be late to class.

He ignored me. "To call something a 'text'—human excrement displayed on the floor of a Soho gallery or Alice Walker's or Amy Tan's or Richard Ford's stereotypes—does not make it art."

"I consider Alice Walker one of the great Black women writers of our time," I said. "She and Amy Tan have both been lecturers in our Celebrity Lecture Series here."

"Exactly," he laughed. "By that logic, Courtney Love is an artist. As for Amy and Alice, I refuse to 'read' all 'texts' at the level of art. A blue tile floor may hide in its pattern the blue of my family, as in The Moor's Last Sigh.[2] But that is metaphor and not necessarily art, and it definitely does not induce me to 'read' the floor mats of my car in the same way. To say 'the world is text' is to obfuscate an obvious and otherwise enlightened idea—that reasonably intelligent human beings try to live wiser, more perceptive lives—with the monosyllabic glutinate additive of a subtle but pernicious assumption: that you people, the critics and theorists, the specialists, are the (only) ones who really know how to 'read' the 'text' of the world. Forgive my particular way of thinking, but all I ask is why you people seem to be so troubled by your lives?"

"No more troubled," I said, "than some couple whose consuming delight is quizzing each other on episodes of the Brady Bunch."

I admit, I was not a little annoyed by the way he was willing to confuse life with theory by conflating the two completely different problematics. I also admit that I was not a little annoyed at myself for sitting there and taking this crap. One could theorize the text of the world without problematizing the Lacanian hermeneutics of post-modern life as the salient simultaneity.

"How many theories would a theorist theorize if a theorist could theorize theory?" he laughed. "Substitute 'marriages' for the first 'theories' in that sentence. 'How many marriages would . . .'"

"I can," I said coldly, "recuperate your metaphor without a direct translation." He was reminding me that I had had five marriages already. Or rather, I was at the moment of this conversation still on my fifth. And he was probably trying to make a joke about the fact that because my fourth wife was chair of another department, and because she was so busy and I had done much of the cooking and cleaning, I had listed the cooking and cleaning as part of my "University Service" on my annual faculty report.

"Good. Then you can understand how for me storytelling and life are the same thing, whether it's Lily Briscoe attempting her 'something' in Woolf's *To the Lighthouse* or Grace Blanket sent by her mother down to learn the ways of white folks to enable the people's survival in Linda Hogan's *Mean Spirit*."

Remembering my first four marriages, I said, "Marriage is different. Marriage is about human relations, about living together in what feels like a nine by twelve cubicle for dullified years on dullified end. It's about pretending to listen when you are weary from grading papers or holding forth on committees."

"I disagree. When it comes to perception, when it comes to wisdom, when it comes to heart, the ability to see yourself in the world is connected at the very source and root to the ability to imagine and to see your selves among the selves of a novel."

"Married partners change over time. They grow together or apart. They develop different interests."

"No they don't. They just lose the veneer of romantic fantasy they've wrapped around their wanting to biff each other, and yet they're stuck with the patterns they established while they pretended to be in love. Take a look at Milan Kundera's *Book of Laughter and Forgetting*. There you have fair warning to new lovers (and future partners in wedded bliss) to be very careful about the things they do in the first two weeks of the relationship, because in a blink of a fortnight, the habits and patterns of a lifetime are made and cemented. Play roles, do or say things you don't really mean just to get laid, and you'll be playing those roles until Tecumseh returns with Lazarus to tell us all. We don't change. Not me. Not you. We play out false roles of selfishness until we can play them no longer. The really interesting thing is that if people separate and remarry (or if an adolescent "breaks up" with a boyfriend or girlfriend) they often separate themselves from false roles they cannot stand by leaving the object around which they've wrapped that fantasy. Then nine times out of ten they go out and make up another romantic fantasy around a person who, except for outward appearances, is the same person they just divorced, and marry them—which, in part, may explain why soon enough the same person divorces again."

He laughed again. God, it was an irritating laugh. "The seven-year-itch isn't a sudden desire to experience new territory. The slow, irremediable wearing away of the fantasy takes about six years. Like a sabbatical, it can take another year for one of the partners to make up his or her mind, get a divorce, and remarry when the divorce papers arrive—because like a sabbatical, most of us are afraid to have too much time on our hands to think for ourselves.

"Books do not change, either. They only reveal themselves. Texts do, because 'texts' are what are studied by people struggling to create a system of certainty by breaking books down into discrete elements or interpretive tasks, much the way industrial production in North America was once broken down into the discrete tasks of labor. Each task is analyzed by movement and distance, timed, and then 'reassembled' into a completion goal and expected productivity with which middle managers could use and abuse labor. Frederick Winslow Taylor, the main proponent and great con artist of labor efficiency, fudged his statistics, reinventing the data or inventing new data to sell his theories, and produced uncontextual outright lies about the scientism of production. Yet fifty years later we are still susceptible to the desire for certainty and the bogus applications of science to human activity—whether it be psychology, sociology, or, not infrequently, anthropology. In literature, linguistics led the way into scientism. Yet for all our theories of literary production and analysis, all our complicated indiscretions about language and sign systems, the best we can do is to say, like separating partners, that we are tired of that kind of reading, that kind of bias, then leave it and adopt a new one. Sure, individually we all differ—but not as much as we would like to theorize. And yes, I am suggesting that to read as a something—an Indian, a feminist, a Marxist, a New Ageist, a performance theorist—is to invent uncontextual and thus false statistics and to play out the false roles Kundera warns lovers against. Though these days books do get published that are more tracts for an agenda—similar, perhaps, to *Lady Chatterley's Lover*. They get used as texts in the classroom, even though labeled as such they are not novels and they not literature but commercial pamphlets that allow the partner-readers, locked in their false roles and agendas, to find self-validation and confirmation of their systems of belief. They don't encourage the reader to question the very foundations of their selves-in-the-world. But the era of self-proclaimed, 'I feel your pain' victimization because I am (a) Woman, (b) Gay, (c) Native American, (d) Chicano/a, (e) Other is coming to a close. Still, when I ask the question Is Book X a good novel?—a question I think needs to be asked—how many times do I have to hear people say, 'It teaches well'?

"The short answer, in other words, at least as I understand it, is 'No.' But as critics, very early in a romanticized love affair with books, you committed yourselves to long answers, not short. This is why it takes six years of articles and reviews for books fully to become texts, objects with which you were bored. Still, even after the divorce you're committed to the illusion of thoughtful (and scientifically logical) consideration. Perhaps Virginia Woolf didn't want to be read at the level of the sentence. But she wrote at the level of the sentence; so it is there, on the ground floor, that another author begins to appreciate what she wrote. If Rosario Ferré's sentences weren't sometimes good, then all the silly and unintelligible statements about her learning to 'write as a woman' won't keep her books in my classroom, no matter how great my empathy—and we live in an age where blinding empathy seems to be a necessary credential for being human.[3]

"But I am not human. I am an author. And as an author, I don't want to write 'texts.' 'Text' (always his son's inverted tyrannosaurical commas) for me is different from 'book.' A book is a story about people or ideas that is printed and its pages joined together. It is not the *book* that I read, but the language inside the book, which is printed but is meant to be heard at the very least with the auditory or aural imagination. The minor keys of telling may change, yes. But your imagination is asked to connect into, and participate in, the same story.⁴ The sentences provide context for each other, and thus it is not a problem of semiotic linguistics but a problem for our imaginations and understanding—not unlike life itself. Theoretically speaking, if we do not hear the story as told but only read it as inscribed, we have already begun to kill the author-storyteller and pick clean the bones. We have begun to make systematic that which is not. We have begun to 'read' what was a book as a 'text,' and a text that is equal in imaginative, linguistic, or philosophical power to any other text and no more powerful than the limits of our own imaginations. A novel becomes a commercial for a preformulated way of thinking, an advertisement that can be described and, after it has been described, analyzed."

"Didn't you once argue that analysis killed literature?" I asked. "Back in the sixties?"

"Which were really the early seventies. Yeah. I did. I was a kid. I was as capable of homogenization as the next person. It took a few years for me to look around and realize that complaining about how analysis killed books was just an excuse for laziness."

"So? That's what I do. I simply try to analyze what texts mean."

"Like the old anthropologists used to analyze what artifacts meant."

"I guess."

"Artifacts don't mean diddly. They let us know about the tools people used, maybe, or whether they buried their dead standing up or lying down. So to analyze them or stuff them into museums is to ignore the process. How the artifact was used was an integral part of how the human being was. And it's somewhere around that dividing line that analysis becomes too much and information becomes meaningless, if not an outright lie."

"And you get to choose where the line is?"

"I am an author. I merely **** around with words. You can analyze how those words work metaphorically in the context of how I'm ****ing around. But take the words out of context and try to analyze their signification and you'll kill the story—the soul of the story, which is its slightly lifelike fluidity and ever-so-slight ambiguity."

"So your friends in the sixties were right."

"As much as I hate to admit it, yeah, they were. They just didn't know it." He smiled. "Because they were too lazy. You critics are not so lazy, always. At least not until you become Somebody and you get fooled into thinking anything you say is correct simply because you've said it. But using analysis, not out of a laziness of mind, but out of extreme and minutely specific application of it, kills the humanity, the novel, and substitutes a mummified artifact, the 'text,' for the once-living body. You separate, disconnect, and describe or analyze—and then with the same animation that Disney uses, you make a fantasy of meaning with which you fool yourself into believing that you know.

"Descriptiveness, your impulse to 'describe' and separate that you discourse about in your textualities, sorts out or removes heart, takes away the difficulties of participating without undue solipsism. But only romanticizers and believers in the falsities of individualism and uniqueness and self-validation, only people given to the nostalgias of their agendas can truly separate the heart from the mind and value knowing about things in a way that Lawrence—in *Studies in Classic American Literature*, I think page ninety-three, maybe -four—criticizes for being 'mind-conscious.' Anyway, David Herbert got some things right. When he says that men (and he should have added women) 'live by lies,' he means that at least a large portion of those lies derive from 'predetermined' fancies and 'innermost . . . self-made-world(s).' He's right that it's 'all a swindle.'[5]

"So, yes, in their self-made worlds, my fellow students saw separation as deadly. And separation, as Wallace Stevens says about death, 'is absolute and without memorial.' It's as though he actually believed that Americans and Western Europeans are the great memorializers of history.[6]

"I saw separation as temporary and useful for knowing of a kind that could reintegrate knowing with the connectedness of the world. And we were both wrong: they, in their refusals, failed to learn the connections of literature and life. But my failure was worse. I failed to recognize the endurance of the ultimate separator, the lover of bureaucratic language who changed *use* to *utilize* and sought out meetings to attend when he(slash)she had none of his own to enjoy, who was then but the harbinger of Zees that would colonize the world of talk and sting those who would did not serve the same critical queen.

"Present-day separators tend, perhaps, to see the resulting systems as all we can really discourse upon. I now see it as talk that, while interesting, has little to do with storytelling (though perhaps much ado about problematizing). *Sometimes* interesting, I have to add, because *Tristes Tropiques* is not interesting but turgid and *triste* in its systematizing.

" 'Discourse,' by the way, from what I can tell (and I do get the gist of it) is the whole schmeggeggy. The 'discourse' of any discretely separated area or period—let's pick modernism—the discourse of modernism, then, says that what is being analyzed and described is the entire project of modernism, including the subtexts and übertexts, though only some of the informing assumptions (admittedly as many of them as it could discover). But 'discourse' is a container that leaks: modernism runs like my daughter's watercolors into pre- and post-modernism and seems, often, not unlike those too-wet watercolor-ings, to make the bright images of art gray or dull, like Michigan or England. Homer, though ancient, is both modern and modernist. Worse (in my measure of things), the 'discourse' of modernism, though it includes the (dead) authors and (not-so-lively) critics and interpreters of modernism, seems to want to take the implied speaker out. It makes 'modernism' the speaker, in a sense, as though there even is such a thing as 'modernism' and as though that thing were almost human. It makes 'discourse' the active subject as well as the passive object. In a sense, discourse kills off the talker and attempts to replace it with a kind of omniscient, fingernail-paring, absent critical matrix that ostensibly objectively presents the analysis of the modernist discourse.

"I am uncomfortable with discourse because it, like the death of the author, insists on the objectification and eventual death of the critic as an individual responsible for the relations and connections established by his criticism.

"So I don't discourse. I talk. And I like to talk about books—novels, essays, poems—a fact that seems to isolate me from literary critics and theorists. Perhaps I am wrong, but few people seem to like to talk about books and would rather talk about office politics or ceiling fans.

"But then," he said, suddenly tired, "who knows? I'm probably an idiot. It's a role I accept: I'd rather be Benjy crying out Caddy's name because of something I smelled, some olfactory mnemonic stimulus, than Quentin. I'd rather learn about the bear while hunting him than study texts that properly theorized the aims of the hunt to be Bear-death and not bear-smell, bear-awe, bear-chase, bear-awareness, danger- or death-inspired (and I mean 'in-spired') identity. Give me Benjy. Give me *Go Down, Moses*. Let's talk. But let's talk about the connections, let's talk about the process of *Spotted Horses*, not what it means (which is, tautologically, process, anyway). Give me the moment training ends and texts become books again, stories to be told and retold, heard and reheard. Give me allusions I can grasp, not the endlessly regressive (and ultimately meaningless) intertextualities that slip through phantastic fingers of most every critical theorist. Don't give me the whimper, give me the bang. Give me, not the separations and descriptions of training, but the messy connections of imagined authority. Give me the fun of books after graduate school has ended. Give me—and for-give me too, if you can.

"Let's talk, for heaven's sake, about books.

"But books, among English professors, are like soiled panties.

"Books are like shit in the woods," he laughed.

"Without the bear.

"So we rarely say shit about books."

"You need a ride home?" I asked. "It's too late for me to make class. The students will have waited the required fifteen minutes and gone by now."

"No, thanks," he said. "I'm waiting for a bus."

"This isn't a bus stop," I said.

"I didn't say I was waiting to catch it."

When I got home, the house was dark. Herself must be still at work. I checked my email, something I do four times a day: once in the morning, once when I get to campus, once in the afternoon, and once when I'm at home. There was only one new message—an apologetic note from him:

"Literary theorists are extremely intelligent. The ones I know, at least. Like you. And I am not being facetious. Not here, anyway. When I sit in a room with you folks and listen to you discourse about Derrida and de Man, Hegel and Heidegger, Lacan and not Laocoon, Reiss and Spivak, I am reminded, sentence by sentence, that I have, at best, an average mind, which, if it has any gifts to give, has them because of the canvas on which I construct myself—that is, I am Nez Perce. A Nez Perce storyteller. As such, I cannot discourse. And depending on your willing essentials, I am genetically or instinctively incapable of separating and describing. For me, there is no before or after to identity; identity *is*, though it simultaneously may be recognized by other selves at the moment one expresses self. One can wave at the figure in the top of the other tree to let him know you know he knows you know he is there and that you are both selves identifying at the moment of being identified.[7] In other words, there is no bullshit about the 'subject-group' relations; the subject and group are not linear, one-directional, and they cannot be separated and talked about as though unidirectional. Subject is group is subject ad infinitum, a problem many (white or Euramerican) theorists seem to have with all their descriptive discourse about Chicano or Native American cultures. Nonetheless, when you folks talk about your own litera-tures these days, calling for Marxisms or post-modernisms instead of the singular Marxism or post-modernism, you seem implicitly to recognize that there is no real group, only other individuals who, being alike in certain contexts fluidly form a group—only to disband *as* group, to dissolve their contextual likenesses when the contexts (which are provided by narrative or story, remember) change. There is, in other words, no such thing as a way that Chicanos think, only, at different times, Chicanos thinking. Indeed, the separation of one from another, the discrete description of one as fixedly different from the other becomes—like the separation of the book from the implied author—the death of both.[8]

"Anyway, when I sit in a group with you folks, my lit-crit friends, I feel stupid. In groups, I tend to keep my mouth shut; it's a form of protest or resistance, if you will have it so. But at the same time, I resist, not the feeling of stupidity, but the drive to separate and describe as though everything were not connected, this to this and each to each. When one of you discourses on subject-group relationships in Native American writing (has the 'subject' died too, thrown down beneath the wheels of a critical semi?), I am willing to try to understand and then to ask what seems an obvious question, Can the subject be thrown down in this fashion? I am—or I was the other day when that job candidate who is an anthropological ventriloquist gave his paper—perplexed by the way in which the speaker can be described as not seeing, in the Conradian sense, that the question just did in his entire problematized framework of 'discoursion.' (Discussion implies

44

dialogue, and as dialogic as you folks would pretend to be, many of you don't seem to give a shit about small questions from average minds.) Anyway, he did not answer my question. He didn't even try, because he didn't seem to take my little question seriously enough to bother. And frankly, my awareness that I am not as bright as you all kept me from pursuing the question for fear not only of being stupid but of my stupidity making everyone kindly laugh—like the kid saying the emperor is naked and making everyone in on the joke or the know laugh—as this ontologically unsound Nez Perce nondiscourser tries to play with the big boys and girls.

"It's okay. You really are smarter. The words you use. The way you change language to mean more. The way you can abstract use and utilize it to give an abstract argument that lacks any relation to what average minds like mine can do. Wow. Just listen to this phrase I read in a recent article: 'A properly gendered situational framework.' Do you hear that? How 'bout that one?"

When herself walked in, hanging her coat on the coat rack by the door while she wiped her feet endlessly on the door mat—she is so assiduous in her foot wiping that she wears out these little throw rugs about once a month—I said, "I've got a question for you."

"Not now," she said. "I just walked in. Give me a minute." She went down the hall. Water ran in the bathroom. When she came back, she was wiping her sweater with a tissue. "We've got to fix that faucet."

"We?" I thought. "You mean me." Why is it that no matter how enlightened we become, when it comes to fixing faucets or hanging bird feeders or standing around a puddle in the basement trying to figure out what to do now, they feel so free to say "We" have to do this, or "We" have to do that, and yet the person they expect to hop to it is the husband?

I was being unfair, to think that way. And I kept it to myself. She'd obviously had a long day. "I'll see what I can do," I said quietly. "Anyway, you ready now?"

She slid off the bar stool from where she usually watched me slice and dice for dinner and went into the dining room and took a bottle of white wine out of the ironwork holder we'd gotten as a wedding present. She came back into the kitchen and pushed past me to the drawer with the corkscrew in it, opened it, and took out the corkscrew, from which she removed last night's cork. (We left the old corks on to cover the tip of the screw and keep us from poking ourselves when we reached into the drawer. Of course the drawer held unprotected knives — old ones that were too dull to cook with — a meat thermometer with a pointed tip, metal and bamboo skewers that we used for grilling after soaking the bamboo ones in water long enough to keep them from charring or catching fire.)

"A red would be better with dinner," I said. "One with body. Maybe a Merlot, or better yet, a Zinfandel."

"I feel like white."

I turned my back to her and went on slicing onions. "So I heard an interesting talk today," I said, sniffing.

"Really."

"About gendered situations."

"Ummm." She poured two glasses of wine and set one near me on the counter before going around and taking her place on the stool.

"Thanks," I said. "The speaker [who was a woman, but you don't *say* that to my wife because she doesn't like women identified by their gender, race, class, or ethnicity; and I tend to agree with her. We are always saying 'a woman said' or 'a Black woman said,' and it's not unreasonable to suspect that by simply identifying her that way we have already put into motion certain attitudes and feelings that are wrong] kept using phrases like 'a properly gendered situational framework.' "

"So?"

"So I got to thinking." You could see the 'Uh-oh' look cross her face. She frowned.

I did my best not to be annoyed. She'd been giving me that look more often these days, though I admit her 'Uh-oh' look was a whole heck of a lot better than the look of resignation that seemed to recognize the sad fact that I might well be in the early stages of Alzheimer's.

"So what the fuck does that mean?" I blurted.

"Ooh. Are we cursing now like a big strong male? Are we to understand that the dominant male has had a hard day?"

"Sorry," I said. "Just that when I stopped and thought about it, I couldn't figure out what 'properly gendered' anything means."

My wife, whose habit is to disagree with me, knew what that meant. When I explained that I sometimes thought we didn't understand what really we meant by "gendered," she told me very well what *she* would mean by it. It made sense while she was saying it. But I was uncomfortable with wondering whether the person who wrote and spoke those words actually knew what she meant and if she could be sure that I (or anyone else) knew that she knew that we knew what she meant.

"It's a kind of shorthand," my wife said. She refilled her glass.

"I understand." I thought about what my friend the author had said. "But when Neihardt's niece took down Black Elk's bullshit in shorthand, was what she took down the same as what her uncle expressed later in longhand? When Schoolcraft appropriated his own (biblical) versions of Ojibway stories, were they Ojibway stories? Doesn't shorthand require not just some familiarity but extreme sympathy and understanding—as when a (happily) married couple uses shorthand to re-create and remind each other of the fullness of discussions they have had? What happens when shorthand is used by strangers?"

"They get the gist," my wife said. I think she began to see my point.

"But the gist is not good. The gist quickly becomes the gist of the gist and then . . ."

"Okay, okay," she said—shorthand for "I don't have time to discuss it right now."

"Take *gendered*, or any other critically acceptable word. Repeat it in different contexts without each time retelling the story of it but using it to give the gist of the story only. Every 'gendered' situation is as different as every human being. The gist overlooks that. And so the shorthand becomes banal repetition and eventually becomes as meaningless as a bumper sticker. And yet one of them uses it, and they all nod as though they understood exactly, precisely, unvaryingly what it means. Are they any better, intellectually, than people who actually stick 'Kids should be seen and heard and *believed*' on their Beamer bumpers?"

"May I remind you that I have that bumper sticker on my car?" she said, icily.

This wife and I had no children. It was my third wife who agreed that, given the way either of our children willfully modified a statement to please the hearer, while we very much wanted to see our kids, listen to our kids, we were not entirely willing to believe everything they said in the way they said it and that anyone who did—in unthematized and unproblematized language—was full of shit and a (dangerous) simpleton. Did that mean that this wife was really a simpleton? With no kids of her own, what did she know about believing or disbelieving kids?

"No," my wife said, almost as though she could read my thoughts, but in a tone that made plain the context of her need to focus on some other matter. It scared me. I realized she had opened the *New York Review of Books* on the counter and was talking back to it, not me.

"What time do you want to eat?" I asked.

"About an hour or so," she said, carrying her glass and the *Review of Books* with her to her chair in the family room.

She wanted to be left alone to concentrate on the task at her hand, and with everything ready to toss into the wok, I went down to Command Central (as, now that I have nice furniture for the first time ever, I jokingly call my study). I went back to the tedious task of answering copy-editorial queries on an anthology of essays I had edited. When I came to this query, "What does 'liberate critical interventions into textual and social space' mean?" I wrote in longhand in the margin, "You know, this is a problem. It sounds as though it ought to mean something, but you're never sure quite what, becoming less sure the farther the writer moves from that which he/she purports to study. Change as noted."

For a moment, I hovered above the page. Something was seriously wrong with me. Then I gritted my teeth and altered the paragraph in which that sentence—a sentence I had read right through when I accepted the essay for the anthology—appeared. I excised the phrase completely and then sat back and lip-read the whole paragraph. The excision altered the paragraph not one whit.

I sat for half an hour staring at the phrase, thinking about properly gendered situations, beginning to wonder if, as Appiah says about race, there is nothing in the world that can do everything we ask gender to do for us, the terminology surrounding words like *race* and *gender* homogenizing human beings and implying that we not only think alike but we see the same things in the same way—until my wife leaned through the upstairs door and called, "I'm ready," which meant that it was time for me to get my butt upstairs and cook.

"You know what," I said as the oil in the wok heated up. "Institutional thinking is like institutional food, full of empty calories and hard to take pleasure in consuming. The difference is that institutional food feeds people to some degree, whereas institutional thinking only feeds itself."

"How do you like this?" I asked, holding out a marinated chunk of broccoli in a wooden spoon, cupping my other hand beneath it in case it dripped. "Careful. It's hot."

That night I lay awake in my bed, wondering just what was happening. Was I changing? Or was I simply coming to realize that the cornerstones of my career were made of sod? I felt vaguely dissatisfied, restless, the way I always felt when another divorce loomed up in my life. My fifth wife and I had only been married six months. We had a great house, which we had divided into halves. Hers was the upstairs, mine the down — except when I cooked, because the kitchen was upstairs. Finally, I got up and emailed my author friend, asking him if he wanted to do lunch.

Two weeks passed. I had emailed him fourteen separate additional times before I finally got an answer. "Who gives a good goddamn. Not eating much. But meet me at Sindhu Thursday, and you can blow yourself up real good," he replied.

I didn't know what he meant by blow myself up and how I should take it. I had put on a few complacent pounds lately, but I doubted that he even noticed that, and as I waited by the coat rack and cash register for him, I wondered what he meant by not eating much. At first, I didn't recognize him. Though dark complected, he was paler, as though the outer layer of skin color had peeled away. His hair was longer. And though he did not look unkempt, there was a small stain over the breast pocket of his shirt.

"Look," he said, gently smiling at me as he set condiment bowls of mint chutney and hot sauce on the table between us — Sindhu was the one Indian restaurant in town. "Once I, too, waxed well-trained. I, too, did theory. I took up the language, pinned a hermeneutical lexicon over my typewriter so I could at least try to remember what the fucking words meant and drew circles and arrows to justify such things as my disappointment as a writer in the end to Hawthorne's 'My Kinsman, Major Molineaux.' It was bullshit. Oh, I still think that Hawthorne, the privileged Nathaniel who wrote at such a distance from our own America, presents a vision of the need for democratic idealism to obliterate all sense of restraint in its delusional belief in abstracts like liberty. But he backs away from that vision and makes it more palatable for his upper-class cronies by inserting the 'are you dreaming' coda at the tale's end.

"That's the short version," he laughed. He shook his head. "The long version became an article published by *Southern Humanities Review* and republished in an anthology called *New Short Story Theories*.[9]

"As a theorist, I might have made a career of it. As a writer, the long answers seemed a waste of time or a use of time aimed at making judgments palatable to my cronies and unintelligible. I wanted to reach a broader audience with my writing. I started to question what I was doing. Things broke down with questions. When a professor I really admired, Tom Hanzo, read aloud a Sylvia Plath poem that metaphorically compares the poet-persona's father to an SS officer, my mind kept asking if it wasn't a little bathetic and over-reaching, a trying too hard for significant emotion in relation to a less significant event, to compare one's father to someone who stripped the skin from Jewish children to make lampshades, pulled the gold fillings out of teeth to trade to Swiss Bankers, or lined adults up back to back to save bullets by shooting two through the head with the same shot. The privileged Radcliffean tormented by the modern world was just a teensy bit hard to take. And no matter what her father did to her, neither he nor she compares in size and importance to Hitlerian death officers or to the millions of innocent people purposely and pointedly exterminated by them. I mean, come on, Sylvia, you're a white, privileged European-American. Shouldn't you learn that restrained emotion is more moving and more true than heavy moaning and on-your-sleeve, feel-my-pain adornment, either by reading Wordsworth or your Bible? As for fathers of women, doesn't Dickenson's line 'Beggar, banker, father, thief' mean a whole lot more than Plath's clawing the blackboard for attention? Where did this need for publicized pain come from?"

Indeed, he did not eat more than a section of nan and maybe an onion bhaji or two dipped in mint chutney. Yet he paid for the full buffet and treated me to mine as well.

On Friday, as a member of the Dean's Fellowship Committee, as I listened to a graduate student nearing the end of her fellowship term,

I must have jotted down ten or twenty questions for her. I felt an almost pathological need for answers to them, and equally important to me was that those answers be short, which is why, though I had these questions, I shied away from asking them.

Her topic was "categorization," specifically the categorization of the concept of "mother" and how the four elements of the normal or good mother—nurturer, birther, etc.—excluded women who had one, two, three, or more of those requisite "elements." What she wanted was to legitimize, by means of an intelligent description of categorization, lesbian mothers, while using the theorized thesis that "categorization" does not account for the complex differences among individuals. As sympathetic as I was to her project, her thesis seemed pretty obvious. "You get a freaking fellowship for this?" I doodled. All she was saying was that everybody's a little different and to categorize them—mother, women, Native American, Chicano, men—is to overlook the important differences among them, to kill the authors of their fates and make them objects. Feminism (since her talk depended like an extra digit from feminist theory) discovered this obvious fact. But wasn't it only after feminism became a canvas of assumption on which very many of our academic discussions were founded that feminism rediscovered this? That women are different, so you need not feminism but feminisms, just as Marxists are making Marxism into Marxisms. I wondered if having removed the complexity by abstraction and description, we weren't now busily retheorizing it to include difference. Eventually, would we be back to knowing what Anna Karenina knew, that women are intelligent and complicated human beings who are not just like men? As though in memorial to my author friend, I jotted, "What the hell, even a fucking Indian has to admit that white folks are complicated and that a few anthropologists are sometimes human, doesn't he?"

This young woman did a very good job at articulating her ideas until a (woman) professor asked, "If a single father fits two or three of these categorical imperatives, can he be recategorized as a 'mother'?"

The short answer, I thought, is "Yes."

The answer the presenter wanted and came as close as Coyote to saying, was "No."

I had to hand it to her, however. She saw the problem in saying "no," so after some hemming and dodging, bobbing and weaving, with Zee words and opaque sentences filled with theoretical terminology, she admitted, "I wouldn't want to exclude the possibility."

Suddenly it seemed to me that if we want to legitimize various attitudes or preferences as "proper" to parents, we don't need all this discoursing. All we need to do is ask two questions: Does the parent love the child? And is s/he willing to spend the time and energy needed to raise—not have, not provide for, not propagandize, but *raise*—the child? (I embarrassed myself by laughing, here, as I remembered a colleague's child who was being raised "free from gendered cultural patterns." When the boy was given his first doll to play with, his father found him using it as a hammer.) Anyway, I thought, smiling apologetically—I felt out of my element for the first time in years, maybe ever—if the answer is "yes" to both, I am for the most part satisfied, certainly more satisfied than with a little girl whose parents abuse her by making her a child beauty queen and more satisfied than two academic parents who enroll the fetus in day care. (Jesus, I realized that when I thought this, I was not entirely joking!)

As I listened to the presenter hem and haw, I couldn't help but think, "All that training and nowhere to use it." All that argument, carefully separated and described—and not uninteresting, mind you—and the results are mixed because things like "love" and sticky, messy representations of authorial or parental intentions were left out.

"Mother effer," I realized. "I have been listening to my friend the author too much. I'm becoming a fucking dinosaur." Nervously, I gathered my notepad with its unasked questions, slid the flyers outlining the two talks to be given that afternoon into my briefcase, and began to prepare an excuse to the dean as to why, regretfully, I had to leave early. The seminar room—the dean's meeting room—was long and darkly paneled, with coffered ceilings and a bank of windows at one end that flooded us with the gray light of Michigan skies that are overcast only one day less per year than Seattle, Washington. The dean sat two padded swivel chairs to my right, and try as I might, I couldn't catch his eye to wink and nod and shrug with apology before he introduced the other speaker, a professor of philosophy whose topic was Socrates.

Back before questions like today's began popping up like cash register tabs—way back in linear time (a time that is, as my author has said, hardly farther than "yesterday" in the time of generations); way, way back when I was but a young dinosaur and had not yet fully become the idiot-savant or ankylosaurus I have become; way back before the ancient history of my student who said, writing about Roethke's poem, "My Papa's Waltz," "The waltz is so old even my grandmother used to do it"; back when I was but a young Salmon-ella sitting with my feet among the salmon like Cinderella's among the ashes and was committed to reading only the great literature of Britain and North America (excluding that insecure country to the north that measures everything in degrees of not-American)—I read Plato, what is commonly known as *The Trial and Death of Socrates*. Though I was bothered by some of the things my teacher told me to think, I did not know why I was bothered. Indeed, even if I had recognized specifically what and where, I would not have had the courage to contest with my teacher. It was not my place to do so; I was being trained. His interpretation derived from and continued to propagate the standard interpretation that Socrates, when he offers thirty minae as a fitting penalty and promises that four of his friends (including Plato, the author) will stand surety for the amount, is ironically or sarcastically playing with the trial's judges by—as the footnote says—offering an amount that is insignificant.

So I was curious about what this professor would have to say about Socrates that was in any way new or different. Imagine my pleasure when he began to use *The Trial and Death of Socrates* as an illustration of how formal academic training can get in the way of true perception.[10] Admittedly, like an anthropologist who wants to find out how much like whites the northwest Indians were, I was ready to be given proof of it. My friend the author said that criticism was supposed to open books up for understanding and that training was valuable only insofar as it opened up stories.

With such thoughts very much in the front of my mind, I listened to the philosopher read the passages surrounding Socrates' proposal of a penalty. He was disturbed by the fact that someone playing with the judges would flippantly set his own ability to pay at one mina and then propose that it be increased thirty-fold, to an amount that required several of his friends to insure it would be paid. The footnote he read—and as my author agrees, that is where training so often finds its elite and proper locus—said that one mina was an insignificant amount. Thirty minae, then, would hardly be more significant. Were Socrates' friends poor like him? The professor asked. Thus it would take several of them to stand for that larger but still insignificant amount?

And that, in part, was what he had discovered. For a hundred years, scholars in their training had held fast to the blind repetitive maze of that footnote, which, it turns out, misrepresented the value of one mina: thirty minae was not insignificant; thirty minae was roughly the payment a juror-judge would have earned for three thousand days of labor. It was, in other words, worth approximately ten years of income. "Now we all know that philosophers are extremely underpaid," he said, "but ten years of income must approximate, in even professorial terms, three quarters of a million dollars." As a fine (for a crime that Socrates does not recognize as truly a crime), even an untrained mind can see that it's a lot of money.

For more than a decade, this professor and his co-author had been trying to return The Trial and Death of Socrates to what untrained readers should have known: that Socrates, as much as anyone would wish otherwise in their romanticization of resistance to authority, is not toying with the juror-judges. He is not being ironical or sarcastic but very, very serious, offering to pay a huge fine for a crime that he does not believe is really a crime and thus by his definition did not commit. For years, this professor and his co-author have been working hard to put Plato back into the process, to return the author to his work; and the way they were doing that was to reexamine the assumptions behind formal, philosophical training. In other words, with Plato still alive, everything must be tested against a kind of commonsense or willing suspension of training.

We can know and do know Plato's intention, which is to represent Socrates as intelligent, responsible, clever, but serious, in part because it is the author himself who allows his name to be included as one of the richer men who will stand surety for his teacher. We know Plato's intention—to make Socrates a positive figure and to question the laws that would make Socrates a criminal—because he could easily have left his name out and made the surety-standers rogues or fools.

He might have done this by description or by report: another figure, even Socrates himself, "thinks" and, as Plato might have told it: "From the look on his face, it was as if Plotinus knew that Plato and his friends were a bunch of snot-nosed fools."

He could have done it by dialogue or reply: "What the fuck, Soc," Judge Aristedes said. "You really expect us to trust the promises of rogues?"

"He could not have done it by theory," I wrote on my notepad. My hand stiffened as though arthritis had suddenly set in when I realized what I had written.

We know his intention by his language and his speaking; this is not discourse, it is a trial with much speechifying. We know Plato's intention—as far as it matters—because in a trial setting he makes a participatory world out of words that demands our participation in order to complete the making. If he is any good, then one thing or another will be what he must have meant. If he is not, well, then, of course he may as well be dead, and he can be thematized as a corpse that has dissolved into uselessness.

For a month, I hid out. I canceled my office hours, and when I walked down the main road that ran along the north side of campus, I wore what I called my Michigan Dufus coat—an insulated nylon jacket the color of elephant—with its hood up, peering out in case I spotted a student so I could duck into a bank's ATM lobby, the Condom Store, or the hip clothing store where once my author friend had said to the clerk, "You'd think you could at least spell Jimi right," getting a blank look from her when he pointed to a poster of "Jimmy" Hendrix. Dark glasses completed my disguise, and it was the rare student who could recognize a formerly well-dressed professor looking something like a cross between the Michigan militia and a bag lady (and these days rare students are very rare).

I skipped department meetings, and I only went to one of the faculty lectures, where I heard one of the crazy old professors who was metamorphosing from an individual into a character muttering under his breath, making what were apparently rude comments about the paper being presented. When I realized that the odd character making noises was me, I panicked, sneaking out of the seminar room right after the paper before the question-and-answer period when I might actually ask some of the rude questions I muttered.

Things at home started to degenerate. Whereas my wife and I had been happy in our routines, I now started to order pizza almost nightly, adding variety by switching from pepperoni to sausage and sometimes adding mushrooms. When she got home, I'd have red wine already opened and breathing without regard to her feelings. And after just a few weeks, I was halfway through the first bottle by the time she walked in, hung up her coat, and sighed her usual preface to the day's complaints. By the time her monthly reading group met, she had elicited a promise from me that I would stay downstairs the whole night, a promise I would have kept if I hadn't indulged in just a little too much wine and if my wife hadn't said over pizza that a properly feminist reading of *Like Water for Chocolate* revealed the encoded textual thematization of the oppression of women by the patriarchy by the very nature of their being forced to cook for men.

I heard someone mutter, wasn't she was making theory a pre-determiner of fate: that in her theory women were oppressed and one symbol of this oppression was cooking for men, and so even though there are few men who matter in Esquivel's novel, a novel so centered on recipes and women must be about the women's need for freedom from this oppression? Indeed, it was as though I was my own author.

Now let me try to be clear—it is what my therapist has insisted I do every time I set out to say something, to make sure that my beliefs and ideas are clear to my audience. I believe that women are oppressed. Whereas out of respect for my author, I am not so sure Sylvia Plath was as oppressed as Sylvia Plath would have us believe, I have faith that Toni Morrison, despite her Nobel Prize and her inclusion in every anthology of modern American literature, remains marginalized, and I know it is my responsibility where the choice occurs to teach Kate Chopin and not Mark Twain. I accept my role in cooking and cleaning for my wife, if only because for hundreds or thousands of years women have been vacuuming and cooking and ironing for the patriarchy.

So why I decided, suddenly, that my wife had a less-than-average mind and that theory had trained that mind to see nothing but the alley and it was an alley that was falsely constructed and falsely painted with overdetermined uselessness, I have no idea. But the longer I sat alone downstairs, the sonorous sound of voices coming down through the ceiling like constant drumming, the more what?—not angry, but desperate, despairing, lost, I became. The stories of the oral traditions—Rushdie, Homer, Esquivel, Graham Swift (*Waterland*), Ralph Salisbury, Tomas Rivera, Toni Morrison, Ron Querry, D'Arcy McNickle, anonymous sagafier of *Njal's Burning*, Chaucer, Mendoza, Momaday, Mendez, Hinojosa, Reveles, Tutuola, Silko, Glancy, and thousands of others—resist these pathetic overdeterminations while they resist the death of the author-storyteller. Killing off the author with a bat of theory does what killing off Indians does for the anthropologist—turns them into a corpse that can be studied, one bone at a time. Though I am not a believer in God, I will venture to say: You can't study God, either, unless you kill him. Beware the priest or critic who says you can, with a result that dissembles the life of stories.

Besides, I had read *Like Water for Chocolate*. Indeed, I had taught it. To make that novel into a tract on the oppression of women required removing Esquivel from her own text—I mean, book. But in a similar way to Plato, Laura Esquivel is ever present in her novel, *Like Water for Chocolate*. Esquivel is there as the person who invented the structure and the technique of the participatory, background narrator-teller of the history of her family (not unlike in the more substantial *The Moor's Last Sigh*). She is there in her choice of the cyclical, epical twelve months ("Christmas Rolls" of January overlapping the "Chiles in Walnut Sauce" of December), and she is there in the recipes.

The recipes are, I realize now, a metaphor for art itself; and they demand, they *require* the presence and our awareness of a cook or an author. No good cook follows the descriptive prescriptions of a recipe any more than a good author follows the prescriptive descriptions of a novel. Rather, the recipe serves as a guideline for the inventive cook, and the cook substitutes more or less salt, more or less chiles, more or less of any ingredient to taste. In addition, the cook's emotional construct at the time of preparation will effect the outcome: Tita's tears fall into the batter of her sister's wedding cake; and when the wedding guests eat the cake, they are overcome with longing. In addition, the recipe that requires the cook also requires the eater in order for the process to be completed. The wedding cake is not finished until the audience for it takes part in the entirety of its process.

The recipes are a brilliant metaphor for the oral tradition, for the way in which orally based literary traditions can dispense with neither the author-teller nor the reader-listener. Oral cultures recognize not *difference* but similarity. We are not very different from our parents (though we can and perhaps should resist becoming exactly like them), and the endlessly regressive differences of structuralism and post-structuralism become, to oral people, the reductions to the absurd of solipsism. The idea in the 1960s that no one could possibly understand what you were really feeling because of the imprecisions and inadequacies of language, was really just the self-inventive pattering of self-loving would-be individualists who were as cow-like as any other set of spoilt children who wish with all their wisheries that they were different, unique, solely and completely themselves. In oral cultures, no one is—not solely and not uniquely.

Moreover, in oral cultures you not only are what you eat, but you are how your stories are told and heard. Rosaura, a picky eater who lacks real sensuality, farts herself to death with a blast of gas that makes her husband wonder in the other room if it's the noise of the revolution beginning. Nacha, the family retainer; Tita, the narrator's great-aunt and main character of the story; and the book of recipes—all survive the changes of time. Indeed, it is out of the inherited book of recipes that the daughter of Esperanza, our narrator, cooks up the art of the novel for us to eat.

But it isn't simply in the structural metaphor that Laura Esquivel is alive and well; it is also in her sentences, in the way she guides, actively, the reader's interpretations with phrases such as "With Nacha dead she was completely alone. It was as if her real mother had died." In "as if" hides the author expressing herself, thinly disguised, if she is disguised at all: we are told to see that Nacha's connection to Tita is more vital, more substantial, more communal and companionable, more understanding and perceptive, more creative, more rhetorically sensitive and participatory than Tita's relation to Mama Elena. We are told to look to Nacha and what Nacha does as meaningful—both to us as readers and to Tita as a character who is, subsequently, more meaningful to us as character. We are told that food is good, cooking is artistic in its relationships, and the oral tradition and food have much to do with each other; that in the oral tradition can be found connection and not separation (or at least that separation and pickiness lead to metaphorically and actually unpleasant deaths, which are a form of authorial presence that no author will readily give up—definitely won't give up if he belongs to an oral storytelling tradition).

Sitting there not a little inebriated, it all became plain to me. Suddenly it dawned on me that I could teach my students to look to the "as ifs" of literature to find—if nowhere else—the self-expressed author. If we want to exercise extreme care, we can say the "implied" author, as long as we understand that it is the author who implies him- or herself, makes him- or herself exist—in the background, perhaps, but nonetheless. Even when the modernist Joyce comes along and claims that the author is like God paring his fingernails, he is everywhere to be found, and found caring, not paring, to an extent that Joyce seems even more present than Laura Esquivel or Salman Rushdie.

So Laura Esquivel is not dead. No more than Alain Robbe-Grillet (who is almost a fascist in his insistent denial of his presence). No more than Manlio Arguetes. No more than I.

No more than I? Hah! That was a laugh. Because I was afraid of these things. Afraid to say them, afraid suddenly that if I tried to say them I would just fuck it all up and allow people who knew better to dismiss me as some crank who was out of touch with his profession. Why—or how—I found myself standing in my wife's living room asking, "Who the fuck cares?" I haven't a clue.

But I could have died.

It was the worst of times. It was the best of times. For three days after the moving van backed up to our house to pack and move my wife into her new apartment, the silence was almost a pleasure. She had arranged the van to come on a day that I was gone for most of the day, from early morning until evening, when it used to be time for me to shop and prepare for dinner; and all that was left in the house when I got home was my desk, with its computer. Not a chair, besides the office chair that went with the desk. Not a pot or pan. Not even a telephone. And even though my computer still connected to email, I didn't bother. Stripped like this was good, and I saw no reason to indulge in nonessentials. Though I felt alone, I felt something akin to freedom. For once I had said what I thought, and it felt, well, good—except, of course, for the fact that I had upset so many people I had considered friends.

As good as it felt despite my guilt, by the fourth day I was sick of eating pizza alone. I realized that things could not go on this way. I had a career. A good career before my author stepped in to screw it all up.

The more I thought about him, the angrier at him I became. It began to seem all his fault that I was about to go through yet another divorce. It began to seem unhealthy to indulge myself in radical fantasies of individuality, as my department chair decided to call it when he called me in for an informal chat.

"Don't listen to your author," my chair said, after I had done what could only be called an inadequate job of explaining some of what had happened. "He's sick. Just between you, me, and the wall, he's about to be let go."

"I thought he was tenured."

"Tenure," the chair said, "is not a sinecure. Especially when you involve yourself in moral turpitude," he added, darkly.

It turns out that in an effort to comfort a student, he had laid his hand on his shoulder. He was arrested, was in jail, and the student was suing him for sexual harassment.

I visited him in his jail cell. The jail was dark. It was overheated, and the air hung heavy, making it difficult to breathe easily. At first I didn't recognize him. "Is it you?" I said. But he didn't answer. "What happened?"

"A story laid in Spain, in Seville," he said, smiling gently.

"Did you do it?" I asked.

"Do what?"

"Harass that boy?" Harassment, especially sexual harassment, is a very serious matter, particularly in universities.

He looked at me with affection and great generosity.

"No. Of course you didn't. You wouldn't. It's not something you would do."

"I put my hand on his shoulder," he said. "I may even have given it a squeeze."

"So you did do it?"

"It's a question of intention, isn't it?" He grinned. "Life and art," he said. "The critics have won. According to them, I am only a perjurer and imposter. But who gives a flying fuck?"

"You know what your problem is?"

"No. But you're going to tell me, aren't you?"

"You asked too many questions."

"I tried to give you beauty."

" 'Beauty is truth, truth beauty?' " I said, snidely.

"Something like that," he said. "I merely tried to comfort the boy."

"For god's sake, why?"

"Because he told me his lover had just died from AIDS."

"Well, you gave up your freedom to try to do it. And you failed any-way. You can't give comfort to someone. Not like that. The world won't stand for it. Ask it why not, give people questions, and they'll lock you up just like they've done and kill you off with isolation, starve you until you give up all that trouble and doubt. How's that make you feel?" I couldn't hide the sound of secret gloating beneath my very real pity.

"Nobody is free," he said. "Only difference between you and me is that now I can see my bars."

I frowned.

"The bars behind which you've imprisoned me get their power and purpose from your delusions of freedom without responsibility."

"I? I haven't imprisoned you."

He just looked at me. "I used to think Sartre's *Freedom and Responsibility* was a very important essay until I began to wonder if we weren't insisting on responsibility so much that the judgments that resulted from an application of Sartre seemed to begin to lose heart and compassion. You chose; you were responsible for the choice. It was a hard judgment to make of oneself, though easier to make on other people; when it was a judgment made by others like the Students for a Democratic Society, it became a judgment harder to accept. So eventually we all let the notion of responsibility atrophy, placing all our emphasis on the freedom of choice. It took years. Decades. But now we've come to a time when young people of the same age we were can claim that any restrictions on their behavior—zoning laws, noise laws, drinking age laws—are oppression, because they restrict their freedom of choice without responsibility."

"Do you ever stop?" I said. "Look at yourself. You're in jail, man. You're as good as dead, if you can't get your story straight."

He laughed. "You and I are in league, aren't we? Our friendship is special, even if it is secret, because we understand each other's necessities. I can be as grim and nasty as you want to be right now except for the fact that I am always secretly happy. You see, I'll go on doing what I do because, like Kafka's Hunger Artist, I am too arrogant and full of pride to stop. And you'll go on doing what you do because you are the only person who can force me to at least feign some humility. You understand that these days, as proud as I may be, without you I am less than nothing. I appreciate that. And I really do give a fuck, you know."

"I know," I said. I would be hard-pressed to describe the sadness I felt at this moment. Finding my fifth wife gone and my house emptied was nothing to the hole that seemed to open inside of me, a hole I tried to fill with a rabbit by saying, "We give them certainties. Systems clothed in the garb of mystery."

"Sort of like car mechanics."

"Sort of," I laughed. "We abstract things for them so they can ignore the particulars. They don't understand a word we say, but they do understand that they don't want to face particulars. We don't always understand what we say. But we say it as though we are certain. They like that. They like the feeling of mystery that opaque abstraction gives them, the aura that if you just have faith in the system, it means something."

"Like cows," he said, "who want to believe they are not tagged for slaughter simply because they believe?"

"Though in what they believe, they aren't sure. Still, they send their children to us to be catechized . . ."

"I'm just an anachronism."

"Yes. And even though, or maybe because, you're anachronistic, we have to lock you up. My god, man, no one touches a student, even out of compassion, even without malicious intentions. Who can prove intent?"

"I could."

"But you won't. Instead, you'll let us put you on display and call you mad for even pretending. Even if it was only for an instant of compassion, you are dead."

"Who am I to justify the ways of art to man?" he asked.

"Bingo. Caught you. That's intertextuality, amigo. Caught you playing our game."

"No fucking way," he said. "Allusions illuminate. They don't complicate. It's not a hall of mirrors."

"Man, you are a waste, you know? What fun is it if your allusion doesn't reflect on Milton, which in turn reflects back on you and your allusion that reflects on Milton?"

"You mean what would you do for a living."

"You know what?" I couldn't help but feel some cruelty behind my words. "No one is ever gonna know you were alive. We'll see to that."

"So? What do I matter? Besides, somewhere out there are readers who know that somewhere in here someone is authoring the world. Eventually they'll find me. Not everyone has been born of an idea like you."

"There you go again. More intertextualities."

"More light," he said, smiling almost apologetically as if he understood that because he keeps insisting like this, eventually we have to kill him off publicly so that we can then mediate between the dead him and the moronic world which we so pretend to love with the bread of our mysterious certainties. "If I refuse to be born of an idea like Dostoyevsky's narrator, I can refuse to die of it. Caveat emptor: beware the person who sells you ideas without connection, whether the idea is of health or knowledge; beware the person who sells you system without heart, certainty without intention, who brings you not only unconnected ideas but their ultimate reductions, agendas. And most of all, beware the ultimate elitist clothed in democratic empathy."

"You know what? You are worse in your arrogance than all those kids in the sixties who spent summers in factories and push-button plants teaching the truth to workers otherwise too stultified or dumbfounded by beer and repetition to even know it. You are nothing more than a conceited autodidact."

"Ah, dismissal. Dante, Virgil, and Homer were autodidacts. But everyone is unworthy who comes before the invention of universities, huh? And universities, as we both know, do strange things to people. Even Dante in his strictures made room for non-Christian autodidacts outside of hell proper. Hell itself is filled with intellectuals who confute and confuse either others' arguments or their own understanding and behavior. But outside hell is a group of people who are not required to abandon all hope, an interesting group of people among whom, if I believed in Dante's diagram of the afterworld, I would be grateful to find myself. But the most elitist among the critics inside the gates and at varying levels of their professional careers, make no room for anyone besides themselves in their assumptive, consumptive elitism. And they just assume that students should be seen, and heard, and believed," he added by way of insult.

That was the last I saw of him.

I'm happy to say that although it took some doing, my author was given a choice of withdrawing from the university or facing criminal charges and that he chose to go. Once I had completed my twelve steps of therapy and was back on course, I finished up my book, *The Intertextual Dualisms and Hermeneutics of False Binaries in the Discourse of Agenda*, which, after my keynote address at the largest annual conference in my field, became a university press best-seller, selling well over five hundred copies. Dare I hope without seeming elitist that most of those five-plus-hundred buyers read and liked the book? It was well reviewed, or rather reviewed well in *Inkvat: A Journal after Post-Modernism*, an electronic journal run by a scholar who, out of principle, remains anonymous, although several of my colleagues believe the one editor is actually a consortium of scholars from very high-powered universities. It was, perhaps, because of my book and its reception, that I became a candidate for department chair and won handily—in a landslide, in fact—and even though there are those who point to the fact that I had no opponent, my friends maintain that it was the general support for my candidacy that prevented anyone else from tossing her/his hat in the ring.

I am also happy to report that I met a wonderful woman. A completely different kind of woman. For one thing, she is not an academic. She was my real estate agent. When she gets home in the evenings, she first likes to run the vacuum before she sits on a barstool and keeps me company while I prepare our dinner. Above all, she has no real preference for red or white, as long as it is wine.

Tradition and the Individual Imitation

I

Cinco de Mayo, 315 years after the Pueblo Revolt. I'm on my way to Santa Fe, although it's my first trip there and so I have no idea how Santa Fe it is. My head and heart are filled with questions about tradition and celebration, answers both wrong and right, brought to mind by the anticipation of seeing my good friend Dave, an elder member of the Santa Clara Pueblo. Things to talk about. Wondering how complacent in my questions and answers I have become, knowing from weeks of dinners with Dave when we both taught at Colorado College as visiting lecturers that complacency is not something Dave allows—not in himself; not in his friends, among whom I hope I'm privileged to count myself; not in anyone who is willing to enter the dialogue about culture and tradition that is like food for Dave.

Since last we saw each other, I have read the books he bought me, or convinced me to buy, a suitcase of heavy books like Michael Kammen's *Mystic Chords of Memory*[1] that made the airline's baggage checker shoot me a herniated frown as I watched my luggage trail off behind the rubber shawala hiding the brute handlers of baggage just waiting to test their mettle against the construction of my imitation brand-name soft-side suitcases patched with silver duct tape.

Cinco de Mayo, the day after hearing an Indian man read an essentialist poem, bad with guilt and New Age prospects, to a mixblood crowd in which the cross-blood Indios remained silent but the non-Indios were staggered in their essentials by what one young groupie afterward (essentially) called "the power of his poem."

It makes you wonder.

It makes *me* wonder, at least, as I drive up the "Turquoise Trail" in my Rent-a-Camry.

I pass through Golden, which is neither golden in wealth nor spirit, given the barefooted babies with drooping diapers; the school bus cabins, blocked up and yellowed by use; the hodge-podge of treadless tires and rusting children; and the plywood windows of houses scraped and peeled by weather that line the road with their porches out—once the homes of immigrants, shopkeepers who came from England and Germany, Holland, Belgium, Scotland, and Luxembourg to lay claim to land. They renamed the place Golden the way they renamed themselves and invented the tradition of Settlers, their movements and manners made manifest by the derivations of these words and names. They opened mines, and then, using the tricks of advertising, they seduced other immigrants into remaking their destinies along with their identities, transforming themselves from eastern farmers into western miners, day laborers, drunks, lawmen, and bartenders. The new immigrants to Golden, who would buy from and vote for the indigenous shopkeepers, and who would labor and remain generations after the minerals were mined and shipped and the rich spare land stripped of all but mesquite and cholla, but only after making the shopkeepers and mine owners wealthy enough to leave Golden behind, abandon these houses and move on—farther west in search of a more satisfied avarice, or back East in search of a consolidated transformation into the heads of established families, less often north along the Makah coast, and less and less often south into the land they cut from Aztlan and de donde they made Mexicans estan.

After Golden comes Madrid (pronounced Mad-rid in one of those ritualized divorces from reality accepted and propagated by the obscure mental processes of the unemployed miners), another mining town. A century after Golden's shopkeepers boarded up their windows, Mad-rid was invaded by hippies looking to get away from anger and truth. Get away they did, inventing a Mining Museum, rebuilding a general store and calling it a Trading Post, adding Art Galleries that sell not art but craft and often not even craft but guile, and installing coffee bars in the living rooms of anorectic houses. In Mad-rid they discovered that though in flight they still could have it all—have the money to send their free-form children to private colleges hidden beneath the veneer of uncon- and unre-stricted liberation, wearing the best of the beads themselves and selling the worst mounted on thin

66

silver etched with only the hint of designs appropriated from those very *indigenos* the shopkeepers of Golden had tried to extinguish.

Finally, I cross beneath the interstate and edge into the outskirts of Santa Fe, past AutoWorld, a sea of autos so large it seems to wave. I pull over behind a Texaco station to use toilets that, like those in Madrid, are for customers ON LY, and to use the pay telephone, perched like a winnowing fan out beside the highway where it's hard to hear. Dave directs me on to the landmark mall with a Red Lobster restaurant, where I park and wait, sniffing at the hint of truth about Santa Fe, yet unable to see right in front of me the Red Lobster's disguise of Southwestern adobe because I'm watching for Dave—who will take me downtown to La Posada for brunch.

II

At La Posada, we're early for brunch. While we wait for the help to set up, Dave draws circles of identities and arrows of influx and fluence on the heavy white butcher paper used to protect the restaurant's linen from people like him as we talk about bones.

Not too long ago, the pueblo to which Dave belongs won the right to repatriate the bones of its ancestors that had been mined, numbered, shipped, tagged, and stored in the basement of the Smithsonian. Some of the bones were older than grandparents or great-grandparents, bones hundreds of years old that had undergone a preparation, ceremony, and burial specific in its traditions, in its process, and in the meaning of the processes which may be called the same as belief. The belief in the meaning of the process was a part of the sacred and secular outlook and worldview of the tribe burying the bones. But whereas, perhaps, the sense of meaning and sacredness had not been lost or altered over hundreds of years, the processes themselves had—as the Santa Clara elders recognized. And now they were faced with a dilemma. Although they wished the bones to be reburied in their sacred or rightful place—the place from which they came and from which they departed on their journeys into the afterworld—would it be right and proper to rebury these bones using ceremonies that, in the time the bones were fleshed, would not have been appropriate, would perhaps not even resemble the ceremonies that were proper and appropriate? If the process and ceremony for burying bones creates and then prepares the way for the spirit's journey, wouldn't the wrong process conflict with the spirit of the bones and perhaps even block the spirit from the path it needed to take? Do the Santa Clara Pueblo people go ahead and risk this, and risk as well showing disrespect and dishonor to the bones of their ancestors by reburying them with rituals that may not even resemble the originals?

Where could the elders turn to find out how the ceremonies were performed?

In the case of bones that were two hundred years old, nowhere. In the case of bones that were one or two generations old, possibly to elders, to the narrative historians and keepers of the kiva. In the case of bones a hundred years old, they could turn to the anthropological cousins of the archaeologists who dug and stole the bones, looking to their records and writings to find descriptions of sacred and private ceremonies where they were allowed to see and hear them. But even given the knowledge that anthropologists, as outsiders, would not have been allowed to know all of the details—that aside, depending on people from outside the kiva to describe what happened inside the kiva was very risky. The pueblo would run the risk of copying or reproducing—imitating, if you will—the representation or imitation "seen" and recorded by people who had little or no idea of what they were seeing but who believed they knew what they should be seeing. In the extreme, the pueblo people might end up burying the bones with ceremonies that imitated the imitation of what a Pueblo ceremony should or ought to be.

What the Santa Clara Pueblo—or the Zuni, or any other tribe—decides is, of course, up to them and not to me or even Dave, individually—as he knows, turning from the problem of bones to dance, to the idea of tradition in dance, a subject not as ossified as the repatriation of bones.

Anyone who has ever seen a ceremony and celebration that uses the Matachina Dance recognizes Pueblo costumes in a dance completely pervaded by Christian, specifically Catholic, images, right down to the Virgin Mary. Indeed, without the masks, the colors, the feathers, and the laugh of movement, one would simply take the Matachina for another Catholic procession.

Slowly taking up this subject, Dave draws a large circle on the butcher paper, the circle of the Pueblo people, their culture and traditions; their beliefs and processes, or ceremonies; their way of looking in and out at the world; and their way of behaving in the context of that world. Beside it, overlapping it in the shape of a football, he draws a second, equally largish circle, which is the circle of culture of what may be called the ways of being of the Pueblo's Mexican cousins, with whom they intermarried, traded, fought, and modified their stories. The football shaped overlap, which Dave shades with angling lines, is the third traditional culture created by the two cultures interacting on and with each other. Gradually, if Dave is right, and I think he knows a lot, about which he has thought slowly and very carefully, the football enlarges; and the unshaded, partly eclipsed circles tend to wither. If for no other reason than to maintain them, the Pueblo (or the Mexican) people would have to rigidly fix the definition of "tradition" and adhere to it without the change that occurs simply by ceremonies being performed by different dancers, different singers, different elders or storytellers or leaders. Without change, things die. That is Dave's foundational thesis for these circles and for the way he shades the butcher paper. It is not Dave's thesis, however, or even a part of it, that change means that things are less—less meaningful, less "traditional," less powerful. In other words, he is not judging the change as reductive or vitiatory, but only as necessary or perhaps inevitable or even desirable.

As our overlapping football enlarges, there comes a curving double line with one large arrow point. A double curve, because it has to be large enough to be seen to influence and modify the right circle of the Pueblos and the left circle of the Mexicans, as well as the already existent intersection of the two. This is the arrow of Coronado, Oñate, and the Castilian *conquistadores;* the *encomienda* system; the slavery, brutality, death; Catholicism and its inquisitional agents, the friars who invent Cibola to get people to pay attention. No one, Dave seems to believe, can deny the power of their influence, negative or not; in some way, the way the Matachina has survived is a hymn to the power of "tradition." But—and I'm getting ahead of Dave here—it is a tradition that has changed so much that possibly a traditional Pueblo person of 1680 would not even recognize it, let alone recognize it as "traditional."

After the double arrow from above, which becomes a part of that enlarging football, Dave draws two other arrows, both double, though (and perhaps he's just running out of room) smaller. One is the arrow of invaders calling themselves "settlers," who bring with them their own attitudes and excuses they call their tradition, whether that tradition is the tradition of the farmer/shopkeeper or the tradition of the scout/soldier backed by armed Protestant mythologies. The other is the double arrow of anthropology and archaeology, the folks who come to study and dig and record, whether or not they speak a word of the Pueblos' language. Like it or not, as the anthropologists spent an entire week or month getting to know the objects of their studies; becoming familiar with their daily lives, their traditions, and the ways in which they perceived the process and meaning of them before recording them; transcribing and then rewriting them with easy interpo- and extrapolation; making additions and modifications and corrections, because like the fabulous John Neihardt they imagine themselves almost to "be" Indian (though Neihardt's worked it out so there's no "almost" in the absolute of his fakery); calling themselves "friends" in the way the people who stole Golden called themselves "settlers"; renaming and recasting their words to trick themselves and their readers—during their week (or month, even) they brought with them influence, seeds, for good or ill, of change.

In a way, given Dave's circles, you could imagine the anthros taking a bite out of the hoop to take home with them, leaving behind filler to complete the circle. Even without imagining that, you have to be able to understand that the very act of being studied (and studied as objects) must have been a force for change, if even to have Navajo people make up stories to tell because the real ones the anthros wanted to hear were out of season and thus could not be told, not even by one Navajo to another. And, if you insist that no Navajo (or Laguna or Pueblo) would have done this, we can only offer the strange feeling of compliment—"We're important enough to study"—combining with the yeast of wanting things to be whole—"We have this opportunity to let people know about us in some possibly 'real' way"—combining with the dough of hospitality and graciousness, the almost Homeric treatment of strangers who were willing to talk and who seemed (at first, anyway, before people realized that a belief out of context was not the same as a belief in context, especially where context—like process—was equal to, or greater than, the belief itself, which suggests how so many Indians did and do manage to be Christians within the context of their tribal ways) to want to understand. Just as the Nez Perce greeted and cared for Meriwether Lewis and his horses, I suspect the Navajo—or most any other band or tribe—were gracious to these strangers.

Anthro, "settler," and missionary all brought influence and change—and who can predict exactly which change is bad? The strength of whatever may be called a "tradition" does not live in a leaden fixity and adamant resistance to change but in its survival and continuation, in the viability of its being handed down grandfather or grandmother to grandson or granddaughter and in their being able to "use" it in the context of their processes, their ways of looking and believing, their ways of behaving.

III

Traditional. Tradition is a word like "civilization," and words are something "they" are always using to trick themselves. For Indians, however, the word tradition involves the debate over bones as well as over art and artifacts and the images or words that are infinitely reproducible, even if Black Elk never said anything like them. Arnold Krupat writes,

> It is also possible, as Karen Warren has written, to conceive "the debate over 'cultural properties' as a debate over the ownership of the past," where "the past" is "understood not only as the physical remains of the past (e.g., artifacts, places, monuments, archaeological sites) but also the 'perceptions of the past itself' (e.g., information, myths, and stories used in transmitting the past)."[2]

When the forces of nature decide to reveal Makah villages five hundred years old, eroding the mud that buried and preserved the artifacts and tools and lodges of an ancient Makah tribe,[3] there seems to be no question that if they value and are inspired by them, the artifacts and tools and images belong to the Makah people to be used, preserved, or displayed or not as the Makah people wish.

What happens, though, when a young Makah goes off to the city, carrying with him his images, his name, his traditions, and has children with a woman who is not Makah but who allows our Makah youth-become-man to raise his children with as much of the tradition and meaning and wisdom as he can in the cities? Do his children by right of a certain blood quantum inherit the "rights" to Makah images? If the eldest son chooses to become a woodcarver and in his artifice uses what are designated as "traditional" Makah images and symbols, is it okay for him to make a living by carving and selling in his artifice in Golden shops that get reinvented as "galleries"? Does the gallery have the right to photograph and reproduce the images of his carvings—even if only for flyers and announcements of shows or openings? Do they have the right to reproduce the images as photographic postal cards or posters? And when our Makah artist is no longer "with" that gallery, has the gallery purchased the copyrights? Or do they revert to the artist, his family, or even as far away in time and space as the tribe?

Sad as it makes me, it seems that the argument may be made that once money or goods exchange hands in a capitalist world, so have the reproductive rights. Argue and fume about capitalism and the Western notions of "progress," no matter what arguments we might present, it—that mass of Jell-O that absorbs pieces of fruit into one big jiggling tasteless goopy mold, IT—does not give a shit. It buys, uses by mechanical reproduction what it has bought ad infinitum or at least ad profitus asymptotem, and then—having approached the infinitely regressive end, the last dot of reduction, having squeezed out the last drop of blood and meaning—trucks it off to a landfill of purchased things to take its imaginary place beside newspapers, loaded diapers, and plastic bottles stamped on the bottom with "1." It buys, uses, and discards. Or, like the trivializing plots of television, it buys, uses, stores, and recycles when it seems as though more commerce may be fueled by its use.

The recycled value of an image bought and used can be increased by authenticating it; and the way commercial capitalism authenticates its endlessly reproduced images and ideas is to certify, to give artifactualities the Good Housekeeping Seal of Approval. In the case of "Indian" art and artifact, that certification is an act of the descendants of "settlers," those very people who returned to the East, after mining the West, to consolidate their gains and use them to be elected to the federal government, one of whose branches is the Bureau of Indian Affairs, which, after taking down names (for relocation, extermination, or slow attrition to the thinning formulae of blood quantum) of Indians, presumes to "tell" them who they are and who they can be, even though identity, real identity, is something that can exist even in disguise, unrecognized by bureaucrats and statisticians who count the heads hanging around the fort. Coyote or Frog do not require traveling papers any more than Moses needs to wear a Star of David.

The individual Makah artist, however, is not the representative of the consensual tribe. So is it in the consensus that the ownership of the past belongs?

What about the other "Indian" artist, a girl of Nez Perce and Osage descent who grew up in Los Angeles with Apache, Laguna, Hopi, Miwok, Costano, Quechua, Mexicano (or Mestizaje), Cherokee, Choctaw, and other mixed bloods or cross-bloods. If her first art images are from all of these people, then when she makes a drawing or painting forty years later and uses some of those images, is she appropriating cultural images? Are the images "hers"? Or is she expressing the growth of cross-cultural influence? If she is appropriating, then do we say that there are images that belong to an identifiable culture or cultural group and that only members of that group may use those images—and for what—for ceremony?

But also for sale?

Thomas Gilcrease, who made his money in Oklahoma oil . . . began to buy rare books and documents, then Indian art and artifacts of the region. The outbreak of World War II in 1939 made him even more cognizant that objects outlast people, and that the surviving remains of past cultures must be cherished.[4]

At the grand opening in November 1924 [of the Metropolitan's American Wing, R. T. H.] Halsey waxed eloquent about the Americanizing role of traditions ingrained in material culture. Somehow, all of that wonderfully glistening mahogany and all of those ball-and-claw feet would make new immigrants into more sober citizens.

—Said Halsey: "Traditions are one of the integral aspects of a country. . . . Many of our people are not cognizant of our traditions and the principles for which our fathers struggled and died."

—Said [Robert Weeks] de Forest: "We are honoring our fathers and our mothers, our grandfathers and our grandmothers, that their art may live long in the land which the Lord hath given us."

—Said Elihu Root (first vice-president of the Museum): Halsey, de Forest, Kent, and all the rest who made the Wing a reality "formed an old-fashioned American community, and in their spirit was born again that atmosphere that produced whatever was fine and warming and delightful in old American life."[5]

Says the literature of dominance: We must form a new old-fashion, that our artifice may last long in the tooth.

Said their Lord, who gave them Indian land: If you build your house on a foundation of sand, then everything depends from illusion.

Said the anthropologists: If you paint, paint brightly, and twirl the Virgin Mary with your Matachina Dance.

But Louis Mumford asked of the American Wing, "What is to keep us from harnessing machine production to a sickly desire to counterfeit the past?"[6]

What, in other words, is to keep and defend us from Disney?

How do we identify those privileged Indian artists—by blood, by community recognition? Or do we let the federal government decide and do it by identity cards: trump cards you can throw on the table to disguise your lack of character and to hide the fact that even you suspect that you are acting in accord with the literature of dominance and not survivance?[7] Is it then okay for a woman or man carrying a card or a certain quantum of blood to knock off jewelry with designs appropriate to his or her people and sell it to the descendants of Golden and Mad-rid's shopkeepers in search of turquoise or general weight?

The problem with some Indian art is that, while some is joyful and celebratory, a statement of color and shape or a joke on Jesus whose face is outlined in gunpowder and ignited, some of the painters (certified by the Heard Museum or by the front men and women for corporate appropriation to the National Museum of the American Indian in the Old Customs House) seem to have bought the fast-drying acrylic and gaudy colors of so-called Indian art as a bold excuse for a lack of training or vision, creating paintings that shout at the viewer that you can have modern traditions in which the modern informs the tradition and not the other way around.

But an Ojibway basket, if it even has colors, is subtle in them; Comanche beaders did not bead for brightness and easy visibility and targeting by enemies on the plains; and a Navajo blanket may have striking contrasts, but the tradition is formal, even staid. Using earth and clay, berry and bug, the traditions of image on rock or in sand seem less bold, more subtle and delicate, less influenced by the bald acrylic cry of modernity.

But—as well as So—like Pow-wows, perhaps, what people take to be Indian painting may be a myth of modernity creating and inventing "traditions." Like most dances, perhaps many of the images are at best reinventions, if not pure invention, which is not to say bad or inauthentic or wrong.

It may be, then, that because of perplexing and perhaps unanswerable questions, some Indians have—the way an artist may let art dealers certify their work as "art," which often seems to mean commercialized trivia—decided that the real question is not "tradition" but an authenticity of "blood," letting the dealers in blood quantum (a.k.a. the Feds or their corporate and collegiate fronts) certify them as authentically bloody enough to be called Indian, a certification that makes one neither more nor less Indian, and trivializes the issues as well as makes Indians into limited edition prints that can be bought and sold for a sum that increases the more the Feds can limit the numbers in an finitely regressive process of defining Indians down to a sum of zero.

IV

The Declaration of Independence is a hymn to Manifest Manners. All men are created equal and have the right to life, liberty, and the pursuit of happiness. Those are the parts we quote, the bones we dig out of the Declaration's grave worldview that, in the parts we are not taught to quote, indicate that it is not only all men—real men, who eat no quiche—but all white men, who are created equal.[8] We cannot blame Thomas Jefferson any more than we should blame Andy Jackson for a worldview that made their sworn and life-pursuing duty the obligation to subdue the barbaros who spoke no Greek or English, the Greek-less "primitive" people who became barbarians because they did not speak British Law any better than they spoke the Latin Columbus had his notaries read to the Indios, giving them the chance to submit to Spain before Columbus had his men attack and slaughter. We cannot blame Thomas Jefferson because that is what he not only thought but believed in a belief system that did not include the systems of other peoples or cultures and that definitely did not include the barbarians as "men" who had any rights whatsoever.

What we can blame, however, is the memorization of the created equal passages in the Declaration and the inability of memorializers to read further. What we can blame are the descendants of Chief Joseph allowing the descendants of Tom Jefferson and his manifestly destined worldview to "recognize" them or not in a way that makes the "recognition" downright Rousseauian: these recognitions are not understanding, they are the romantic nostalgias that invent the "noble" savage. To let Jefferson or Rousseau "recognize" who is "Indian" is a simulation of dominance created through Manifest Manners.

Gerald Vizenor used to say this.

Gerald Vizenor once quoted Standing Bear, who saw Sitting Bull, invented as the man who killed Custer, appear in a theatrical simulation in Philadelphia:

> Sitting Bull "addressed the audience in the Sioux tongue" and then the white man, the interpreter, misconstrued his speech in translation. "My friends, white people, we Indians are on our way to Washington to see the Grandfather, or President of the United States," and more was translated as the story of the massacre of General Custer at Little Big Horn. "He told so many lies I had to smile."[9]

Faced with imperialism performed as benevolence, as the kindness of strangers toward childish old men after the inevitable events of Destiny are manifestly concluded, Standing Bear can do nothing else but smile. It is time we learned from Standing Bear "to hover at last over the ruins of tribal representations and surmount the scriptures of manifest manners with new stories . . . counter the surveillance and literature of dominance with . . . simulations of survivance."[10]

Videotapes and images are artifacts. And artifacts—what one card-carrying, supposed "Indian" bureaucrat proudly claims as a lot of "stuff" with the kind of ludicrous and absurd pride that goes, not with ownership, but with working for the owners—are the bones of old stories no longer heard in the heart, which we don't have the ceremonies to tell.

In "Postindian Warriors," Vizenor's terminologies became their own definitions reflexively, the way a poem becomes its meaning in the dialogue between images and lines. Every time you were denied an absolute certainty, you were rewarded with a possibility; and it is in the mirrored images of certainty and uncertainty that the possibilities survived like the strobes of theatrical performance. The possibilities are stories that survive in dialogue, simulations of themselves. The "theater of tribal consciousness is the recreation of the real, not the absence of the real in the simulations of dominance."[11] These simulations of dominance include the acceptance of future events as though they are inevitable, true, but they also include the acceptance of un-recreated past events as though they are not only inevitable, but in some way good or necessary: without European encroachment and conquest and annihilation, we would not have had the smallpox vaccine. Possibly, but perhaps we would not have had smallpox either. Without the superior minds of the Europeans, we would not have had the weapons to defend our nation against the Soviet Union when it was soviet and union. Besides their attitude, the superior weaponry of the invading Europeans was, without question, disease—as they themselves recognized when they infested blankets with the smallpox virus and gave them out to starving and cold Indian women, children, and men. With the return of millennialism—which might have been expected, given the Yeatsian arguments over when the millennium occurs, 1899–1901 or 1999–2001, as well as the psychological concept of Endspurt, a renewed energy and creativity countered by a doomsday deathwishfulness at the close of centuries, especially millennial ones—fertilizer and disease remain the weapons of dangerous choice; and you don't have to introduce a disease to a colony to act in accord with the literature of dominance, you may just let it go to run its course.

The simulations of dominance are complicated, and the theater in which they are performed seems absurd. One thing we can be certain of is that remains are not survivance. To cherish them too much defines their pastability. Civilization becomes a spaghetti with simmering sauce to be consumed. By whom is a factionalism.

⋆

In the spring of 1995, Dave gave me a copy of an editorial by George F. Will. Faced with the continuing immigration and survival of Latinos and Chicanos and the changes coming about in Norte Americano society that from his perspective are "non-traditional," Will called for the forsaking of factionalism and a return to "traditional" American civilization. *Tradition* and *civilization*—these are the catchwords for historical revisionism, revising the truth back into the beloved falsity of invented historical consciousness in which Betsy Ross is not the self-promoting agent of icon, but a sweet colonial lady who sewed together stars with stripes.

"For all its faults, X is better than Y" is not an argument but a consolidation; and to the people who built the Alamo, the changes that have occurred and will continue to occur are not acceptable unless the "factionalists" act like those Indians who propose New Age solutions to impossible problems—become an Eco-Injun, for example, or a channeler who haunts the "new" artifactuality of the National Museum of the American Indian, which is housed so appropriately in the old Customs House in New York. Only then can he or she become acceptable. Only then will she or he seem consistent with the values of a traditional "civilized" society, which are commercial fabrications and not good.

The fabrications of Will's argument take protean shapes:

After Woman Killer lost at Big Horn, the banner headlines called it a "massacre," as if it were the Indians and not the cavalry that had surprised the encampment. In the literature of dominance, the image of the battle is linear, whites ranged defensively against mounted Indian attackers; while in the literature of survivance, the Lakota image is confused—soldiers mingled among soldiers, their allegiances distinguished only by their uniforms in a running dogfight.

The continued use of "settler" (as Senator Bill Bradley used it recently) describes people who broke their word and the rule of their laws to do all the things that have been done in the name of Our Lord Civilization, who gave his only begotten Progress, that we should be free from History.

The words they use every time they fear losing what they may not well deserve to have or use, or what they may never have had at all but for a trick of the light.

*

What George Will means by "civilization" is not what I mean by "civilized."

And even a simpleminded and cursory glance at American history makes you wonder when America ever comprised more or less than factions. When, since the immigrants first arrived on the shores of what became America, have those in power not pitted one faction against the other in order to maintain their power? World War II? Americans of Japanese descent might quibble there. The Civil War? Even limited by a degree in Domestic American Studies, you can think of at least a couple of largish factions. Vietnam? The maudlin sentimentalism and thoughtless patriotism of our late century may fool some into believing the modes of change are all acceptable. Or now? Pitting Indian against Indio?

George Will is not a fool, and he is not being fooled. In the post-Vietnam Age of Homogenization, every curd looks like a faction to those like him who own(ed) the process.

George Will is an object.

Two scholars collect and edit an anthology of women poets. Regret-fully, these scholars are forced, because of the number of women poets, to leave out Joy Harjo, not to mention Roberta Hill Whiteman, Linda Hogan, and a bunch of other Native American women; and it is in this regretfulness that they reveal how the literature of dominance continues to repeat itself.

Selection and inclusion is based, not on the poems so much, or on the audience, but on the poet's reputation. They overlook the fact that many Native American poets—women and men—choose to publish their poems with small and alternative presses, select a smaller but possibly more attentive audience, and by doing so, limit the range of their reputation—which is sometimes gained in the mainstream by hiring photographers or by sticking one's head in an oven like the perennially manipulative and self-proclaimed victim Sylvia Plath, one of the great self-pitying monologists of our millennial century.

Regretfully, these two scholars leave out more than one important voice in Native American poetry as easefully as they leave out the wonderful poems of Carter Revard or Ralph Salisbury. There is nothing new to this repetition of dominance and simulation of reality that comes out of a profound insecurity or uncertainty.

Like them, George Will's banalities result from insecurity. His debate over the remains, which he sees as uniquely factional, leads to a repetition of the argument over false correctives.

The respected and respectable Richard White tells the audience that the traditional view of the Alamo or Custer's "Last Stand" is primarily defensive, the innocents being attacked and massacred by the implicitly guilty. These defensive disasters have been made into icons of tradition.

Bemused, White adds that now it's the Indians at Wounded Knee or Sand Creek who are being reinvented as innocents forced into a defensive posture as history attacks and massacres them. They too are mythic inventions of the same order, according to the way White tells it.[12] The implication is that both versions are equally false, and yet this equalization is falsehood itself: Colonel George A. Forsyth was no innocent, no more than Chivington or Strong Arm Custer, who, given his lifetime subscription to the Buffalo Billed belief that Indians were savages to be subdued and eliminated, got a better afterlife than he deserved.[13]

At Sand Creek, the Cheyenne and Arapaho bands believed they had made peace with the whites:

> [T]he army might have been justified in attacking the hostiles. Unfortunately, the ones who had surrendered were easier to catch. . . . [Major Scott J.] Anthony encouraged the Indians to remain near the post, in order—there is no doubt of this—to have them available for massacre. About forty miles northeast, on Sand Creek, a wide, almost dry watercourse, there were about one hundred lodges of two hundred men and five hundred women and children, ten lodges being Arapahos under Left Hand, the other Cheyenne under Black Kettle, White Antelope, and other peace chiefs. . . . Chivington marched [600 to 625 men] to Fort Lyon . . . joined [by] Anthony with 125 men from the garrison, saying, "I believe the Indians will be properly punished." . . . They marched all night and

reached the camp at dawn on November *29* [*1864*]. *Some of the women saw them, but Black Kettle said there was no danger. He ran a large American flag and a white flag up on a lodge pole in front of his tipi and he and his wife and White Antelope took their position under it. Then the soldiers fired. . . . "We, of course, took no prisoners," wrote Anthony. Terrible things happened: a lieutenant killed and scalped three women and five children who had surrendered and were screaming for mercy; a little girl was shot down as she came out of a sand pit with a white flag on a stick; mothers and babes in arms were killed together. The pursuit [of the fleeing] continued for about five miles. Then the soldiers turned back to the camp, stopping on the way to mutilate the bodies. . . . [Colonel] Chivington and his hundred days' men returned to Denver, where they exhibited more than one hundred scalps and were lauded as heroes.*[14]

This is not historical revisionism, the rubric under which people dismiss the fact that their traditions are brutal, dishonest, and corrupt, and excuse the greed and murder that motivates them the way it motivated their ancestors. This is not reinventing the posture of the Cheyennes and Arapahos camped at Sand Creek as "defensive." It is recording the actuality. By implying that it is a reinvention, Richard White merely renews his subscription to the literature of dominance—which, take note, is not "the dominant literature" but the linguistic tricks that create an attitude that perseveres.

What Richard White implies is revisionist is not revision but revelation. He would be correct only if he illustrated how Sand Creek can be made an icon, a mythic competitor with historical time, and a source for false historical consciousness that can lead to many things: to the belief that things have changed, that greed and commerce do not use brutal means to justify themselves; or to Indians staying near the fort, hoping the white flag of their identity cards will protect them while they, themselves, thin their own numbers into nonexistence. Why else does the federal government encourage the Laguna people to identify and certify Laguna people on the basis of their having one-quarter Laguna blood? Because many Lagunas are of mixed Indian blood and thus would be disqualified in this generation, being one-eighth Laguna and one-eighth something else. Because if the Feds can get the people themselves to hang around the fort, in one or two generations there will be virtually no Laguna people left. They will have been annihilated, and the crazy thing is that they will have helped themselves be revised right out of history by peaceful acquiescence; and the federal government will be able to take away benefits, rights, and land belonging to the sovereign Laguna nation.[15]

V

Recently, a friend told me about an Indian writer who, partly out of youthful thoughtlessness and perhaps partly because he smells commercial gain as long as he can be packaged and sold as Indian, has called people to ask how dark their skin was and if they carried in their pockets The Card.

Nota Bene Descendants: the "Indian" writer is what gets sold, not the writing; and the writer is transformed here into the primary salesman, selling the writer's talent, which will be trivialized by commerce like the Indians on display in Buffalo Bill's Wild West Shows.

Indeed, this Indian person reproduces the self as "Indian" writer in the image of "Indian writer" that those editors and agents who tell him he has "commercial possibilities" already possess. He goes about imitating the imitation of the romantically represented noble idea much the way, as Richard White notes, Indians like Sitting Bull acted out the roles of "Indians" in Cody's Wild West Show, and in doing so imitated the imitations of themselves.[16] His writing need not be good, and it need not have any connection to the oral traditions or the speaking truly and well of Native American storytelling—it may confuse the end of commerce, which is gain, with the end of story, which is unending process, and become an end in itself. He may lose sight of the fact that Talent is not only a means of exchange that integrates the self into a community and the individuals of the community with each other, Talent is also a burden—literally—a responsibility that must be wisely used and maintained.

He may well find himself like Coyote, who says:

> "I'm the Coyote.
> And I am lonely."

He says,

> "I can't . . . use my powers anymore,
> and people,
> they ignore me now

they don't depend on me
and nobody will pla-a-y with me
nobody will listen to my stories!"[17]

This Coeur d'Alene story ends with the idea that if you give something to a white man that's going to do him some good, "he'll skin you alive!"[18] What the mostly white and mostly still dominant mainstream culture of commerce wants are the authentic pelts of Indian stories, in this case; and in selling his pelts, the writer may end up skinned alive, tied up and dead, needing Fox to step over him five times to bring him back to life. And even then, if he's like Coyote, he won't admit that he ever died and went to artifactual heaven.

This same writer is reputed to say that other mixbloods do not "write Indian"—whatever that means. And when called on to answer this question, he says that their writing doesn't "speak to the Indian" in him.

Sort of like a young woman writer saying Flannery O'Connor doesn't "write woman"—is that it?—or Katherine Anne Porter doesn't "speak to the woman in me?"

Or Richard Wright doesn't "speak to the homosexual" in me—or is it that he doesn't "write Black"?

Or Buchi Emecheta doesn't speak to the "African"?

Or Ngugi wa Thiong'o doesn't speak to the prisoner of politics in all of us?

Europeans are not the only people susceptible to confusing consumption with experience or the experience of being consumed with authenticity. And in this unimagined argument over authenticity, the issue becomes no longer an issue of imagination, which is a large part of identity or self-identification, but a problem of fantasy—a fantasy of blood and birth and ownership, a romantic nostalgia.

Consider the "Sweat Lodge," as told by Jim James, in which Sweat Lodge says, "Whoever desires to construct me will have the right to do so. / The one that builds me may pray to me for good looks, / or whatever he may wish, / the one that made me."[19]

"Whoever"?

Evidently. As long as "who" treats the Sweat Lodge with prayerful respect. As long as he or she "makes" it, does not simply buy it or reproduce it, but enters into the respectful construction and therefore meaning of it. As long as this making is personally involved and not a making only for public consumption.

Combine this with the Coeur d'Alene story "Cosechin," in which it is customary for the Indian who is going to use something from a tree (or fish, or whatever) to "ask permission first . . . / 'Mr. Tree may I use some part of you / or I need it . . . for warmth for my children."[20]

Last weekend, I was outside pruning some rather bony spruce trees, talking to the pair of them, explaining how I thought this would make them happier, help them grow taller and fuller, help them take advantage of their situation. My neighbor came over to see to whom I was talking in such a solicitous voice. After she left, it dawned on me that the argument can never be over who is Indian, who is an Indian artist, but over how—never over which images are whose, but how anyone makes those images their own, with respect and bearing the burden of talent's exchange and integration. Wasn't that why the Cherokees could adopt someone into the tribe and consider him or her fully a Cherokee because in spirit they were? If so, then they were not Cherokee for the public, but for themselves by integrative extension for their communities. And if they "taught" about being Cherokee after that, they did not organize New Age encounter sessions of forest excursions of tree hugging, they did it instinctively and humbly by example.

VI

The argument over who owns the past is an argument bureaucrats want Indians to engage in, especially if they'll engage in it with other Indians. It helps them trick themselves, like our lonely Coyote, into thinking they not only have something other people want, but worse, trick themselves into believing that by providing that "thing" they can control not only the process but the result. The result for Coyote is that he is flayed alive, abandoned by the one he gave himself to, dead and needing Fox to bring him back to life by stepping over him ritually, respectfully, prayerfully, five times (and even then Coyote, as charming and likable as our exemplary "Indian writer," refuses to admit to Fox that he was dead, claiming he was only asleep).

To frame the argument as an argument over the past, especially the "authentic" past, is to memorialize memorized images, stories, and meanings of the past, which is to memorialize Coyote as dead or flayed as though he were not dead, not flayed, which is to memorialize a fantasy. It is to come to inhabit a millennial, end-approaching delusion:

> Even as the erosion of millennialism caused people to contemplate the nation's past and future in terms of historical change and hence historical time, the proliferation of historical tales and anecdotes made mythical time—that is, heavy reliance upon sacred stories related to such moments as 1492, 1607, 1620, 1630, 1776, etc.—a genuine competitor with historical time and a complex source of false historical consciousness. Americans believed that they knew much more about the past than they actually did. Not only was the very basis of belief undergoing change, however; so was the place of belief itself in the nation's sense of its own traditions.[21]

After our first child was born, even though she was not particularly difficult, especially in relation to other children, my wife and I used to videotape her during the day; and then, exhausted, glad when she was finally down for the night, we would watch the tapes and tell each other how delightful and precious she was, how much she was to be cherished.

America has videotaped itself from here to the moon. Some people like to watch the tape and tell themselves how delightful America is and how much whatever remains American is to be cherished.

In the past ten or so years, Native America has been getting videotaped (again), and the possibility exists that what is recorded (memorized) and stored (dead, but for the sentimentalism that passive audiences "feel" re-watching them) are the manners that the arguers over the past cherish.

In seeking the "real," Indians, like all Americans, may be creating a fake.

By memorializing the real—not just dates, but the intangibles of blood—we are memorizing stories and not remembering them. Frey says, "Stories are always remembered, never memorized. Memorization results in a rigidity that can inhibit participation in the story.

Remembering encourages spontaneity and thus greater immediacy with the listener . . . [it] reunite[s] with the reality of the story, . . . reestablishes membership with the characters of the story . . . for the listeners as well as for [the storyteller]."[22]

The membering of identity demands re-membering. Membership demands re-membership. It cannot be legitimized by cards, numbers, or Stars of David. You may achieve the recognition by the community as a member of its story, but you cannot stop being a part of that community. It's this latter that makes "Indians" fearful of Wannabes. People who Want-to-Be Indian, Want-to-be-a-Real Indian, or anything else never involve themselves in the processes. They do not remember anything but nostalgias, and once membership is no longer popular—as it will not be—they will not only let their membership lapse, but they will move on to better facilities, newer clubs. The community is shunted aside in a process of dis-membering and disremembering.

VII

In the Heard museum, hidden in the glare of all those big paintings, is a colored pencil drawing, framed along with the artist's pencilled note saying how surprised and honored she was to have the curator ask to display her work in a museum. It is a moving drawing—evocative, delicate, and true—and true is all I care about, not whether the government certifies her as authentic or she sells herself as Indian, or whether she has "less" blood in her veins than one of the other represented artists.

A supposed Indian with the trumps of identity would not question these paintings' authenticity or traditionalism. But a supposed Indian, whatever machinations produced the ace of his identity, has already allowed the federal government to determine what is or what is not Indian without considering that if he lets the government do that, he has accepted the government's final and inevitable statement that a particular tribe or people are no more. That's what the government wants from the Laguna people. It wants them to subscribe to the literature of dominance. That's why the Santa Clara Pueblo invites the young people home.

Identity cards, like pow-wows with "traditional" dances and art museums with "authentic" paintings, may be a subscription to the literature of dominance, not survivance. Survivance asks Indians to burn their cards and dodge the BIA draft—or at least to doubt and wonder at them, to refuse the federal definition of their anti-selves in the absence of the real, to stop harvesting the contempt of millennial imperialism.

> "For anything I see," said Dr. Johnson's friend, Old Meynell, "foreigners are fools." There has probably never been a time when the majority of Englishmen would not have agreed with this sentiment, adding, perhaps, that most foreigners are frivolous and lubricious rascals. Certainly at the end of the nineteenth century this insular mixture of contempt and suspicion was general at nearly every level of English society. No doubt a connection exists between England's imperial expansion at that time and the intensity of national insularity that accompanied it . . . splendidly isolated from . . . the great intellectual ferment on the continent."[23]

The ferment is intellectual now, and it is also cultural and axial. A journalist's call for everyone to join his isolation and submit to his mixture of contempt and suspicion of the so-called factions that are growing and changing is a sign of his class, not his national, insularity.

The problem is that everything is connected like dandelions. Painting, speaking, dancing, and storytelling, like all the other things that may be called "Indian" (or specifically called Nez Perce or Choctaw or Osage or Miwok or Costano), embodies change. Especially in the written literatures derived from a highly oral tradition in which the story told contained within itself the seeds of change according to audience, according to the corroborators who attended the telling and could interrupt and modify at any point along the story line, according to circumstance. The story loses its ability to change when it becomes memorized, memorialized for recitation; when it loses its ability to accept its origin in change and growth; when it mythologizes time and ties event to the leash of the myth. Indian stories of survivance are comic as myths are never comic. To call traditional stories of creation, of adolescence, of living and dying, of the journey onward "myths" is to call them dead, like the Latin mass of Catholics or the anti-comedy of George Will calling on "us" to act like "him" in a hyper-reality of simulated civilization and the ruined representation of renewed millennialism in which he wants "us" to believe that "he" knows more about the past than we.

Comedy, comic stories, do not search anxiously for the real thing and do not submit themselves to the melancholy of dominance. Doubt and wonder produce laughter. Doubt and wonder are comic, not tragic. Doubt and wonder mean that the argument is not over the ownership of the past, but over the processes of the future informed by the changed and changing past.

Rachel Antonia Penn, six years old, saw two Quechua girls dressed up all in white one Sunday morning as she was riding the 85 Toyota with her mom. Wondering why they were dressed like that, she suddenly said, "I know, Mom. They're on their way to their First Confusion."

The Matachina Dance may have been the Pueblo People's first confusion, but they have made it their own, and it survives.

William Anthony Charles Penn, two years old and named for grand- and great-grandfathers with as many handles as William Penn Adair Rogers, bounced on the bed where I had folded his clothes, packing a suitcase for our journey, and began to knock the folded clothes onto the floor.

"Stop," I said.

He didn't.

"Willy, stop! I'm serious."

He stopped bouncing up and down. "Don't get serious, Dad," Willy said.

"Okay. I won't," I said when I stopped laughing.

But how can I not when downtown Santa Fe is about as close to the real thing as Disney is to Pocahontas, a place the first immigrants to Golden may have emigrated to, and it makes Dave and me a little serious? Overwhelmed by the truth, over-represented by the made-for-tourist kitsch of the downtown square and the noise of clicking cameras as loud as a tour bus, I can't help it. It reminds me of Umberto Eco's statement that in seeking the authentic, Americans invent the absolute fake. Dave can't help it because he has friends from the pueblo who can no longer afford to live in the place that is theirs, has been theirs, and in all likelihood may well not be theirs in the future. Even if these friends of his were to change, they could not adapt, not to this—because to adapt to this you have to counterfeit the future and adopt a commercial fantasy, become a middle man or middle woman who sells channels through crystal skulls purchased at Tiffany's or wears a Pendleton blanket in the National Museum of the American Indian and lectures tourists on how "they" have fucked up the world and now it's up to Indians to help them rescue it, or adopt unimagined poses like William Least Heat Moon and Jamake Highwater, or package and sell your "Indian" or "Indian writer" self to the mainstream and then deny that ever you have been dead. You have to trump with your identity card or trumpet "civilization" and call for a "domestic Ethnic Studies" program because the "domestic" leaves it not only in your control but also unchallenging. And it too, like American Studies, can intensely study nostalgic fakes.

Baudrillard writes in *Simulacra and Simulations*, "When the real is no longer what it used to be, nostalgia assumes its full meaning. . . . There is a proliferation of myths of origin and signs of reality; of second-hand truth, objectivity, and authenticity."[24]

These myths and second-hand truths are all around you, especially in Santa Fe, having proliferated around Taos with the strangely impassioned dullness of D. H. Lawrence's late sermons and the bright vaginal kitschiness of Georgia O'Keefe's unimagined paintings, and having flowed downward like water seeking its lowest level to be dammed in Santa Fe by middlemen, under-dealers in second-handedness who argue that in destroying the ability for people to live in Santa Fe they are actually helping Santa Fe move forward into the twenty-first century. As much as the "Song of Hiawatha," Santa Fe is a memorial to dominance, to the manners manifested by the Dutch-American who says on camera that we have to limit immigration to preserve America for Americans. *Ratio obscura*, indeed.

So when we claim that the world has changed, we are claiming that some people out there know all too well the attitude of dominance and how it works to continue the invention of Manifest Destiny with its emphasis on the axis East to West, its assumptions that without the generous contempt of the English, or the sometimes self-hating contempt of the French, or the burgomaster contempt of the Belgians and Germans, this continent would never have had A or B, let alone X and Z; the continued stereo-mythologizing of the lazy and greasy

Mexican or Guatemalan and his or her need of the CIA at home and abroad; the refusal to understand that hundreds of years ago indigenous people began scientifically engineering better crops, like corn, by cross-breeding and grafting, and better ways to grow them by enclosing food crops with pest-repelling plants or irrigate them in tiers descending a hillside, or to realize that Bayer did not invent or discover aspirin but only patented and claimed what *indigenos* had already discovered.

American Indian people themselves, along with their cousins on a North-South axis, have the most difficult job of all. They have to maintain their knowledge and awareness of this attitude without succumbing to the instinct to mythologize history and life. They have to find a way to not get serious and to aim the argument, not at the ownership of the past but of the future; not at the images themselves, but at what the images mean; at the process, not the artifact. They have to be careful not to revise history or tradition, and at the same time to allow it to reveal itself—and tradition, like history, reveals itself not by mannered manifestations of artifactuality that try to tell us what we have been, but by humorous suspicions of how we can continue to be.

Leaving the Parlor

José Saldívar quotes Kenneth Burke's *The Philosophy of Symbolic Form* to describe what he calls the "conversation of American culture":

> *Imagine that you enter a parlor. You come late. When you arrive, others have long preceded you, and they are engaged in a heated discussion too heated for them to pause and tell you exactly what it is about. . . . You listen for a while, until you decide that you have caught the tenor of the argument; then you put in your oar. Someone answers; you answer him; another comes to your defense; another aligns himself against you, to either the embarrassment or gratification of your opponent, depending on the quality of your ally's assistance. However, the discussion is interminable. The hour grows late, you must depart. And you do depart, with the discussion still vigorously in progress.*[1]

Saldívar calls this a "wonderful allegory," which

> "*depicts the cultural conversation as a series of rhetorical exchanges, with people asserting, questioning, answering, defending, attacking, and sometimes changing their positions. It is an unending conversation . . . [and] so that we don't become too entangled, with pistols in hand, Burke supplies a nice twist in his discussion of the cultural conversation: he places the verbal contests in a genteel parlor setting.*[2]

The quotation may work as a framework for Saldívar's discussion of Texas border narratives, but as a description of the cultural conversation as it continues to exist, I am struck by other possible variations. For while José Saldívar uses Burke's parlor gentility to mean a conversation among friends, the question arises: What if they are not friends but strangers, or even antagonists struggling for the same cultural space? Like a parlor, the space available for occupation by the conversants is limited, and it becomes a matter of comfort.

Once there are too many people to sit comfortably in the parlor, the noise level rises to a din. People apologize or fume as they bump first into one conversant and then another, and stentorian voices turn raucous or even thersitical.

Imagine that the parlor is the United States, enduring all the pressures that "border narratives" implies. If we bring the quotation from Burke to bear on the broader cultural conversations entered into by the diversity of Americans, we can discover some of the assumptions and presuppositions as well as some of the hidden forces still at work on those people who once were excluded from the conversation—Chicanos/as, Latinos/as, Blacks (African-American, as well as African or Caribbean or Latino/a), Asians, and Native Americans—and even perhaps touch implicitly or indirectly on the similar experiences of European immigrants as they came to the United States—Jews, Irish, Poles, Italians, and so on.

For three hundred years the parlor, built on stolen land, has been occupied mainly by white people calling themselves Christians, who derived their descent, their plantational assumptions, and their initial rights to power from Britain.[3] At least in the academic parlor—and I suspect in the world at large—the primary dominance of the "conversation" was British, not "European." British Literature was the "great" literature that all of us had to learn about. American Literature was a younger sibling rival for attention that, as it grew up, continued to define itself in opposition or similarity to British literary value. The very image of Ralph Waldo Emerson calling for a specifically "American" literature in a speech at Harvard to a bunch of pure-bred WASP males makes a metaphor out of my problem with Burke's parlor conversation and its supposed gentility. For I suspect gentility, though it may derive from "civility" and a sense of propriety, always derives in part from the assumed power of those in control of the definitions of "culture" and "civilization." In other words, to tolerate Emerson's call for an American literature is somewhat like tolerating the appearance of your maid asking for an hour free to take her kid to the hospital. It is easy to say, "Sure. Just be back in time for drinkies?"

British literature proved a remarkably flexible umbrella, reaching out to bring into its civility incomplete, fragmented oral narratives such as *Beowulf*, the "first" epic composed in English. To call the

Anglo-Saxon of the Beowulf poet English is a real stretch, even to someone like me who considers Shakespeare the beginning of "modern" English and who finds Chaucer and Sir Thomas Mallory eminently readable in their originals. It is such a stretch—it helps to have studied German, and the older the German the better—that you could argue that anything with a Sanskrit language base could qualify as being composed in English—all you need to do is go a bit farther back in the history of European literatures. Indeed, the argument seems to be made even without acknowledging it. Somehow, too, the Icelandic sagas got invited into the parlor: my favorite, Njal's Saga is brought in, I suspect, because it implies or hints at the oral, anonymous poet's record of the "influence" of Christianity and the so-called change from "Pagan" to "Christian"—so-called, because the change recorded in Njal's Saga is more superficial than substantive, reminding me of the converted Catholic Lakota elder, chided by his priest for making a venison stew on Friday, who tosses water at the stew and declares, "I baptize thee fish!"[4]

However, like most of the British Christian assumptions, they succeed only if the participants in the genteel parlor conversation are kept to people who want almost genetically to accept, believe, and propagate the same assumptions: that "pagan," like "oral," is somehow less than "Christian" or "written." Not only to propagate these assumptions, but at the same time to remain continuously flexible, allowing the ever-wider circle of "English" literature to include anyone they like—as long as he is white or he can be made to resemble white (the great Russians, Dante, the Bible, and the honored Homer). Homer is decidedly "oral" in his augmentations, circularities, formulae, his economy and scope; but we forgive him that orality because he was pre-Christ. After all, in a strange irony, Dante forgives Homer his "barbaros" paganism—his otherness and non-Christianity—simply on the basis that Homer could not have known better. Indeed, Dante places Homer in the only region of the afterworld that would be either interesting or fun. When asked, I have always said that if the afterworld resembles Dante's configuration, the only place I would like to go is to the circle outside the gates of hell where Plato, Aristotle, Homer, Odysseus, George P. Elliott, and Grandfather all pass their spirit days. The Inferno itself is too tormented, Purgatorio too much like modern life, and the Paradiso too sensually insensate and dull for the non-Christian stuck like the Midwest with a bunch of homogenes who run on C-type batteries.[5]

Evidently, the priests of English literature are willing to overlook the barbarity of Homer because, well, eventually it was written down. And I guess they have to forgive his orality as well because after all, their Bible is a set of oral stories that, not unlike the Odyssey, got written down. Homer at least was, if you stretch it, white. Though three thousand years ago he may have exhibited a much stronger melanin content in his Mediterranean skin, over the passage of linear time he has paled significantly.

As for Njal's Saga, while it may record the "influence" of Christian whiteness, from another point of view, it also records the cultural resistance to the colonization of Christian missionaries. Structurally, the saga does end synthetically with the call for peace among the fighting factions and familial "tribes" of Iceland. But though Christians would take credit for it, this is not Christianity but self-preservation, the quite-logical stated supposition that if they don't achieve peace, they will wipe each other out of existence. If they wipe themselves out, they will wipe out their culture. Even if they wipe out only their warriors, they will erase their ability to resist colonization. Though a Christian critic would see it otherwise, the writing down of this oral saga or legend may well be an anonymous poet's warning against the invasions of the monks, who are so certain that their way is the right way that they will kill anyone who remains too insistently "barbaros." It may not be recording the gradual influence of Christianity but celebrating the Icelandic resistance. And thus the funniest, most lively parts of the saga are moments such as when two "families" are fighting:

> When his enemies came up to the house they did not know whether Gunnar was at home; so they wanted someone to go up to the building and find out. Meanwhile they sat down outside. Thorgrim the Norwegian climbed up on the roof. Gunnar saw a red coat appear at the window and lunged at Thorgrim with his halberd and struck him in the middle. Thorgrim's feet slipped from under him, he dropped his shield and tumbled from the roof. He then walked over to Gizur and the rest of the group who were sitting on the ground. Gizur looked at him and asked: "Well, is Gunnar at home?"

Thorgrim answered: "Find that out for yourselves! All I know is that his halberd is!" With that he fell dead to the ground.[6]

In the age of Disney, where Pocahontas is transformed from a thirteen-year-old who is kidnapped, forcibly converted to Christianity, and married to John Rolfe, into a consenting woman of age in a rocket bra and Macarena skirt, I realize it is difficult for most people to see this as funny. But it is.

This same resistance is in the celebratory novel by Tomas Rivera, . . . y no se lo tragó la tierra.[7] In Tierra the orality, the anonymous near-absence of the narrator, who "overhears" a "lost" year's worth of his community's conversations, creates or envisions the survival of his community, his people. He does so in the face of children being shot by playful field bosses or of adults and children being required to work exceptionally hard for substandard wages while living in substandard housing or riding dangerous flatbed trucks standing up all the way from South Texas to Michigan to pick crops for the descendants of the "Christian" immigrants who "influenced" the indigenous culture(s) of the Americas, killing or enslaving anyone who was too resistant to the firepower of their assumptions.

Equally dangerous to resistance, however, is compliance.[8] What Rivera exhibits in Tierra is not the compliance of the people his narrators record. Although the voices have a what-can-you-do attitude much of the time, these are not voices of submission as much as the orally produced communal voice of survival, of a generational understanding of how one person is less important than the whole collective of the community. It is a powerful voice that resists the perceptions and self-perceptions that colonizing whites produce and reproduce—Mexicans as passive and easily manipulated—and it is a resistance we are allowed to overhear as though we stood just outside the place of Chicano cultural conversation.

Tomas Rivera's narrative control is astounding. Here are the boy's and father's voices, followed by the narrator I have described as overhearing his community:

"I'm very thirsty, Dad. Is the boss gonna be here soon?"
"I think so. You can't wait any longer?"
"Well, I don't know. My throat already feels real dry. Do you think he's almost gonna be here? Should I go to the tank?"

"No, wait just a little bit longer. You already heard what he said."

"I know, that he'll fire us if he catches us there, but I can't wait."

"Come on now, come on, work. He'll be here real soon."

"Well . . . I'll try to wait. Why doesn't this one let us bring water? Up north . . ."

"Because he's no good, that's why."

"But we could hide it under the seat, couldn't we? It was always better up north . . . And what if I make like I'm gonna go relieve myself by the tank?"

And this is what they started doing that afternoon. They pretended that they were going to relieve themselves and they would go on to the edge of the tank. The boss became aware of this almost right away. But he didn't let on. He wanted to catch a bunch of them and that way he could pay fewer of them and only after they had done more work. He noticed that one of the children kept going to drink water every little while and he became more and more furious. He thought then of giving him a scare and he crawled on the ground to get his rifle.

What he set out to do and what he did were two different things. He shot at him once to scare him but when he pulled the trigger he saw the boy with a hole in his head. And the child didn't even jump like a deer does. He just stayed in the water like a dirty rag and the water began to turn bloody . . .

"They say that the old man almost went crazy."

"You think so?"

"Yes, he's already lost the ranch. He hit the bottle pretty hard. And then after they tried him and he got off free, they say he jumped off a tree 'cause he wanted to kill himself."

"But he didn't kill himself, did he?"

"Well, no."

"Well, there you have it."

"Well, I'll tell you, compadre. I think he did go crazy. You've seen the likes of him nowadays. He looks like a beggar."

"Sure, but that's because he doesn't have any more money."

"Well . . . that's true."

It is a compliment to Tomas Rivera that I feel compelled to quote at such length from his short but lyrical, orally founded and orally structured and presented novel. It is also a comment on our age that my students don't quite get it and sometimes don't care. And it is a comment, as well, on the terminologies of the cultural conversation.

Rivera's narrator subscribes to the Dandelion Theory of the universe: everything is connected; connections do not need us to occur, they only need to be perceived and celebrated, though there are people who see no beauty in the connectivity and so would kill them. Where water metaphorically connects life and spirit as well as the religious life of the narrator's mother with the actual, real thirst of her son, it also connects us to the field boss who, meaning to scare him, accidentally shoots and kills a boy who goes too often to the water tank to drink. Not only do we have the modulations of the voice in our ear—the slight but so effective question of the thirsty child, "Is the boss gonna be here . . . ?" repeated in "Do you think he's almost gonna be here?" with that word "almost" tucked in to give us a sense of the child's despair and beginning of the loss of hope but willing to cling to his father's belief. In Spanish, this "Ya" (almost) combines even more effectively with the "Usted cree" (Do you believe). Here, as with other resistant oral cultures, thinking is creating is believing (it makes the world and makes it one's own), and this watery scene connects to the (false) spirit-water of other chapters, which begins the boy's loss of faith in the things his mother believes and leads to the title's meaning, which is that when he doubts the devil and God, the earth does not open up and devour him alive.

Rivera refuses to editorialize, his narrator saying only, "Ni saltó como los venados" (he didn't even jump like a deer does), offering us the colonizer's reduction of Other to the level of an animal hunted for sport, which has become a necessity because of the colonizer's tampering with population controls in nature. The horror of the scene: the attitude that allows a boss (viejo)[9] to think of Chicanos as nothing more than labor to be used and cheated, and that allows him to see the Other's child as nothing more than something that can be toyed with, and with the usual violence of the colonizer's playfulness that is not unlike the sudden striking blows of four-year-old boys at play; the feelings of the fathers and mothers and other children in the field; the comparison of the child's body to a dirty rag (trapo sucio); and the water, the water that begins to turn bloody—all of this is left to us and demands our active, imaginative participation in the rhetorical process. The impulse to editorialize here would be extreme, to make sure we get the full force of this scene. But it is actually in staying out of it, in keeping his thumb out of the pan, that Rivera makes us feel the most.

"And the child didn't even jump like a deer does."

Capitalism—which in some ways I am not entirely opposed to—reduces labor to human units and then removes the humanity from the formerly communal relationships of production. The boss wants to wait to catch his workers breaking or disobeying an inhumane or absurd rulishness so that he can fire them and not have to pay them after they have done most of the work. The resistance to this tendency of capitalism is community—Burke's and Saldívar's parlor—and humane humor that does not sugarcoat or hide the truth. In *Tierra*, on one of the trips north in a flatbed truck, a voice says, "What a stupid woman! How could she be so dumb as to throw that diaper out the front of the truck."

Most important, Rivera refuses to allow the disconnections that the culture of the field boss would make: we hear two people talking, one trying to "buy" the sympathetic misperceptions that the boss, after irrationally killing the child who was thirsty, even though he got off scot-free, jumped out of a tree because "they say" he wanted to kill himself.

They say?

I'll bet.

Let me ask you: if one person consumes a bottle of aspirin and another puts a loaded pistol in his mouth and pulls the trigger, which one really wants to kill himself?

The truth: "But he didn't kill himself, did he?" answered by the reluctant, "Well, no" and the return comment by a voice, "Well, there you have it."

Or the subsequent recognition of the truth, when the first voice says, "He looks like a beggar," as though we are supposed to buy into what "they" say and feel sorry for this guy because, already beggared by his inhumanity, he has murdered an innocent child and now is incapable of functioning well in the world he took active and violent part in creating. We are not to pity him. He looks like a beggar because he doesn't have money, not because he is accepting responsibility for his actions or because the social contract has forced him to accept responsibility for his actions. Indeed, the social contract, the parlor in which this murder is contextualized, lets the former boss go because all he has done is repeat the very actions that built the parlor itself.

"Well . . . that's true."

The contained emotions are striking. But the containment is the implied author's and not ours. Below the horror we feel is a kind of matter-of-fact humor in the interplay of these voices, a bemused, if not amused, humane, and calm recognition of the truth. In the context of this parlor, the field boss's supposed pain is an invention, a sympathetic romanticization (he was suicidal, poor man) that reveals the bathos of a world that gives up its humanity and then creates lies of humaneness to fill in the hole of loss.

This parlor, where Chicanos have been commonly thought of as little more than interchangeable labor that can be treated like a hunted animal (and commonly thought of as a slightly higher animal than Native American people, even including the latest romance with Indian things), is a hole, an emptiness that is dark. For the narrator of *Tierra*, the locus is beneath another family's porch, where he can overhear the voices and where he is *outis*, a no one — much like Odysseus, the clever *outis* — until the children discover him and throw rocks at him and the dogs keep barking at him and he has to come out and reveal his presence:

> . . . Everyone was surprised that it was him. He didn't say anything to them, just walked away. And then he heard the woman say:
>
> "That poor family. First the mother and now him. He must be losing his mind. He's losing track of the years."
>
> Smiling, he walked down the chuckhole-ridden street leading to his house. He immediately felt happy because, as he thought over what the woman had said, he realized in reality he hadn't lost anything. He had made a discovery. To discover and rediscover and piece things together. This to this, that to that, all with all. That was it. That was everything. He was thrilled. When he got home he went straight to the tree that was in the yard. He climbed it. He saw a palm tree on the horizon. He imagined someone perched on top, gazing across at him. He even raised one arm and waved it back and forth so that the other could see that he knew he was there.[10]

Connection. The dandelion theory of all with all. The discovery and rediscovery. And how is it done in this darkness? By the spoken word, the orality of communal and participatory narrative, storytelling. Bartolo, the troubadour who records peoples' lives in his poems, tells the people to "read the poems out loud because the spoken word was the seed of love in the darkness."[11] This is the same spoken word of other cultures that are now resisting their treatment under colonial capitalism, the same creation and recreation, the same humored way of survival. The cultural conversation begins with imagining that there is someone else perched across from you, gazing across at you. You begin by waving so that he can see that you know he is there. You recognize your self and recognize the presence of another self with which you can form a community, which in turn creates other selves, other voices that enlarge the community that creates even more other selves and voices until the parlor has to be expanded.

In terms of labor, the resistance to Christian capitalist assumptions begins with movements such as the Farmworkers Union in California. It happens again with other people who resist the loss of humanity inherent in bureaucratic power relationships—the lost humanity of field bosses, middle managers, and lunchroom monitors. The people who resist find themselves willing to walk out of the parlor and have the conversation in places that are not sanctioned by the WASPishness of Harvard, the canon of British literature, or the church that in one way of looking substitutes mystery for humanity—to sit in the tops of trees and rediscover the connectedness.

Indeed, it is the Chicano and Indian resistance to being made into Other and categorized as cheap labor to be used and cheated that has revealed to so-called white males in their beleaguerment how they have allowed themselves and their children to become nothing more than interchangeable human units. It surprises the white males that it is Tomas Rivera or Linda Hogan who emerges from the darkness, having begun the connection of this to this and that to that. The white males feel sorry for themselves. Now that they are conditioned to being interchangeable parts, those who are given to it resent anyone's refusal and resistance, because deep down in that hole they wish they could have known what those who know the spoken (or the written-as-though-spoken) words believe, that (orally used) words are the connecting seeds of love in the darkness. In his condition of loss and emptiness, the field boss feels that his masculinity is at stake, so he crawls on the ground to retrieve it, and it misfires like a rifle, killing an innocent child and leaving the field boss alone in the pusillanimous dark.

It is hopeless for the field boss. For all field bosses. But white is not a color, it's an attitude. People are not born into psychological whiteness, and thus not all so-called white males want to be field bosses. These, too, can resist. They need not feel resentment. I have great sympathy for the fact that—as people inured by their history of assumed superiority and willingness to inflict their assumptions on Others, as people who were in the parlor when José Saldívar arrived and who stay in the parlor long after Tomas Rivera has left—to reexamine their assumptions way down where the dandelion roots tap into the aquifers takes something akin to a leap of faith combined with exceptional trust in themselves, both of which muscles are weakened by their history of assumptive superiority and power.

The main framework, the necessary musculature, is oral: words, the seeds of love, used to rediscover the connections of storytelling, of creating a livable world and making it everyone's own in participatory words. Listening, but with imagination, as though the story was a matter of life or death. For that is, ultimately, the answer Rivera offers us: voices speaking, reading poems aloud, talking.

And that is why José Saldívar likes the quotation from Burke's Philosophy: because Saldívar—coming from an oral culture that continues to survive the field bosses and their assumptive attempts to destroy and maim, coming from orality, which is more able to survive than the formerly supposedly "superior" written culture of British colonization because orality strengthens both the speaker and the listener and joins them in perhaps not a genteel conversation but an engaged, passionate exchange—is a person who loves creative talk.

To rewrite Burke:

They have to imagine that they are in the parlor that Rivera enters late. When he arrives, they have long preceded him, and they are engaged in a mild discussion. They pretend that it is heated, too heated for them to pause and tell him exactly what it is about. . . . He listens for a while, feeling a little out of place, until he decides that he has caught the tenor of the argument; then he puts in his oar. No one answers, though some are embarrassed by his insolent intrusion. Rivera, made aware by the sudden chill of his idiomatic difference, feels equally embarrassed — it was not his intent to cause discomfort. He leaves, goes out onto the porch, and the conversation regathers its inertia and continues, an interminable discussion about whether or not Rivera should have been allowed into the parlor in the first place. They needn't worry. If Rivera has the audacity to return another day, he will leave once again, feeling some humiliation, perhaps, but also some determination, which he will use to build an open gazebo, to find people who are not embarrassed to talk with him, even heatedly. They will build the gazebo right next door. And then the people in the parlor will begin to hear laughter and argument coming from outside their parlor, and they will envy the people having so much fun. Bored, perhaps, with the footnoted ennui of their own repetitious discussions, they will go to the gazebo where they, too, are welcome to talk and enter the discussion. But when they put in their oar and discover that it is only an oar and not the sole method for the boat's propulsion and movement, they will take their oar and go back to their parlor, wait until it is dark, and then sneak next door and beat the gazebo to pieces.

But the gazebo is strong, and it is easily rebuilt or repaired as long as it maintains its narrative orality, its sense of community, its refusal to be drawn into thinking something interesting is going on inside the parlor, and its sense of balance and humor. Combining humor and balance with narrative may turn over the coin and talk, not about resistance but about survival; and it begins by reimagining that large Dominant Other as something much smaller, much more equivalent in size and power, and even weaker in terms of survival. And thus Peter Blue Cloud really can be taught in equal measure to John Donne. While the gazebo, too, looks into the past, it does so less for instances of victimization and more for connections, for continuous examples of survival. From those connections comes an active participation in continued survival. The gazebo tends to emphasize a creative, active role that is almost celebratory. It gains from the realized continuousness of that past a tremendous sense of power and expectation for the future. In short, Indians, Chicanos, Blacks, and Asians are still here, still doing things, still contributing; and if my daughter and son have their way, they will still be here when the anecdote that is me is gone.

In *Killing Time with Strangers*, Palimony Blue asks, "Mom, what's a minority?"[12]

Mary Blue replies, "It's what we are in this city." Then she laughs and adds, "It's what they are in the world."

Donne Talkin'

I

It happens—not in spring, but sometimes at Christmas, when all the world celebrates—unless, of course, you are Jewish, Moslem, Buddhist, or something other people don't recognize at all, like unconverted American Indian.

Some of my Indian relatives have been missionized and have converted to Christianity (Protestant and Catholic). Some of these are given to telling me that "If God found them, then God can find X," the f(X) being equal to whomever God needs, in their reconverting opinion, to find. Besides the fact that at twelve I tried to stand stock still in the open and let that God find me—as though standing, washed by rain in an open field, waiting to be struck by lightning—in the end my problem with all this is that god, the Christian god, cannot "find" what he has not "lost."

Others—indeed, the extremely few Christians I know who are not baleful of hypocrisy—when things come round to fitting their enduring and often resilient views—like to say, "You see? God will provide." These latter I can understand, as an optimistic cynic myself whose worldview demands that one continue to participate in the processes of life and that if this participation is willfully hopeful, it can create the possibilities for things to work out. When they don't work out, then perhaps they were not supposed to. This is not so different from my relation's God providing, and if it is suffering he provides, then that too is a good thing, meant to toughen you up for the long haul.

Nonetheless, even though some of my friends and relatives are Christian and I can understand, even relate to, their ways of seeing, I remain (apologetically but insistently) an unconverted non-Christian. I remain not unlike the narrator of Tomas Rivera's novel, *And the*

Earth Did Not Devour Him, who has realized what he has known from childhood: if the Christian God exists, he is absent, powerless, or just plain out of gas. Like him, I have tried to convert myself into Belief with all the romantic intensity of early adolescence. And like him, the evidence against Belief has been so frighteningly plain that I have been and I remain unconverted. Each year I wait as the earth cycles into winter and prepare to withstand the choric carols of the Christian Christmas fueled by food and family, gifts and unrestraint. For the sake of my relations and you who are like them, then, I beg you not to take any of this to heart and let it offend you, even if you cannot understand how much the notion that your God will "find" me alarms me.

To an anti-Christian—as to a racist, I guess—They, Christians, all look alike. And in the Midwest, where Protestants are closed, narrow, exclusive, and as parsimonious with smiles as with human feeling, they not only look but act all alike.

Still, I hate groups. I don't want to include myself in any group, politically correct or not. So even here in the heart of the heart of the beast, I refuse to inhabit the position of anti-Christian as a general rule, and I remain respectful of Christians who act and think the way Christians should, according to their stories. It usually doesn't take much time or effort.

But now it's Christmas, and with all the whispering about the baby Jesus, weakened as I am by all that history and the sheer effort of being agreeable, I can't quite help remembering, and the process of this remembering sometimes makes me angry, even shrill. Though some of my friends are Christians, just as some of my friends are Blacks, I find myself willing to inhabit an individualized stance: he or she is a lousy Christian; he or she is a lousy person; he or she is a frigging racist, even if he or she is a WEPOC (we persons of color) or PORC (person of reddish color or, as my friend David joked, "the other white meat").

As Alley Hummingbird is told by a Black man in my first novel, "Nigger ain't a color. It's a state of mind."[1] I know plenty of niggers, in that context, except Indians like to call them "Apples," and Asians, "Bananas." At the moment, I can't recall what my Chicano friends call 'em. Doesn't matter. It doesn't even matter that most of the Indians calling people "apples" are often niggers themselves, doing riverboat antics in Redface to please the Massa (and what pleases the Massa most is to tell Massa how bad he is, how great a guilt he or she bears).

The point is that we have all sorts of words to describe that sucking state of mind, except for white Christians.[2] Heck, in the case of Jews, here in lovely downtown Michigan, the word "Jew" can be used with very slight tonal modification to mean something as despicable as nigger, though when they use it in Michigan they, like Richard Nixon,[3] tend to picture "rich nigger" in their minds because, as everyone knows, Jews are rich and they own Hollywood as well as Holland, Michigan. But what do you call a white Christian who pretends to accede to the Ten Commandments and yet lusts after power and closeted fellatio with adolescent girls or who kills directly or indirectly every day? What do you call a white Christian child who goes to church and yet not only does not honor her father or her mother but downright dishonors them?

A "hypocrite"?

Oooh. You dirty hypocrite.

Has punch, doesn't it?

It interests me that we have words for every group we want to bunch together and discard in a grocery store dumpster like bananas, apples, and Oreos ("vanilla cremes"? Is that what Chicanos use?), except for white Christians. And it occurs to me that we do not have such words because it seems to have been Christians who controlled not the actions so much as the attitudes of the Western world, and out of essential attitudes come the names we use to praise or denigrate. Christians somehow have achieved the psychological coup of making all the rest of us struggle against their assumptions and making us look narrow or foolish for the struggling.

When I walk into a lecture hall and use the term *myth*, I have to carefully explain to all the little Christians out there that their stories (let's ignore how all the Bad News is removed from the *Good News Bible* and pick the King James Bible, okay?) describe their world and their position in it in the same way the frog songs and Nez Perce stories describe my world and my position and function in it. Jews seem to understand the importance of stories, though they might disagree with my insistence that all stories of a people become legends and eventually—if the resonance is large enough in both quality and quantity (i.e., over historical centuries or millennia)—myths. Abraham and Isaac as myth. But myth, then, is not falsehood or unreality. It is total connection. And to have a "mythic mind" is to have a mind that connects all things, especially oneself, with one's ancestors and descendants.

Jews of my acquaintance might argue that the Old Testament is the word of the prophets as given them by YHWH; they might take offense at my claim that Yahweh is a word describing that which makes words which make stories possible. Yahweh, from my point of view then, might be called "boundless imagination." Even Christians believe that "In the beginning was the word," even though it requires an absolute or fundamentalist belief in a literal six-day creation to not wonder if in the beginning there wasn't a lot of grunting and pointing and not very many distinctive words, much like today. Christians, however, no longer seem to believe that the "word" was also more than language—"wyrd" or "fate" or "destiny."

But Indians do. At least, Nez Perce, Laguna, Osage, and a lot of western people do. We believe that language, the word, makes the world in the fullest sense; and if the word makes the world, it makes, in some sense, destiny or fate by giving context to our lives. It makes me wonder why, when the Christians cut their God from the whole cloth of the Fertile Crescent and Egypt, they dropped that understanding of "word." Didn't some Christian wonder what "the word" was, even then? Did it need a few thousand years before Physics proclaimed their Word as "Bang"?

There is a Tohono O'odham story that tells how the Great Mystery Power "sent the locust flying far across the eastern waters, to summon a people in an unknown land, people whose faces and bodies were full of hair, who rode astride strange beasts, who were encased in iron, wielding iron weapons. . . . [It] allowed these bearded pitiless people to come in ships . . . permitted them to come to Montezuma's country (not the Montezuma of Cortes and Montezuma, but the one chosen to lead humankind by the Great Mystery), taking away Montezuma's power and destroying him utterly."[4]

It is a story not unlike the elder Joseph telling Chief Joseph the younger of the Nez Perce that there would come a time when the white people would take away the Wallowa Valley from the Human

Beings who had occupied the Wallowa nearly from the time when white people were black, darkened by the Lucyan sun of Ethiop. And it is a story that sticks with me, not merely because of the differences it delineates between Europeans and Tohono O'odham (and Pueblo and Nez Perce and Shoshone and . . .), but because they wield iron weapons and they are so pitiless as to raise the hair on their own heads.

But then pity is not only a feeling of compassion for someone else's suffering but, like charity, is a state of mind that allows you to feel good about yourself while temporarily doing a little (but a good little; yes, better this little than nothing at all) to stave off what you take to be inevitable for the sufferer (starvation, disease, death, shotgun-shack poverty, or the tastelessness of tattoos). This compassion also includes an attitude of unexpressed and unrealized (right to) appropriation. One's concern is for someone less favored or privileged and, as the concern atrophies, the feeling of privilege ossifies into an assumptive right so that the concern can be nothing but condescending. Witness all the middle-class kids who have condescended their way into trailer park aesthetics, taking away even those obvious class distinctions so that you can no longer tell if someone has grown up in a double-wide with a biker mom or if he is just an angst-ridden Yute trying to disguise his four-point average in the Honors College as unwanted cargo in its baggy pants. Witness the uncreative, unimagined hauteur of the funless coyote whose arrogance combines with appropriation—appropriating the stature and importance of coyote without the sheer creative force of Coyote that demands so much work and risk.

This is Christian charity. Much of it does some good, and yet it is always from the point of view that we (Christians and non-Christians alike) are better off than they and secretly proud of it—a pride we have to disguise by feeling that we, like a CEO or a sports star, deserve to be better off, have earned our betterness. And it is an attitude that makes me laugh. Makes me laugh when I find it in you, but more when I find it in me. For I, like many Christians, have a similar feeling that in the end I am stronger than they, more able to survive, more worthy to resist their attitudes because—because—imagine!—I am Nez Perce. I have history and the patience of Joseph on my side.

But they have history too, the patience of Snopes and shotgun weapons stronger than iron. Which is why I am Frog and not Coyote.

No one notices Frog. Certainly no one shoots at him or tries to kill him, except for little boys with firecrackers.

And they have their gospels. Where the Tohono O'odham or the Nez Perce have only stories that tell of the coming of pitiless people, they have a book of stories they underline and capitalize — Their Bible — that tells, not of pitiless people coming, but of their arrival and their right to arrive with attitude.

That is probably why, when I quote the Tohono O'odham story, I leave out the description of European firearms as "magic hollow sticks" that spit "fire, thunder, destruction." I wish I had left the phrase out of my collection of Indian stories, The Telling of the World, because it not only allows but invites, indeed forms, the attitude of unconscious appropriation and better-than assumptions. "Magic." How cute these primitive people are. They believe in magic. Poor people in need of our correction: they should believe in miracles, not magic.

It is possibly why, when the Nez Perce speak of the creation of the Real People, the Human Beings, the Nu-mi-pu and their nearby neighbors, the Assiniboine, Shoshone, Pueblo, Flathead, and others, they leave out any asseverations of "god." The unprovable fact of a Great Spirit, a God, a Great Mystery Power is unimportant. Proof of the whatness lies in the howness, and the howness can make even a Christian worthy of respect. A Nez Perce does not concern himself with declarations or proofs of the Great Spirit, and the presence of that spirit does not make for a destructive bill of rights. To a Nez Perce, while the Tohono O'odham's "pitiless people" are not exactly cute, most of them are a little quaint and more than a little needy and insecure, worrying over the existence of the tri-cornered god of their stories and trying to prove it with the serio-impact of their fantasies cum assumptions on Real People.

God, the pitiless people's god, is mainly irrelevant, except for the impact of the attitudes they take from him.

II

These assumptions are as violent as my resistance sometimes seems shrill. Stephen Jay Gould, the brilliant and wonderfully agreeable natural historian, has said he feels somewhat uncomfortable that because the Dodo was unusual in its appearance and physiological structure, evidently clumsy and slow, easy prey for hungry Spanish sailors who had not eaten much meat lately, we accept its extinction with something resembling an almost perverse delight. Yet the Dodo was clumsy and slow because it did not need to be fast and defensively quick: it lived in its own version of Eden, with few or no natural predators until the Spaniards showed up.

Gould seems to find a metaphorical relationship between the Dodo and the Lucayan people, the Taino Indian people of the Bahamas who were completely wiped out by the Spaniards.[5] A gentle people, unarmed because they lacked unnatural predators until the Spanish showed up, they were used as slaves and called "willing" servants, beaten, raped (but the Lucayan language was not spoken by Spanish sailors, so perhaps it was understandably easy to think that "no" meant "yes"), starved, punished (a foot or hand cut off of all the young men in the village kept them "willing" in their servitude, like the fear of an angry god), and finally made extinct. Completely extinct, like the Dodo. That was the Catholic Spaniards, though, right?

The Western world of 1880 was, as Gould says, "at the height of colonial expansion, . . . untroubled by a history of exploitation (even genocide) against 'inferior' peoples of other cultures, prepared for celebrations to mark the 400th anniversary of Columbus's landfall." At the same time in the Western world, one of Gould's favorite scientists, W. K. Brooks, linked his discussion of the fate of the original inhabitants of the Bahamas to these Columbial celebrations, lamenting the brutal destruction of the Tainos, locating the "focus of tragedy in the extreme paucity of remains," and expressing "special pleasure in the task of rescue" anthropologically. But then Gould notes how Brooks's essay follows a "standard pattern," disparaging the Lucayan or Taino peoples "as if to suggest that the native Bahamians had been doomed by their own inherent inferiority" (31).

Disagreeably, it remains a pattern in the 1990s. People disparage Coyote (or Raven, Bluebird, Rabbit, and Tarantula) as the invention of doomed and limited minds.

Gould has trouble reconciling "the two invariant and contradictory themes of early literature on preserving the remains of our initial depredations: the fervor and nobility of rescue, even for the merest scraps; with the disparagement of organisms so preserved as artifacts, and the attribution of extinction, in large part, to these supposed inadequacies" (32). In a very agreeable way, Gould suggests that "we need new concepts and metaphors to replace the false and constraining notions, however comforting, of predictable progress in the history of life (with sad but inevitable loss of inferior creatures) and sensible causality for all major events" (32). Using the example of Lewis Carroll's dodo—with which Carroll, a bumbling and ungainly man, identified—Gould suggests that "life itself is more like a caucus race than a linear course with inevitable victory to the brave, strong, and smart. If we truly embraced this metaphor in conceptual terms, we might even find ourselves in a better position to consider the moral consequences for human actions" and, "when we talk about the intrinsic and ultimate worth of a human life," find ourselves, like Carroll's wise dodo, with "no judgments of superiority or inferiority among participants; no winners or losers; and cooperation with ends attained and prizes for all. . . . The death of the dodo really doesn't make sense in moral terms and didn't have to occur. If we own this contingency of actual events, we might even learn to prevent the recurrence of undesired results. For the Preacher of the Ecclesiastes wrote: 'I returned, and saw under the sun, that the race is not to the swift, nor the battle to the strong . . . but time and chance happeneth to them all' " (33).

In other words, people who claim to believe in the Christian myths and legends should begin with the humility that passes much of their understanding: they are not here because they are superior, nor should they be trying to maintain their illusions of superiority at great human cost, like Proposition 209 or 187 in California.

Ecclesiastes is Old Testament. It is in the sacred, Old Testament that the virulent violence of Christianity and its lack of humility valorizes the arrogant destruction of species and cultures by Spanish inquisitional sailors, men descended from seven hundred years of aggregational belief that it was their duty, given to them by their god, to drive the Jews and Moors from Spain.[6]

Why do the heathen rage . . . ? I will declare the decree: the LORD hath said unto me, Thou art my Son; this day I have begotten thee. Ask of me and I shall give thee the heathen for thine inheritance, and the uttermost parts of the earth for thy possession. Thou shalt break them with a rod of

iron; *thou shalt dash them in pieces like a potter's vessel. (Psalm 2: 1, 7–9;*
King James Version)

On Dasher!
Merry Christmas to you, too.
The British sectarians, who were such royal pains in the ass in their
homelands before they emigrated to the Lowland European countries, romanticized it as "religious freedom." But they had "religious
freedom" in tolerant Holland, even though their harsh attitudes and
proselyte views made them less than well liked—about as well-liked
as Scientologists in Northern Europe or Survivalists in rural Montana
today. They did not come to the New World for religious freedom.
They came for commercial opportunity—land and wood and cotton
(the silky long-strand cotton Indians had developed, not the short,
hair-of-the-dog cotton that Europeans in their superior advancement
had produced)—and they came with a violent willfulness and with
assumptions they would not allow to be assailed. One was that
the "heathens" were primitive, barbaric, and without stories that
mattered. The other, or part of the same one, was that their Christian
stories, their literature, being superior, was central to the intellectual
geography of wherever they happened to end up.

The Tohono O'odham story needs to be retold:

Long ago, there were pitiless people. These people did not like things to
be disagreeable, and it was disagreeable not to know how the world came
to be. So they looked about and found a god. The Jews' angry god of
retribution was disagreeable. And yet it was easier to remember one god
and not several, so they borrowed the one Jewish god and made him
forgiving—enough to let even the arms dealers and fornicators among
them hope for, indeed expect, forgiveness. To make sure, they decided
that you could repent pitilessness in the instant before you passed into
another world and all would be forgiven. That way, you could do
pretty much anything you wanted up to the last moment, which was
certainly agreeable. The only remaining problem was that like Santa
Claus, they had trouble imagining this one god being everywhere and
doing everything, so they looked to Egypt and perhaps to Odysseus's
descent into Hades to find resurrection stories that could be modified to
make sense to them. As for the third part of their three-part one god, well,

there was a vestigial memory, a blood memory of a time when the lands of the earth were one and the people were not yet pitiless. In that time, some had believed in a Great Spirit. So they took the Great Spirit and made him a ghost, but since they did not believe in ghosts, they made him a Holy Ghost to excuse the fact.

(As you can see, language was already becoming confused enough for modern politics.)

Anyway, having pirated the design and stolen the parts for a god and assembled them in their assertions, the people desired more. More of anything. More of everything. So they decided to build ships to go out upon the waters and find more. Men of courage set sail, and though some of them missed their targets by thousands of miles, they did find more. More cheap and tractable labor in the Bahamas. More silver in Potosi, more Incan and Mayan Gold, and, though it did not please Coronado's men who were searching for Cibolan gold in Nebraska,[7] more land. Though they were courageous, which means they had strong hearts, their hearts were not pitiful except to other men like themselves (and even then, not very). Their hearts were brave but untrue. They took the gold and silver and, driving the inhabitants off, killing them, enslaving them, they inhabited the land. They looked about themselves for government, and remembering how they came to godliness, they borrowed from the inhabitants they were driving off, and they made a country out of the land and word of other people. The land was cleared, and they made Ulsterous plantations; the words were changed, first in their meanings as the words of treaties lasted only as long as Chemlawn fertilized and the hose was on.[8] They looked about, and wanting words that were flexible, they created new words that housed in the one the son of the word as well as a holy ghost of words. And lo! it came to pass that they made bumper stickers, and in the banality of bumpers they returned their thinking to its primal state, its Eden, its first movement of grunting and pointing; and everyone was blessed in the name of Big Bang. God was Big Bang and Big Bang was god, and if you did not like it, they called you bitter—or worse, they turned the words on you and called you "immigrant," they who in their second generation called themselves "native."

In this state of mind, which to you may seem bitter but to me and others like me seem amused, when my son at four years of age started

114

saying, "Oh my god!" I began to teach him that he shouldn't say it because it is not agreeable.

Why not? he wondered, with his untainted, four-year-old sense of wonder.

I didn't have an answer, except that it offended people who were offensive. Although mutual offense might give substance to resistance, it is not a solution; and in its worried concern with Other, it is a false way to survive. So, as a compromise with my converted relatives, I began to teach him to say not "Oh my god," but "Oh your god."

Oh, your god! in an implied recognition of the very fact that the believers in Bumper Stickers, the white Christians (in general, remember, with deepest and sincerest and heart-feltest apologies to those of you who particularly do not fit) ask us to capitulate to their assumptions, to beg forgiveness from them, to be properly colonized in our psychologies, and not to say anything that might offend them while any old time they'll offend us if they feel like it by superciliously "knowing" that if god found them . . .

III

My need to shout has another context, different from the blanket of religiosity protecting the Midwest, and that context is the other one in which I live or exist, the untroubled attitudes of the world of academe where the fervor of rescue and full-of-excuses identity creates the illusion of matterful perceptions and understanding. Nowhere else is the fervor and assumed nobility of rescue so pervasive. Nowhere else do people love Indian things beyond measure. A critic like Mr. P. C. loves Indian novels so much that he ignores good Indian novelists.[9] Here in academe they just love the frog songs, and every time I hear them say how much, the Menominee story "The Man Who Loved the Frog Songs" starts echoing through my mind, making me want to cry. The story goes:

> Once an Indian had a revelation. . . . In the early spring, when all the frogs and toads thaw out they sing and shout more noisily than at any other time of the year. This Indian made it a practice to listen to the frogs every spring when they first began, as he admired their songs, and wanted to learn something from them. He would stand near puddles, marshes and lakes to hear them better, and once when night came he lay right down to hear them.

In the morning, when he woke up, the frogs spoke to him, saying: "We are not all happy, but in very deep sadness. You seem to like our crying but this is our reason for weeping. In early spring, when we first thaw out and revive we wail for our dead, for lots of us who don't wake up from our winter sleep. Now you will cry in your turn as we did.

Sure enough, the next spring the Indian's wife and children all died, and the Indian died likewise, to pay for his curiosity to hear the multitude of frogs. So this Indian was taught what has been known since by all Indians—that they must not go on purpose to listen to the cries of the frogs in the early spring.[10]

The academy loves us to shout. It makes it feel liberal and good because it gives us the freedom to do so, and it can dismiss us as shrill when they tire of it—and in most cases it (the academy) is right in its dismissal. Where I am now, however, they love a little shouting, as long as it is only the distant cries of one who can no longer make war, who is only a tiny animated figure in a diorama of academic attitudes. So shouting continues to be a dangerous activity. Like too-loud rock and roll, it can become a dangerous din that first, prevents thinking, and second, replaces it with noise so often that the sheer noisomeness begins to seem like thought. If you shout, you become predictable and inhuman. In short, you become an idiot to be silenced by diverse indifference. However, if you always refuse to shout, you are mistaken as one who is "reasonable" if not compliant, and, refusing to take everything personally as though every possible comment just has to be an insult to your grandfather, you are seen as taking nothing personally at all. On the one hand, no one dares say anything important to you, and certainly never dares to joke with you—adding to your increased humorlessness and jowl-heavy injured seriousness. On the other hand, people feel free to assume that you, like them, believe all that shouting is without cause or basis or reason; they nudge you and say anything that comes to mind—further weakening your already atrophying ability to laugh (atrophied humor often seems a prerequisite, these days, to rising in the academy, and Oh! Your god, I'm rising!).

Somehow, there is a balance to this, but it requires a constant reevaluation and return to that which begins the shouting. For me, this balance is represented by the brilliant, jewel-like story by George P.

Elliott, "In a Hole."[11] Readers should read it for themselves; however, the first person narrator, at forty, is caught in a hole by an earthquake, a hole in which, at first, it was "a sort of relief to be." He feels relieved of the anxiety of wondering when he is going to be caught by trouble, having lived in this "great and strong" city where people grumble and question the wisdom of the founding fathers who built a city in such a location (one can't help but envision San Francisco as this city). "But we do not seriously complain, we have no real intention of rebelling, even if we did it is dangerous to say anything but what is expected" (285).

The hole he falls into is funnel shaped, with the wide-mouthed end down. The chimney is five feet above his head, and the rubble on the floor of his hole is too small to use to build a platform from which to reach the chimney. Determined not to die alone, he begins to yell for help, but without getting any response. Then he begins to complain "in a loud clear voice and complete, rather formal sentences," and large rocks, even boulders, begin to fall, which he can use to form a pile. However, if he complains too loudly or shouts, huge boulders that he cannot move fall from the chimney, enlarging it, making the task of saving himself all the more difficult. To make a short story shorter, with "ordinary words used with care," and pretending that someone is listening to what he says, imagining an audience even though he knows that he is in fact complaining without one, he manages to modulate his complaining voice to the right wavelengths to dislodge the stones he needs. The story ends with his getting on with his complaining while he has both the strength and time.

The academic attitudes I complain about occur like this: In 1995 I applied for a research leave to collect, select, and edit *The Telling of the World*, a collection of Native American stories and art. My goal was to try to show how storytelling creates the world for many Indian peoples—a broader, but similar process to the idea that the reality in which you live is created and transmitted by speaking. If you say it, you make it be.

It wasn't funded. That didn't upset me. Michigan State University has been good to me, generous with time as well as money. I've had my share, some enviously would say more than my share of rewards in a world where limited money and respect (and even more limited respectability) has to be shared. It was in that spirit that I received the notice of my rejection. I only cursorily read over the reasons colleagues gave for it. You don't win, you go on. But my eye stuck like your god's eye on the sparrow on the phrase, "There are too many of these already." As a sealant to the window of his views, someone I was forced out of genteel agreeability to call a "colleague" very clearly believed that of collections of Native American legends and stories, we have too many. His (why do I assume without evidence that it was a "he," or am I merely succumbing to the absence of a grammatically correct collective pronoun?) assumption seemed to be that there are a limited number of Native legends and that the work done by early anthropologists and translators was more than sufficient to the breadth and importance of the subject.

Even that did not bother me, did not make me want to shout too loudly, even though I had just lectured (with specific examples) to a class (or that portion that was still awake after having spent the all-night demonstrating their right to Brew) on the interesting way early anthropologists recorded Indian stories while knowing little or none of the tribe's language or customs and then freely altered them, even using biblical language, to fit the Western (biblical) sense of "moral" endings, closure, or meanings, and then—and Then!—actually decided and eventually proved to their anthropic satisfaction that these stories, because of their biblicality, must have been influenced by early contact with missionaries.

Or, to be more accurate, at first, it did not bother me. I was working on assimilating the action of rejection, and a personality like mine that never really thinks its mind is as good as other people's takes other people's rejection seriously and is slow to assimilate its meanings. So it took some time, the way it takes time for the flowing tide to turn to ebb and pull away, revealing the driftwood and detritus left behind on the sand, for me to examine the dead jellyfish and oil-slicked auks of my colleague's thinking. In terms of the action of the rejection, my attitude toward it is much like my attitude toward death: out of it, something better can come, if we are willing and if we have prepared the way for that betterness, like my grandfather's death. How often I have walked the mile and a half home, asking grandfather to please stay with me, to speak to me, to help me past the anger and disappointment I felt, usually for even temporarily fooling myself into believing that something as large, impersonal, inhumane, and bureaucratic (the latter three, I realize, are synonyms) as a university might behave justly and well. How often I have needed grandfather to help me regain the peace and contentment I felt before my own croaking and shrill self-deluding, to help me, in other words, return to the proper preparations that are beyond anger or hurt.

(If my own death can leave behind it love, respect, re-membrance and re-creation, identity, and a love of stories in my children or grandchildren with as much power as his death did, that will be something better, proof that progress lies with the generations—if only because his great-grandchildren [the extreme joys that are my daughter and son] already show signs of becoming better than I could ever hope to be. From—or if not from, then after—rejection, in my life, has come the full measure of everything good. At the moment rejection seems about to bury me, to make a landfill of failure out of me, if I complain in the right voice to grandfather, the ground shifts and the garbage moves, and yellow and white flowers rooted deep beneath the junk poke up their heads—sometimes in surprising numbers.)

So it bothers me, I guess, after all.

MEMORANDUM I
Faculty for the Literature in London summer overseas study program may no longer teach Shakespeare at the 300 or 400 level unless they are qualified to teach Shakespeare.

QUESTION
Isn't it possible that the overseas experience of being in England, seeing plays by the Royal Shakespeare Company, having backstage tours or lectures by producers and actors in that company doesn't more than compensate for the so-called lack of expertise of faculty who are not hired to teach Shakespeare?

MY ANSWER
Yep.

THE ANSWER THAT HELD SWAY
Nope.
(Or: Shakespeare is a complicated subject that can only be taught by someone who has had years of study or training in the reading, production and staging, or criticism of Shakespeare plays).

RESPONSE
[Unuttered to avoid shouting the obvious]
Guess Shakespeare wrote and produced plays for experts only, eh?

TIME PASSES
[Okay, three years to be exact]

CONVERSATION
[With department bureaucrat who helped instigate Memo 1]
Crat: I see that you've applied for a research grant next fall.
Frog: Yep.
Crat: What will you do with it?
Frog: Take time off to work on a new book.
Crat: Umm. Well, what about your Oral Tradition class? [A large lecture of 200–300 that looks good on the bottom line.]
Frog: What about it?
Crat: If you're not going to teach it, I want you to get Prof. X [the other "Indian" on the department's faculty] to do it.
Frog: Can he do it?
Crat: Of course he can do it.
Frog: I mean, is he qualified? I've spent three years developing the course. Do you think he . . . ?
Crat: Bill. Anybody can teach that course.
Frog: [Silence. Bitten lip imitations of Potted Plant. Refusal to leap from chair and turn seventeen-inch computer monitor into bureaucratic necklace.] You think so.
Crat: I know so. Otherwise I wouldn't have called you in.

The unconscious racism that assumes any "Indian" can teach the Oral Traditions of Nuestra America also presumes that the literatures of the Americas, which are recognizably founded in oral traditions in large part, are lesser than the "written" literatures of Europe, and in particular Britain, or North American as it derives from Britain in both its literature and its pilgrim attitudes.[12]

The irony is that, as in Stephen Jay Gould's discussion of the Dodo and the attitude that assumes the Dodo should be extinguished because it was not fit to live in the technological world, it is the inflexibility of the "written" cultures that makes it difficult for them to adapt to new technology. For that, in part, is what the argument over such things as euthanasia or abortion is: Christians of Anglo Descent (a.k.a. CADS) who used technological "progress" to justify their ascendancy sometimes find themselves embattled against the results of the very technology that they believed justified their behavior (I won't even bring up environmental damage). In this world, as it changes, they could be seen as unfit to survive. And, in the extreme, they are just as violent, just as willing to transform the word-stories of their god(s) into an explosive exclamation of absolute truth outside an abortion clinic.

In this frame of mind, I heard a colleague express his fear at the increased emphasis on "Cultural Studies," and I could not help but whisper, "Oh your god!"

My colleague was afraid that "Cultural Studies" meant that the Johns of Donne or Milton would no longer get taught.

"You're already done," I thought, grinning. Childishly grinning, as though now I could use the Frog Songs to show how now it was their turn to suffer, because for too long he and his kind had ignored both the grief and the joy of enumerating remembrance of those very songs. After all, wasn't the world out of balance? Given its assumptions—and I think they are primarily Caucasoid Christian—hadn't the world been out of balance for a long time?

"Out of the window / I saw how the planets gathered," and I remembered the cry of Wallace Stevens's peacock.[13] I gloated that I was not afraid. My colleague was right to be afraid. He had caught a glimpse of just how out of balance the world has been and for how long, how since Copernicus his planets had been gathered around the only begotten sun of British literature (and of course they don't really "gather," they expand until they appear to fill what appeared to be a void, an emptiness, a need). But to him, the increasing valuation of Cultural Studies was the cry of the peacock in his ears, and his fears were derived from the assumptive fact that for too long now British literature has held sway and dominion over the English departments of our country, and now that affirmative action has done much of its work, or now that the demographics of both the wider and the narrower worlds of literature have changed, Donne's place (and my colleague's, in turn) may well be smaller, look less like a plantation house and more like a row house or condo or, in the case of lesser figures, like a coal bin or potty shed out back. For too long some of my colleagues have assumed, the way they did with the Big Bertha of "Civilization," that British (and Western European) literature was superior to the (oral) *barbaros* of Latino/Chicano, African/Caribbean, or North and South American Indian literature. They assumed their stories were like the children of Abraham. Meant to multiply, and to gain dominion—like a jar that's round upon a hill, in Tennessee.[14] And anyone like me had felt, perhaps as they wanted us to feel, as though I was sticking warts on the Leviathan's face by teaching Latino novels, or as though a novel by a Native American was merely an accessory to the emperor's fashion of English literature. Like Queen Elizabeth's handbag—which, while always there, goes largely unnoticed—minority literature was an accessory in which to carry small change. But the empress's clothes, expensive as they may be, have become dowdy; and hidden in that bag we might find the keys to the kingdom, now that we cultural studies people knew to and how to look.

The temptation, then—and although it is childish, I think it is a very legitimate one—is to "repay" the British literature specialists, the people who, despite what I earlier noted as the ironical call by Ralph Waldo Emerson for an indigenous literature of the new United States of America, have controlled if not the actual subjects then the attitudes of college English departments. We could repay them by trashing British literature in a riot of sudden uncontrolled and uncontrollable license fueled by long resentment—not unlike the Watts riots of the 1960s or the Big Ten Beer Riots of the 1990s. The temptation is to repay the British specialists by tossing out their specialties and substituting for them our own "nueve specialties"; and for at least two decades, if not more, that seems to be what we have been doing— substituting modern cultural perceptions for the assumptions of the culturally British (and, I would maintain, the Christian or Judeo-Christian) past.

We have all heard the cry: Alice Walker is taught in college English courses more frequently than Shakespeare. And we have heard Saul Bellow's rather assumptive and smug support for that crying in his silly statements about when "they" produce a Tolstoi, then he'll read "them." We have all seen the bookshelves at the college store change.

Walk, as is my habit, down the English and humanities aisles, and you can see the material and perceptual change: Americo Paredes, Tomas Rivera, Carter Revard, Ron Querry, Linda Hogan, Gerald Vizenor, Maryse Condé, Toni Morrison, John A. Williams, John Wideman, Shawn Wong, David Mura, Amos Tutuola—these are just a few of the authors who showed up on last semester's shelves. Compared to historical British (or even nineteenth-century American) authors, it is obvious to even the most modern person that modern minority literatures far outnumber all other categories combined. And last, we all have colleagues who have unearthed or rediscovered writers out of the great well of history: Indian writers, Women writers, Black writers, Chicano/a writers; and we have all had contact with students whose dissertations have specialized in subsets of those (Immigrant Women writers was the topic of a close friend and very bright Ph.D. candidate not long ago), so the balance continues to tip toward the *renovado*.

Renovar, in its political meaning, means to reform and also to replace (*remplazar*). And although my Spanish-English dictionary gives *renovador* as the Spanish word for "new broom," I suspect this is not unlike the instructions to a Japanese-made VCR that tells you to "intercourse" the male lead with the female receptor and that by "new broom" is meant reform and replace in a clean sweep of the past or the previous and preceding.[15]

That is, of course, what has been going on and what we have been helping go on with all the religious zeal, the self-justifying assumptions, and the (intellectual) violence of the Christian Old Testament and Psalms. For all our talk about "the canon" as though it were something bolted to the terreplein of Fort Sumter, there has been no such thing for decades; indeed, the readings for English courses are a virtual riot of individual professorial expression and, in a few instances, good taste.

These are what, given his long history of experience with Christian attitudes, my colleague is "afraid of" both in substance and in feeling: both the payback and the riot. As a Jew (and I, as a non-Christian), he (I am speculating; I haven't asked) does not fear the philosophical Christianities of St. Augustine or C. S. Lewis. As a Jew (and I, as an Indian) with thousands of years of experience at survival in the face of deadly persecutions, he does not fear the philosophical Christians anywhere near as much as he fears the Christians bearing the Good

News with violent attitudes and closed minds that are definitely Bad News for anyone who isn't willing to subscribe to their way of believing. He does not fear the more intelligent voices of minority literature and criticism as much as he fears the voices that accuse anyone who criticizes minority literature of a kind of intellectual fascism, using the Tarot card of race to discount opposing opinions. He fears—although he might not put it this way—the self-righteous narrow-mindedness of the foot soldiers of reform who would shift the meaning of *renovar* to "clean sweep" with a "new broom."

IV

John Donne feared—or given his faith, perhaps it was less fear than amplified recognition and warning to those who would be intelligent enough to listen—the same thing. In Donne's "Paradoxes and Problemes," the second of his "Problemes" is "Why Puritans Make Such Long Sermons?"

> It needs not for *perspicuousness*, for God knows they are plain enough: nor do all of them use *Sem-brief-Accents*, for some of them have *Crotchets* enough. It may be they intend not to rise like *Glorious tapers and Torches*, but like *Thin-wretched-sick-watching-Candles*, which *languish* and are in a Divine *Consumption* from the first minute, yea in their *snuff*, and *stink*, when others are in their more profitable *glory*. I have thought sometimes, that out of conscience, they allow *long measure to course ware*. And sometimes, that *usurping in that place a liberty to speak freely of Kings*, they would *reigne* as long as they could. But now I think they do it out of a *zealous* imagination, that, It is their duty to Preach on till their Auditory wake.[16]

One can hardly resist the very modern sense of irony or satire in that last line, the doubled meaning that adds to the waking of the collective listeners the meaning that their very ability to listen and *hear* (in that old black magical "I hear you" [he said deafly] way) eventually may awaken if they speak long and loudly—though it is doubtful, given the austerity of their attitude and intentions.

More to the point is the idea that, having usurped a liberty to speak freely of the predominant figure or ruler, they would reign as long as they can. In our case here, the predominant figure is represented by the fantasy of a fixed "canon." To reign (as long as they can), Native American writers or scholars chronically have to play the Indian the white people want them to play and salt their novels with the white stereotype of the modern Indian. Caught in the trap of obligation, the self-appointed duty "to Preach on till their Auditory wake," they trap themselves in the role of puritanical preacher, missionizing the white people soft enough in their hopes, faiths, and charitabilities to be converted to worshipping the Indian icons the missionizers identify as worth the worship. It is this power that some Native Americans become enamored of and that they want to maintain by whatever method, by whatever delusion, even if they have to give up their creative powers and jump from place to place, college to college, position to position to feel this power in the continual reestablishment of it. The power doesn't change; but the feeling of reigning does, renewed at each different place and enlarged to the limits that place can stand. It is nearly a matter of time and space: if the space is limited, then the longer the time one can feel power, the greater a power it can seem to be.

Reigning—the sense that one has at least personal power, if only the power to whine and accuse, like the little humanoid lemmings who, in their rush to the sea in the parental SUV stop long enough to wail about how the community police "oppress" them because the police ask them to follow the civic laws and to accept responsibility for themselves—becomes an end without process, a "human right" without ever demonstrating any humanity, something one "has" without ever learning how to have more than the appearance of it. It is all marketing. And the brilliance of marketing is not only to make our youthful lemmings think that fingernail polish "expresses" a real identity, but that dying your hair black, donning a half-ton of turquoise and silver, and wearing aviator sunglasses to hide your scrutability proves a real identity ("And did I mention my 27-city book tour?").

Reigning: thus, instead of D'Arcy McNickle, we get the Public Indian, who, if you do not agree with him (or her), uses racist fascist tactics to sell the white CADS the privilege of overlooking disagreement or disputation. Instead of Dr. King or Bayard Rustin, we get Al Sharptons or Carol Moseley-Brauns out of Chicago. Instead of Cesar Chavez, we get . . . well, I don't know just who we've gotten, as yet, there. Instead of the Tale of Genji we get the Fails of Amy

Tan. We get celebrity, not substance; sermons, not paradoxes and problemes, "rude pretenders to excellencies they unjustly own who profanely rushing into Minervaes Temple with noysome Ayres blast the lawrell which thunder cannot hurt" (5).

We get Native academics who invent the frog songs and then teach soft whites to love them too much.

VI

John Donne may be white, male, and (as Dean of St. Paul's) Christian, a member of the exclusive Patriarch's Club (on Lusty Mews, just off discrete Bond Street), but he is also thoroughly modern. True, he believed in the Christian God. That he feels called upon to say, "It is the foole that said in his heart, There is no God" (297; in "Juvenilia: Or Certaine Characters, Essays, and 'Conceited Newes' "), suggests that many a one in his mind has already said it, that Donne bridges between a world of faith and a world in which faith is thought and felt, a world that is losing God, and possibly a world in which even John Donne himself has had his thinking doubts. Nonetheless, he remains a philosophical Christian "in an age when anything is strong enough to overthrow her [truth]" (364; in a letter "To Sir Henry Wotton"). It is an age that more than resembles our own post-modern confusions of feeling with thinking, of notions with opinions, of theoretical expertise with human understanding. Try explaining to your eleven-year-old daughter the paradox of "he is wise who understands he understands nothing," an epigram she extracted from a book of hers; try getting a twenty-year-old college student to care, when "wee, by providing every ones selfe, divinity enough for his owne use, should neglect our Teachers and Fathers" (292; in "Problemes").

Imagine someone saying we live in a time when people seem to have a faint weak love of "vertue," where the lethargic world has lost its strength by (over) confidence, imagining itself safer because it has tolled the dangers and diseases of the old. Imagine him criticizing the rampant neutrality of people, asking if there could "bee worse sickness, than to know / That we are never well, nor can be so?" (188, "An Anatomie of the World"). Or pretend he says that information can be (and often is) as nothing, that information does not mean understanding and that in fact too much information can focus the mind so much on the short limitations of the Here and Now that it becomes as concentrated and as heavy as lead. As his world began to lose the very god that now, having been lost for several hundred years, is supposed to find me as I hide behind the contradictions and ambiguities of my own prose, John Donne saw and understood and said all these things. For the wisdom of these things, John Donne's poetry and prose should continue to be taught, even by someone such as me, who is for Cultural Studies—the comparative investigation and understanding (note, not "excusing" but "understanding") of various ways of understanding, perceiving, and believing or refusing. Not only does Donne represent philosophical Christianity, but his dialectical ability to question his own valuations and thereby open his attentive reader to entertain and consider, not just the opposites, but also the modifications, which are not so much oppositions but finenesses of perception, makes him interesting.

Where, exactly, is this philosophy? In the process of Donne's poetry and prose, in the structure that is both a part of process and the control of the reader's experience of process. In his sense of metaphor, which some call "metaphysical conceit," but which I call "connection." For that is what metaphor does, it connects, and an extended metaphor connects more—more complicatedly. Metaphor moves us outward beyond the Here and Now, the "contracted to an inch" (189, "An Anatomie of the World") of space and time. It is not genetics that makes us like our grandfathers and mothers, it's metaphor: we are as they are and only a Here and Now—some would say paranoid—mentality deludes himself into thinking that the world has changed so much that he is nothing like his grandfather(s). Genetics, in other words, only describes, and in some ways explains or excuses, what we already (should) know, at least in those relations between ourselves and the generations past and to come.

When I call modern Christians non-philosophical, I mean that they have lost this sense of metaphor and tend to treat images as literal. Yet the Christian God is nothing but metaphor, and his reported activities can be understood only by means of metaphor. To believe—which, granted, is not based on thinking—that the universe, the planet Earth, or even the flat dullness of the Midwest was created in 144 hours followed by a 24-hour rest period requires the believer to suspend, if not forego, all sense of metaphor. To believe that the Great Mystery actively created the United States is shallow and self-loving. It is this loss of metaphor that the schismatic churches represented to the young Chief Joseph when he "observed that churches would only teach his people 'to quarrel about God'."[17] Instinctively, Joseph, whose heart and mind were not separated, understood that the Great Spirit, or God, was a metaphor integrated into process; and no Dreamer Nez Perce ever believed that arguing over God was worthwhile. Whether the world was created by the Great Spirit and made better by the antics of Coyote or by a Christian God made better by the (less enjoyable) antics of Jesus Christ did not matter. The Dreamer Nez Perce were an integrated part of nature; only if you wanted to subdue nature and lose your part in it would you become a praying Christian. Only if you devolved into literality could you believe that whites were superior to Human Beings and that the only hope for Human Beings was to make them like European whites; only literality lets you live sufficiently in a limited Here and paranoid Now to bomb an abortion clinic or a Federal Building in Oklahoma City or shoot up a Baptist Church youth prayer meeting.

Outside of religious belief in the wider civil world, it is literality that forgets that Law is only a civil description of the what and how that the metaphorical heart knows. You do not need sexual harassment legislation, or the quisling Clintonesque thinking of third-wave feminists who call his immoral behavior "consensual" and therefore legal, to lose respect for a middle-aged man who allows himself to be seduced by a girl barely older than his own daughter. To not be bored by someone half your age, either that someone has to be extremely wise beyond her years (which seems, in the case of the presidential blow jobs, highly unlikely), or you have to have that kind of literal mind that separates, divides, segments, and pigeonholes so that sensuality and sexuality are divorced from mentality, so that the heart, no longer knowing, sleeps in a separate compound from the wife of its mind. And of course, as I've said all too shrilly elsewhere, in the academic world, where highly intelligent critics and even many of our resident writers have lost their sense of metaphor as a real and functioning way of knowing, one needs "theory" to excuse unclear writing and "Cultural Studies" to excuse bad taste.

One reason the academic world (and this is only one reason) wants demarcation, separation, and division, instead of connection is to rid themselves of their problems of "taste." Something they rarely talk about, a lack of "taste" excuses the inclusion in their courses of "one-time" books, Here and Now novels, as an entry into browbeating students to believe what is politically correct. Topical novels are one time. Good novels are novels that can be read a second, third, or fourth time with increased pleasure and increased understanding—increased Human understanding, that is, or of how we are connected to the world over (not in) Time And Space. And increased understanding demands metaphor as well as an active assimilation or living of metaphor and the wise connections metaphors provide. (Bad metaphors, obviously, are attempts to provide connections that are insincere or untrue, such as comparing a dying mother's heart to a dieseling internal combustion engine because it compares the human to the mechanical.)

Literature meets Gaston Bachelard's dictum that the correct thing to do when you finish a great book is to begin it again, immediately. Literature not only invites rereading, it demands it and rewards it. That is the simplest definition of literature that I know, and it is not to say that I favor only reading literary novels. I don't. I understand that reading a good mystery novel can be fun. Rereading it, however, once you've found out who done it, seems possibly enjoyable only if the mystery writer approaches literariness in her or his metaphorical and sensual prose (e.g., a mystery about identity such as Paul Auster's *City of Glass*). If it's like most mysteries, however, I frankly don't see the point. There is an end to mysteries; there is no end to a literary novel. Not only should it be reread and reimagined and reenjoyed, but the connections it makes of writer to reader to world of human beings continue even if the action of the novel or story is "closed."

In addition to mysteries, I am for reading anything and everything, including cereal boxes. But just because the copy on your *Cheerios* was written by Duane Eagledroppings, that doesn't make it literature, even if it wins a National Book Critics Circle Award, a Pulitzer, or a Nobel Prize. In the academic world, where colleagues want to be able to include virtually all Native American writers among the literary and therefore worthy of teaching, people don't want to make or to allow these distinctions, and if you continue to try to make them, they accuse you of all manner of prejudices and failures. I, unfortunately, lack the heart not to make these distinctions. I am incapable of discussing books I've only partly read or have read "around in" beginning at the end and taking up the middle, coming to the beginning whenever, although I do understand why someone would only skim a book of criticism for its argument. It requires too much separation, too much loss of metaphorical connection.

The loss is not recorded by John Donne, but he signals the beginning of the loss. For all that he records dialectically the increased dissolution of communities and institutions, for all that he forewarns us, not unlike the late de Tocqueville, of the problems inherent in rampant individualism (especially, de Tocqueville says, in a democracy), he also complies with one of the prerequisite changes in the Western European mind. It is not merely a loss of church or soul. It is the ability to separate heart and mind that, like the modern separation of criticism from literature, creates a bifurcation as well as an unrootedness, a loss of the autochthonous whole, which culminates in a wandering literality.

For thirty years, since the wonderful, brilliant professor Lindsay Mann introduced me to John Donne, that famous compass image in "A Valediction: Forbidding Mourning" has troubled me, and it is only now that I begin to see why. There is the brilliant extended metaphor: "As virtuous men passe mildly away . . . / So let us melt, and make no noise" (38). Would that President Clinton understood that "T'were prophanation of our joyes / To tell the layetie our love" (38), even though love in our Here and Now world has been reduced to the simple solipsisms of sexual gratification. I can go along with the expansion "Like gold to ayery thinnesse beat," although using a soft precious metal that cannot be beaten in its purest form to much of an expansion begins to worry someone who sees love or soulfulness as unrelated and unrelatable to the objects of greed. But then comes that compass: two hearts (or souls), one rooted, the other wandering in a circle around the fixed point, joined at the head, in the intellectualized aether; and yet even when the "I" comes home, for all his growing "erect," still joined only at that head. Perhaps I make too much, in this poem, of the hint of separation of head and heart, the Cartesian split that people had to adopt first as metaphor and then as literality if they were ever to believe (and excuse) the changes they called "progress." Donne's image of twin compasses as the condition of the lovers themselves becomes, in the end—and perhaps for me alone—a metaphor not of connection but of separation. The "foole that said in his heart, There is no God" is more the fool, because once separated, he will spend his time proving or arguing about the Great Spirit in his mind, while his mind atrophies, unfed by the justness of the heart.

VII

The heart of criticism should be literature. Should be. You all know (and thanks to you who have come this far) that few are the critics who read and talk about anything but other critics, gleaning the gist of the gist of the gist until absolutely anything may be said as though it is theoretically true. I've said enough about critics to leave me friendless—and rightly so. I don't know why I ever thought there should be more good critics than there are good writers. It was a fantasy of hope in the Here and Now.

The heart of literature is metaphor and the spoken word (or the word used as though it were spoken). Metaphor connects image to image, character to character, whether in "real" life or not (and thus the fun of asking who is more alive, a character in von Rezzori's *Memoirs of an Anti-Semite* or a person—who is very real—who "sleepes as hee goes, and his thoughts seldome reach an inch further than his eies" [298, Donne's "The True Character of a Dunce"; note that a dunce does not see with his heart]). Metaphor expands a person's understanding; it does not simply describe the immediate world around like so many contemporary novels do. Metaphor, as I said above, connects even more; and where we learn this "more" is in the honest thinking about the oral traditions of the Western Hemisphere, indigenous or not.

In his reflections on the short story, Julio Cortazar says, "As is natural among younger literatures, in our countries spontaneous creation almost always precedes critical examination. . . . [W]riters themselves don't have to be theoreticians and critics, and it is natural that the latter enter the scene only when there exists a body of literature which permits inquiry and clarification of its development and its qualities."[18]

Along with the short story, this applies to specific literatures and implies that the stages of critical inquiry into literatures that have flowered—like the past twenty-five years of Native American and Chicano literature—come to the moment in which the flowers need taxonomy, which involves, at least in part, keeping some in our arrangements and letting others go. But for this taxonomy to occur and not succumb to the historical assumptions that permeate the understanding of even the most sensitive critic requires a (spontaneous) refusal everywhere those assumptions appear.

British literature is not used to being in this position. Neither is it prepared or supple enough in its American critical form to occupy the position. For too long we have been too kind and let British literature feed off the vanity of its own dominance as the canon expanded. But just as when, during Christmas, a converted Christian may whisper about the "baby Jesus" to the children of non-Christians, or when someone writes a book about Why America Needs Religion and people assume it means Why America Needs Christianity (no one, not even a Chinese person, reads the title as meaning that America needs Buddhism), the vanity of white Christian dominance becomes almost sad and sadly apparent.

So at Christmastime, when I teach my son to say "Oh your god," I am doing more than simply being disrespectful or funny. I am reminding him that their god is not the one and only god, no matter how much it might expand to include anthropomorphic sons or non-Western but holy ghosts. I am teaching him that foresight—a value in Homer, *Njal's Saga*, and the Coyote cycles of the Nez Perce—requires hindsight, and the hindsight on Christianity is not a pretty picture unless you like a lot of reds soaking into the background of browns—and that if he wants for religion and a peace that comes with it, he can choose his own. I am preparing him to understand that it is okay to begin reevaluating the canon of his understanding, teaching him to admire the influence that British literature has had in its great writers like John Donne but not to overvalue that influence by allying it with the assumptions of Western Christianity. I am telling him to hand the English don or the American Nobel Prize winner who denigrates non-British literature by means of his assumptions a toilet seat as the don staggers drooling into the gray drizzle of an English sunset. For that is Herman Melville's image of Christ as he emerges from a ship's cabin, painted with the stars of the galaxy and wearing a toilet seat about his neck that he believes to be a life-ring.

But I am also telling him not to love the frog songs too much and certainly never to love them just because they are sung by frogs and not zebras. Perhaps I am hoping that he, along with my daughter, will be thankful to those who have helped, as Carter Revard, whose poems are everywhere equal to the best the West has to offer, encourages us to be.[19]

Above all, I am telling my children that before we can find new metaphors (which is the same as revitalizing old ones, since nothing changes, really), we have to try to give up the metaphors that have died and gone to literality. In religion, the dead voices of the literal Bible; in literature, the dead voices of violent assumptions.

Peter Blue Cloud's stories speak just and well, but Donne ain't done talkin'.

Killing Ourselves with Language as Such

A notion is often a fantasy or ignorance, either wishful thinking that cannot be supported or vicious viscous thinking that is insupportable. Notional thinking leads to bumper stickers and issues du jour and requires a critical mass of misused language. We all complain about how our students do it, reducing complex novels like One Hundred Years of Solitude to a study in "dysfunctional" familial love.[1] But we rarely take a look at the wearing away of our own thinking by the repetitive slow drip of the words we use, words that are given and not made, words (and phrases) that are reproduced like footnotes to a confused dream and that do not poetically make an idea or a contextual world in which old ideas take on new life. "Poeticizing," in the given language of people who want to seem as though they know something the rest of us don't.

Some of my favorites that I would like never to hear again?

Problematic, as though it means something problem doesn't—and if you say it includes the notion that the problem has been identified and formulated, I suggest that problem identifies the problem and, given Susanne Langer's statement that the way in which a question is asked contains the restricted implications of its answer, to identify a problem is to implicitly formulate an approach to solving it, and that approach may blind more than illuminate.

Zee words without necessity or thought: utilize began the movement from the direct and simple use to the important-sounding bureaucratic back in the classic 1960s, and now it has infected even transistorized minds with a virus that spreads to thematize, problematize, and the like. I recently heard a conferencitizing academic (he was engendering col-loquializationalism and trying to be one with the peoplizers) enlarge thematize to "thematicizationalize," carrying academic pidgin English to what I hope is its outer limits.

Space. If you want to talk about critical "space," would you please stay in yours? Reviewing an article for a prominent literary journal recently, I encountered the idea that a Native woman writer needed to "transform her alterity in conventional space." Meaning what? That as a mixblood she needed to learn to live in the world?

Interrogate, as in "interrogate" a question, an idea, or a novel. Inquisitions and military dictatorships interrogate people, and it is not often pleasant; how do you interrogate an interrogation (question), a thing (idea), or a contextual framework that questions (novel)?

Intervention, whether the intervening is critical or authorial. The "author's intervention" into his own novel is just a silly way to avoid using "authorial intention." But authors do not "intervene" in their own work. They write with intentions that they either successfully or unsuccessfully manage rhetorically. And as for "critical intervention," well, it has all the pomposity of a medical doctor trying to cure a disease he can't diagnose or the arrogance of a Catholic priest "intervening" between a Nez Perce and his Creator or the profit motive of an art dealer "intervening" between the painter and a buyer of art.

And, I would add, all words that use novels as sociopolitical or cultural "analyses," a truly overreaching (but undereducated) way to ignore rhetorical structures and methods and to perpetuate the notion that living things can be completely objectified and used.

In *Beloved,* Toni Morrison's narrator (who at this moment speaks from Sethe's point of view) says, "Clever—but schoolteacher beat him [Sixo] anyway to show him that definitions belong to the definers— not the defined."[2] Definitions are language, and language is power. Given language may be false, but given power is most often false—so false that the givers invent words like *empower,* which is used most often in relation to people. Women are "empowered" to refuse the patriarchy. Blacks are "empowered" to resist racism. Indians are "empowered" to run casino gambling in Michigan. Children are "empowered" to disobey parental dicta and treat their bodies as pincushions of revolting fashion.

But power comes from within the self, at best an expression of having drunk from the one main source of one's person and identity. I drink from a mixblood pool, which means that, being part white, part of my power comes from recognizing the whiteness and letting it mix with the so-called redness, refusing essentialisms on either side of the buffalo-head nickel. I am not empowered by anyone else, either white or red. You are not given power, allowed power; you earn it, envision it, and raise it like a child to adulthood. The people who offer "empowerment" and give you its language don't want you to know this; they want you to remain a child and accept on faith the noddle-empty notion that you are "somebody," that you are, by virtue of a specific and highly limited current reality, empowered.

Indeed, just look at the grammatical construction of sentences that use words like *empower*: there is rarely much agency—no one gives power; there is no activity or work involved. But rather it is passive—it is a given; it happens without description or effect. Indeed, the construction comes to mean that if one is "empowered," then one is "allowed."

How would you like it if you were Black and I came along and said, "Okay, I'll allow you to talk endlessly about racism. I empower you. In fact, I'll set up an 'empowerment zone' in which you can talk about race and racism all you want. I'll even put you on TV, and only the people who want to agree with you will watch" (but I as giver will go right on being racist).

What is an empowerment zone? A ghetto or a reservation upon which People of Problems are permitted by some other unspecified Overpower (*Arbeit*) to practice (*macht*) the limited politics (*frei*) of the notional thinker. It makes you free, all right, even and especially from the burdens of reality.

Recently I hired and heard a writer who describes herself as a lesbian Native American woman read from her work. Though singing titled one of her books, there was no song, only preaching of the worst kind, which used easy notional words like *oppression, homophobia, rape*, and the repeated statements that she was a lesbian Native American woman. She got up, after I introduced her, and said that normally she read with other lesbian women, lesbian Native American women, but that she rarely got the chance to read with a gay Native American man and that she was especially pleased to be reading with one this evening.

Why? What if the gay Native American writer were bad? What if he hated women? After all, a lot of Indian men have some real problems with women.

Did she assume that gay men, gay Indian men, have the same politics as she? All gay people think alike? She became angry when someone from the audience implied that all Indians thought alike, had the same politics as one another.

I have thought a lot about these and other statements she made from her diaconate podium. I have thought a lot about both her first and second pieces—her second being a prime example of stereotyped, easy, empowerful emotions, using big unpoetic (unmaking) words, not to evoke, but to demand emotion from the audience. A piece that, in my opinion, ratifies once again the suggestion I make to my writing students to consider carefully whether deep emotions unexpressed do not seem deeper, more courageous, more, if you will, real. Thus, a father who has lost a son and sits in silence on a hill overlooking the gnarled oak tree planted above his son's grave moves me because I know the inarticulation of grief (which may be why many grieving people resent, slightly, too many words of condolence as though they are false—which, to the grieving, of course, they may well be—even when their offering is true). It also moves me because intuitively I pick up on the age of the tree in its gnarliness and thus feel the power of a grief long endured. The clicking chant or wailing song of a mother over the body of her daughter can also move me, but by its simple inarticulate repetition and piercing dissonance, by its ritualized behaviors, not by its personal attempts to articulate that which is inarticulable. In either example, we have the distant, lasting grief that I, as a parent who has lost family and friends before their time to unexpected aneurysms, suicide, and the slow starvation of cancer, can measure and imagine (or approximate since, having two children, I am unwilling to imagine completely that loss at all). Just as you, even if you're not a parent, can measure and imagine, if you do still have an imagination—a (if not the) prime target for destruction by schooling and television. In the other example, we have the immediate grief, the expression of which is ritualized, given context by the culture from which the griever descends. I, who have heard chanting and singing, can feel it because of the wordless music and the ritual that connects this singular grief to all griefs come before and yet to come that resemble this one.

In both cases, I feel the music—the chant or wail and the silence that makes up two-thirds of all music and that in vocal music is sometimes called "phrasing"—and it is the music that plays across the chords of my humanity and allows my imagination to hear the grief. In both cases, I am called upon as a human being who has an active imagination and whose identity is not limited to a singular (or at best dual) notion that I am "empowered" to wear like a tattoo or a birthmark.

When a person who calls herself a writer stands up before her audience and says she is especially glad to be reading with a gay Native American male and then goes on to blazon the tattoos of her identity by repeating the stock phrases she is "empowered," permitted, or allowed and even encouraged by the allowers to use, demanding that I feel what she has convinced herself she has felt in the iconographic language of the romanticizer, I am moved, but not in the best of ways. I remember Sethe's words. And I begin to understand that she has extrapolated one current reality to a characteristic situation in the history of human beings, and she is deeply fooled.[3]

This extrapolation of current reality does not know its limits. At a writing workshop the next afternoon, I listened to this same writer angrily tell a white woman to write from her own experience as a white woman and not attempt to use a narrator who was (in this case) non-white, an "Indian." The white woman had read aloud a piece in which she eulogized All of Us as Human Beings in a way that made my grandfather—and the grandmothers and fathers of all the Indian and Black people in the room—turn wooden on the porches of their Cigar Stores or disappear as though erased from history like the Fundamental Militial erasure of the Holocaust. She defended her piece in terms that meant my gay friend's homosexuality was erased right along with his Creekness. His response to her "We are all human beings. We all look alike underneath," was to lean over and whisper in my ear, "Are there glasses for that?"

However, my other friend, the Indian woman, was insistent and dogmatic: Write from whiteness. To which one of my students—a woman (if it matters), returning to college after thirty-eight years, who happened to be one of the most interesting and perhaps the most able writers in my advanced creative writing seminar—replied with a gentle question: "Someday I might want to try a piece from a man's point of view, though (?)."

"Ah, but you can do that because we always know the language of the oppressor," replied my angry colleague.

We do?

The language of the oppressor. Whose language is that? Am I to envision a trilateral commission of white folks who decide that this is the linguistic currency of the day? Or am I to realize that I am the oppressor, or in part the oppressor, by my complicity in using ever more debased language, whether the elitist twisted language of French or German or American critical theory or the vague and guttural implications of the pointy-headed, ill-liberal anti-educated? The latter is what I tell my students: as professor, I am that which "oppresses" you; I work for the university and thus am an extension of it in both its good and its bad aspects; I use "standards" as a winnowing fan to separate the wheat from the chaff of performance. I give grades. In turn, my students are responsible for being there in my classroom: they choose my course and in choosing it agree to abide by the specific regulations of it (whatever attendance, essays, examinations, or other requirements there may be). Moreover, they choose this university with these requirements, so complain as they may about the specifics of those requirements, they are as free as a Catholic to seek another cathedral; they—not I alone—choose grading as a way of evaluating their work in a shorthand way (a.k.a. Grade Point Averages) that can be put in relation to all other students quickly and easily by administrators and acceptance committees or future employers; and they, indeed, want grades—especially if they are high ones. Take a vote at the beginning of a class, and the majority of students may opt not to have grades put on their assignments; run the class for six weeks with only comments that evaluate the work in words, and these same students start showing up at your office asking what their grade "is" so far. This can lead to the impression that they—students, their parents, and the government, local, state, and federal—are not interested in education anyway. Of course, they're not. But that's another essay.

The point here is that "oppression" sometimes requires the participation of the self-identified "oppressed"—even colonization, which involves both theft and oppression, requires the colonizer to create the complicity of the colonized mind, whether it is by force: Montezuma's thousands surrendering to Cortes's hundreds of stranded Catholic soldiers; or by guile: the careful and purposeful destruction of Mayan books and records of phonemic writing and language as though one silly day they would want to assert that Indios were more primitive because they lacked a phonetic alphabet.

Taking off on conquistador methodology, the white Europeans good-heartedly relocated hundreds of Indian kids in boarding schools, separating them from the practice of their language and beating English into them with the passion of an embittered nun who still mourns the death of Latin. At least these kids could recognize the oppressor, and, because English was a different language altogether, perhaps these kids in their confusions and misunderstandings could be said to "recognize" the language of the oppressor. But by time they came to "know" the language of the oppressor, it was too late. What was lost—a part of their way of making and living in the world—was lost. The only activity open to them was to attempt to re-create that world by re-creating language, whether that meant reestablishing fluency in their native tongues or using the language given to them in their own adaptive way to establish a world in which they could live, dodging the manipulative assumptions of their "oppressors."[4]

In some ways, that is what the Indian woman writer, insisting on writing from ("real" world, unimagined) experience, believes she is doing; and she does not even realize that she's fudging her own prescriptions by saying that women can write from the point of view of men because they "know" the language of the oppressor. It is also what the white woman thought she was doing, writing from the ("sympathetic," unimagined) experience of her mixblood adopted grandchild. One is a reactionary position; the other a nostalgic one. Both lack imagination. The reactionary Indian woman's position demands the same lack of imaginative vision that the reactionary white male (poor *pendejo* that he is) displays with the cry of his peacock, who thinks in his privilege that he is being picked on unfairly. The Indian woman claims that being picked on unfairly gives her privilege—and the privilege in the extreme case is to reproduce the actions of the oppressor by judging people and telling them what they may or may not do. The nostalgic woman's imagination is less circumscribed than her Indian counterpart only in that her imagination is for all intents and purposes dead, or at best unfocussed, like a wet night fog in which she must dodge the rush of headlights. Sensing that her world and the assumptions on which she has been fed are as nutritionless as commodity cheese, by creating or re-creating new assumptions, she unwittingly destroys the very things she would appropriate. Both women's imaginations have been damaged, if not destroyed, by TV and talk shows and sitcoms and advertising and empty talk, all of which give us the currency of language that we can exchange for thought. Reaction and nostalgia both forget the rhetorical nature of their constructs, which "have been forgotten by convention and habitual use."[5]

Walter Benjamin says, "Mental [being] is identical with linguistic being only insofar as it is capable of communication,"[6] and we might well add that only insofar as it is capably communicated can it be said to exist. Language that communicates is poetical: it makes a world of mental being in which we are pleased to live, even for a time. Dead language is dead because it does not make a world, certainly not one in which one could be said to be pleased to live, even for a moment. The pleasing world is the context of communication and therefore as important as the heart is to mental being. It runs the processes that allow the mental processes to exist and to be capably communicated by language. So language that communicates little or nothing may be called "dead." It belongs in the office of dead letters and should be refused with all the strength of Bartleby's "I prefer not to."[7]

To reexamine what the Indian woman was saying, then, if the oppressed "know" the (dead) language of the oppressor, isn't what they "know" the very dead language given to them by the oppressor? After all, the oppressor certainly must control if not the production of language then its distribution—not unlike the Spanish controlled the language of the Maya by preventing its distribution. The "oppressor" cleverly distributes to the "oppressed" the very language by which the oppressed would know the language of the oppressor. We can, then, use the words the "oppressor" gives us to know little more than what the "oppressor" wants us to know—which in this case is to give the veneer of value to interchangeable low-level workers and give them the mock appearance of importance as the owners get richer and the rest of us cling by our fingernails to the middle class. We often help create this appearance by using language given to us to describe difference and then waddle in the difference as, not seeing what is on the backside of the parchment of fate because of our lack of candlepower, we attempt to imitate the powers and positions of the colonizers and owners. Declaring ourselves "marginal," we perpetuate the very distinctions that the "oppressors" depend upon for their power and oppressive success; and we begin to exclude from our ranks anyone who dares to disagree with our faith of and in marginality.

Changing the words does not change the assumptions but often only reduces the skeptical response and significance of understanding while letting the imagination—which is the a priori to compassion and understanding—become dull and voyeuristic. As Henry Louis Gates seems to recognize by his preference for "colored" over "Black" or "African-American," "people of color" is a grammatical construct that still means "colored people." Because it's a new construct it may sound better, unless you put it the way I did to a colleague who spoke of sending colored writing by email.

"Please, Diane," I said. "It's 'Writing of Color.' "

A dangerous joke, these days, in a room full of academics. However, Diane, a Cherokee mixblood, laughed.

Whether colored writing or writing of color, it means the same thing. And the attitudes of historical oppression, repression, or unjust discrimination haven't changed any more than the "east to west" and "lower to higher" articles of faith upon which America is founded.[8] In the "long delay" (is this Linda Hogan?) between past and future, we need to examine "Not Ideas about the Thing but the Thing Itself" (Wallace Stevens), and the way to overcome being a colored person is to be comfortable with our colors. Only people afraid of the truth lie in the sun, proof of their unhappiness with being pale-faced like white people, translucent like those plastic models of the circulatory systems in biology class, or of their falling for rainbowed essentialisms.

"Truth waits in the creek," Roberta Hill Whiteman says. She's right.

In all our drive to make language less descriptive and less emotionally active and more "correct," are my objections so far from Jorie Graham's poem "Self-Portrait" in which "something difficult is disappearing from our lives, something critical / like emphasis / or the blue / deep-grooved river currents now reduced to pattern / in the ice"? The so-called oppressor wants us to have patterning words that reduce emphasis and that etherize and besot our critical ability to discern attitude and meaning from empty generalizations.[9] In accepting the language of the oppressor, we not only obfuscate, but we participate in our own oppression. In the bodies of adults, we often act like day-care children; we are, in other words, retarded in the development of our attachments to thinking.

Thus, to say that one must write from actual experience (is not what is imagined experienced?) and not appropriate points of view not rightly "ours" is to speak with the voice of the (self-)oppressor who lacks imagination. We have no real point of view until we imagine it.

Still, appropriation remains a complicated problem, and like a person waiting for acceptance into Kenneth Burke's genteel parlor of cultural conversation, I want to put in my small oar and keep stirring the waters even if I don't get anywhere. For sure, there are a whole bunch of white guys and gals (for lack of a better term) who want to play at sympathetic understanding while the market's hot, who—and I do not doubt this—are sincere in the belief that they are understanding, and yet who cannot give up their deep-seated generational and foundational training that puts them in what they presuppose to be a position of needing to sympathize rather than be sympathized with (for their lack of understanding). White guys and gals who do anthologies about the meaning of ethnicity with mainly white guy and gal writers; white gals and guys who anthologize modern American women's literature and leave out Linda Hogan or Roberta Whiteman; or white guys and gals who reproduce the valorization of the colonialist by telling a graduate student that Diane Glancy (three books of stories, two books of essays, seven books of poems, a play, and several novels) is not important enough for chapters in his dissertation.

One thing the "oppressor" (who gave us this very word to use about her or him) does is appropriate the things and appearances of others while propagating the same assumptions that he and she came with to the New World. Simply the notion—which is still held and still virulently continued in so many provable ways—that the European in his literature and culture and point of view is superior demands an overwhelming sense of, or belief in, linear progression, even to the extent of calculatedly wiping out superior and more advanced civilizations like the Maya. Roy Harvey Pearce calls it the "progressivist pattern of pity and censure."[10]

We can say that the American [by which Pearce means the immigrant European], as the self-consciously civilized and civilizing man, could envision the possibilities of a life free from what he somehow felt to be the complexities of civilization. Envisioning that life, he might very well yearn for it. But seeing it, as he thought, in disturbing actuality to the west, he hated himself for his yearning. He was tempted, we might say; and he felt driven to destroy the temptation and likewise the tempters.[11]

Pearce possibly misplaces the self-hatred of the European who keeps fleeing one location for another because he can't stand himself, "progressively" taking on newer or changed appearances and making up his reasons after the fact, reasons such as the phony fantasy of a need for religious freedom or a nostalgic fantasy of explorers needing to "discover" routes to the Indies. The contemporary self-hating Euramerican demands and uses a sort of reductive evolution of awareness and thinking: he teaches his children to think of the Maya in comparative, equalizing terms; he teaches his children that even if the Maya are proven in the new historical narratives to have been more advanced, such proofs reveal only the problem with "narrative" and not "fact"; or he teaches them that the Maya were more advanced than was formerly thought, but of course not more advanced than Europeans in literature, science, art, agriculture, and even political organization, even though they were, in many ways. Coming himself from an arrogant, self-righteous religion that reenacts cannibalism every Sunday, eating the body and drinking the blood of a sacrificial victim, he says:

"And besides," (there is always a besides), "didn't the Mayan priests cut out virgin hearts?"

"No," you say. "That was the . . ."

"Oh, right. Aztecs. Well . . ."

And yet the Maya remain comparatively sullied in the parlor air by the blood sacrifice of the Aztecs as the parlor's habitués congratulate themselves on having never been as bloody-minded as those ancient Indians.[12] Where the Maya originally were wiped out by a burgeoning population, overuse of land, and war, these days they get wiped out by the sense of temporal distance from us, combined with comparative misrepresentation, as though human beings have progressed in a line from Lucy to mom, homo erectus to homo the wise and knowing.

Similarly, their literature and history. By comparison (2000 with 300 CE), the literature of the Mayans was pretty backward (we have Gutenberg and Disney, after all); no one asks what kind of grunting Europeans were doing around 300 CE in the depths of the Porchean forests. Moreover, in the Mayan world there is no linear descendency and linear influence as in the gradual influential development of English literature, and their histories record only events important to the Maya in a way that is culturally nuanced—a criticism that only recently has turned less critical with the realization that culturally nuanced history may be a better history than the plain and simple lies some people call facts.[13]

In fact, isn't it the false sense of linear development that can so depress an intelligent reader these days? He or she expects literature to be improving, and because it isn't, he or she falls prey to the despair of public reputations. Really what he needs to see is that literature does not improve but remains the same. There is not more good literature just because there is more published writing. But with all those books available, it becomes difficult to judge. Thus, the idea of "good" as defined by the definers becomes entangled with money or prizes. When Oprah Winfrey (as competent and admirable a person as she is) selects books for people to read and turns them into best-sellers or when Richard Ford, whose solipsistic dullness seems to feed like bacteria on the mold of praise, receives a Pulitzer Prize, the state of literature can seem pretty bleak. And yet literature is still there, still being written and read, published by presses you have to seek to hear of—Arte Publico, Permanent, Mercury House, White Pine, Curbstone, Sun & Moon, West End—or the university presses—Nebraska, Nevada, Michigan State, and Arizona. Some literature makes it into the mainstream—Vea, Garcia-Marquez, Swift, Querry, Silko, Morrison, Reveles, Williams, Munro, King, Szanto, or Vaz—but it makes it as commodity, not as literature. Still, the state of literature is like the state of college students: there is the same number of good ones, but since there are more students, it looks as though they are getting worse.[14] In other words, art and the use of the imagination seem to be a numerical constant, more or less, and will survive, like Native Americans or Chicanos, and periodically seem to revive. Perhaps—imagine this!—right now, art and literature's revival is being driven by the survivors in Native America or the Latino Community.

Art does not develop like a time-line; art is like a bush, with new branches sprouting and growing while others wither. Art and literature, in other words, are like the evolution and natural selection of human beings. Strong and enduring work occupies the same geological time as that which will disappear by natural selection. Even among natural historians, the true believers in linear evolutionary relationships (like C. Loring Brace) cannot bring themselves to reimagine the evidence that "two (or more) human species might have interacted in one place."

> He [Brace] even invents the label "hominid catastrophism" to stigmatize the view (now favored by most paleontologists, particularly for the replacement of Neanderthals by moderns in Europe) that a temporal transition from one species to another might arise by immigration of the latter species from another region (followed by local extinction of the original inhabitant), rather than by linear evolutionary transformation. . . . Our present reality of one worldwide species is the oddity, not the norm—and we have been fooled by our bad habit of generalizing a transient and contingent present.[15]

Now we—lesbian Native American writer or confused mixblood essayist—must be careful not to generalize too much from the transient and contingent present. Yet it is fair to say that if literature develops similarly to the hominids who make literature, then Faulkner and Garcia-Marquez are branches of the same bush. The same bush. Indeed, if I may stretch the metaphor into an almost metaphysical conceit and invert John Donne's famous Valedictory compass in which the lovers are joined in the air, each with his or her compassed foot on the ground, Faulkner and Garcia-Marquez are branches pushing out from the trunk of an Oak as ancient as Penelope and Odysseus's bed. The two writers are not joined in ethereal spirituality, nourished only on the wishings of the air that can (and do) sometimes bear beauty and truth; they are joined in the dirt, the soil, in the traditions that come from the earth and that, planted and tended, bear beauty and fruit to nourish the teller of stories. It is the same foul rag and bone shop Yeats stayed rooted in; the soil of Homer who planted Odysseus's oak; and the earth of those civilizations that have always told stories as though they were equal in truth to narrative, "nuanced" histories—Nuestra America. Whether it is the Maya, who record events with narrative nuance, or the Nez Perce, whose histories bear in the moment of telling the corroboration of two, three, or four other people who were there or who heard it told from their grandmothers and grandfathers, narrative is a process that bears fruit and nourishes the autochthonous whole hominid, the indigeno, the mixblooded survivor whose endurance surpasses all time-bound understanding. And though they speak the truth as they know it with "authority," they hold within themselves a humility of approach, a humbleness toward their object that creates an attitude of gratitude and respect and honor that those joined in John Donne's aether no longer seem to have.

It is indignation and anger at the arrogance of non-indigenos who, like rich kids raised to expect the world, never expect their assumptions to be open to question that leads us adopt the superficial language of the "oppressor" and claim that writing from experience means that not everyone or anyone can write about Indian or Black or Chicano or Asian things. As much as I recognize (and sometimes feel) that anger, I am obliged to take a contrary position to the notions it generates or produces. Taking off on Stephen Jay Gould's ideas about evolution, we can say that the predominant way of thinking—which is east to west, primitive (or savage) to civilized, lower to higher—fools us by generalizing the very transient and contingent present that it would overcome. It is a fashionable language, with about as much meaning as the length of a hem or the doubling of a blazer breast. It takes a contingent and, if observed in relation to the seven gener-ations forward and backward of indigeno thinking, utterly transient notion, and gives it a word or a grammatical construction, making an iconographic symbol of the passing notion, oftentimes inventing a holographic binary of opposition and mutual exclusion.

This kind of thinking (if "notion" and "thinking" are not mutually exclusive, the latter canceling out the former by simply occurring) is the real, fully colonized substitution of notion for thought, and the fully colonized notioner remains one who wants to hunker down in the gazebo as it gets battered by the "enemy," who wants to maintain a defensive position (usually by aspersive names), who wants to romanticize their defense, make an icon of it, and talk about it—not until, but even though, at the outset, the talk is empty. Just as I suspect Roy Harvey Pearce misplaces the self-hatred of the fleeing European pilgrim, taking on ever newer appearances (which finds its apotheosis in "fashion") and ever newer terminology or language, we want to be careful not to misplace the reductive self-hatred of the colonized person who proclaims himself or herself a "victim" of the "oppressor" and flees from one "victimization" to another, all the time reinventing a more bureaucratic and less personal language along the way. For although he and she do not seem to know it, in their self-proclaimed victimhood, they stand on the steps to the gazebo right alongside the dead white guys and gals against whom they live their fantasies, accepting the tools of oppression as the tools of their resistance to oppression, accepting the meaningless words and metaphorically allowing their enemies to use those very words, which are the length of two-by-fours and the weight of a sledge hammer, to batter the gazebo. It's what the dead white guys and gals want; it's what the notional thinkers who call themselves victims are allowed or empowered by them to do. It is this linear and causal, defensive, self-hating and self-pitying posture, which sees everything as happening to us as though we did not help it to happen, that we need to abandon, once we step inside the gazebo of literary and cultural conversation.

Inside the gazebo, the only true power must be the imagination. From the active and full imagination comes empathy, compassion, the "something difficult" that is being human, and understanding without appropriation. And the active imagination prefers not to indulge itself, bury itself with the meaningless currency of a bureaucratic or academic televised language given by oppressors to the oppressed.

Moreover, imagination, not fantasy, is the soil of identity. If power comes from within the self, the self comes from within a real but open and changing community. All of us in our language as such can imagine a culture or community that does not believe in European "progress," enduring the contingent and transient (three hundred years is little more than the blip of my lifetime) overlay of a dominant, "progressive" mainstream culture. When that dominant culture—as is the fitting end to commercialism—recedes like a tide, it reveals bedrock that has been there for all time. We call that survival, the end result of a timeless endurance.

Since the time when conquistadors attempted to "prove" that Mayan culture was inferior to theirs by purposely destroying the Maya's books, ignoring the "civilization" of Tenochtitlan, an American "theory" that is connected to an American art and artistic tradition has endured beneath the overlay of European theory and art. This is not to devalue European art or theory. It is only to envision the probability that as European dominance recedes and takes its proportionate and rightful place in the history of human beings, what was here when the conquistadors arrived will be revealed as having endured and survived, but only if we survivors stop adopting the language of the oppressor to try to describe ourselves as oppressed, only if we refuse to give up the power of imagination, which is not limited by blood or race or parentage but only by our language as such.

Con safos

In the Gazebo

I

If one refuses to be "empowered" by the "oppressor" and to use his or her language to delude himself with the very notions, such as freedom or power with which the "oppressor" wants you to delude yourself—living in a kind of static time of fashion in which the fashion seems to change but the time does not, and everything goes round and round like a wheel whose axle is slowly wearing away until the wheels fall off, and one is left holding the empty bag of afterbirth—then one is also refusing to be "oppressed."

Refusal is very different from "resistance." For one, resistance tends to be made up from anecdotal foreshortened narratives that are all about "us" and especially "me." We live in an age when the focus of time is so foreshortened and the sense of our connection to our grandmothers and fathers and great-grandchildren is so atrophied that an elfin figure from Northern Europe called Bjork can say in a television interview that she writes songs about "me learning about me" and expect the interviewer and the audience to actually care. "Me" establishes its supposed import by making its insignificance seem large against a fantasized Great Other—a fantasy of resistance to hegemony and homogenization that means that "me" in many ways has to behave just like that fantasized Other in such ways as not listening to anyone but one's self (or with one's "we" group of agreement or "agweement"), almost as well as literary critics who must listen to themselves alone if they are going to continue their ignorant appropriation of minority literature while wearing the transparent cloth of liberal guilt. Me stops listening and plows straight ahead with actions that may injure but that are justified by the fantasy of the injuries being inflicted upon what me knows of me without connection or understanding drawn from the continued perceptions of connections with all the others the Great Other comprises and without any wisdom that comes from realizing that one is at the very least co-responsible, if not for the historical events, then for the continued effects of those events. Behaving like the Great Other means, in other words, that you *are* that Great Other since behavior, the process of being, is who you are; near-absolute resistance is not very different from near-absolute compliance.

The absence of an aggressive or loud resistance suggests that the "Me" or the "We" has cultivated an extremely difficult flexibility and tolerance even for insult that may seem like a resignation to fate or destiny, a lack of caring or involvement, or an absence of sensitivity. Really, it is the transformation of resistance into refusal that allows the Me *and* the We to survive in a positive way that is not always limited to defining itself in opposition. We get hurt. We get angry. But we get over it (because we have a life).

Of course, if you are not loud and aggressive and always opposed, then in the United States the agents of government (television, the FBI, bureaucrats) will try to make you loud—either to cause your self-destruction by encouraging you to occupy yourself with paranoid conspiracy theories or to co-opt your resistance into the endless illusions of adaptability that are task forces and special committees. To be formed or to form yourself into a loud and continuous opposition means not only that you are safe and safely recognizable, virtually every movement and moment predictable, but also that you define yourself in relation to the Great Other like iron filings that have attached to one arm of the Great Magnet. Moreover, it means that you accept the fact that the Great Other not only exists but has a kind of legitimacy—without it, you would lose all definition—and often it is this legitimized Other (Euramerican cultural theorists) that takes over defining us as *oppositus extremis*, as a way of defining the liberal necessity while at the same time defining themselves as not Great Others but Great Sympathizers (who are not, of course, according to them, really like that awful Great Other they so easily and banally represent with sad straw men like Newt Gingrich).

And so, even if the Great Other does manage to change (or to pretend convincingly to have changed), you are forced to find something else in the Other to define yourself against in an endlessly reductive denial of self-responsibility as well as increasingly absurd arguments and descriptions of your own supposed "otherness" or "marginality."

An anecdotal example of what I mean is my grandfather telling me and my sisters, the first time one of us was surprised by the backbiting of Indian politics, that he moved out of Indian country to get away, not from the abuses of Indians by the Feds, but from the abuses of Indians by Indians. It surprised me as much as my sisters then. Nowadays, though, I tell jokes that go like this: if you want to be sure an Indian does not get hired, put five Indians on the hiring committee. We can further the joke by adding that if you want to make sure that the mediocre or even stupid Indian gets hired, put one Indian and four Euramerican sympathizers on the committee.

When the federal government approached my grandfather and told him he needed to enroll, to get a number, like a Star of David, he refused with the simple wisdom—with which I have tried to live all my life and have tried to pass on to my children—that no one, not the government and not any other Indian who fantasizes himself or herself the "head" Indian or *Reichsfürer* of Identity, can tell you who you are or how you are supposed to be. Though I have relatives on the rolls, though I have been invited to enroll as well as to receive a name, the name is the only thing I would not refuse, not because I believe it is somehow wrong to be enrolled, but because I have no choice or desire but to honor my grandfather.

When an Indian who bought his enrollment card with Kellogg boxtops tries to tell you who you are (or are not), he is acting like a weak and ineffectual Fed. When a colleague tries to disregard your work, implying that it gets published because you are Indian, he too sounds like a weak and ineffectual Fed. Together they are like seed potatoes for Congress in the midst of an Irish potato blight. To such people one can only say, Get your own potholes in your road of life and don't try to fill in mine with your dirt.

Humor is the first tool of refusal, and it can only really be developed by a "we" when the community recognizes its own responsibility in the things that have happened to them, even if that "responsibility" is the recognition of a kind of naivete or even foresightless stupidity. Certainly, it was kind of naive of the Pueblo Indians to think in 1692 that Diego de Vargas's promises of peace were anything but a false trick, or that once defeated by the great Pueblo Revolt in 1680, the

Spanish who left would be any less cruel or violent when they returned under de Vargas. That naivete, however, while the immediate senses of perception and forecast understanding illustrate it as a failure, in the longer term of the history of the Pueblo people, it colors their success and survival because their worldview connects of all things, including even the Spanish Catholics, by using their humored adaptability to change—without enthusiastically subscribing to any immediate change. In fact, it is giving up humored naivete that, in specific instances, causes one Pueblo person to battle another in skirmishes of identity politics and political "power" on the campuses of New Mexico and Arizona, and thus it is the loss of that naivete—or, better, that wise innocence—that threatens the modern Pueblo.

Not unlike the Pueblos, the Jews of Germany seem, from my vantage point and only in these very limited terms, naive. Even though exiled, driven, excluded, denigrated in Europe for centuries, Jewish people believed that their German neighbors and even friends would not do what they did. In regard to the unspeakable horror of the Holocaust, there was a kind of blinkered responsibility in this, with blinders that, as with Indian people, got torn off or very actually cut off.

Briefly—my point is not history but humor—despite the virulent anti-Semitism that in all likelihood still exists even below the surface of tomato Salsa commercials in which—and it's certainly true in Michigan—"New York" means alien and Jewish, a place where "real" romantically individualistic "Americans" don't live, Jews, like the Pueblo people, have survived, and this survival demands a sense of humor. "Jewish" humor may be dark humor—how could it be anything else? Often Indian humor is mistaken by non-Indians as being "bitter," but it isn't bitterness but simple and straightforward recognition of the things that have happened while trying not to be buried by the negative anger and horrible sense of hurt and injustice.

Other groups of people depend on humor to allow the transformation from resistance to refusal. The Irish have it (though in Northern Ireland the IRA and the Unionists seem to have lost it); and anyone who thinks Chicanos don't should read Daniel Reveles's essay, "Of Time and Circumstance," or José Antonio Burciaga's essay on "Pendejismo."[1]

At this juncture, I am tempted to use humor and Roy Harvey Pearce's *Savagism and Civilization* to divide people into two groups: the "savage," who have humor; and the "civilized," who want to acquire the humor, make an icon of the humorous and then try to destroy its sense by calling it "dark" or "bitter." Lately I have noticed angrily defensive speeches coming from white males about the "transparency" of the false metaphor of "whiteness," asking what does "whiteness" mean? If I could joke with them, serious literary people that most of my friends are, I'd say it's the colorless all-color of disbelief that causes them, the white guys, to be so palely portrayed and joked about.

After all, race is (and whiteness is) an invention. But who was it that invented colors to use to classify whole groups of invented people—black, red, yellow, brown? White guys. In Germany, Mexico, the Bahamas, Ethiopia, China, and the United States, who used colors to classify and associate the colored with the savage, the primitive, the unwashed and uncivilized? Who made propaganda films making "dark" Jews into vermin? And how many SS officers were filtered through the Vatican or Radio Free Europe offices to escape to South America or the United States? Who made Andrew Jackson into a hero? Or Custer? Who emptied and filled the so-called frontier of Indian people according to mineral or budgetary need? Who purposely and systematically destroyed as much as they could of Mayan culture? Who enslaved the Indios of Potosi to mine silver so they could switch from a barter, feudal economy to one of monetary exchange? White guys and girls. It's pretty funny, if you think about it, and there's a whole lot of honkin' going on about making these historical opacities of whiteness transparent.

But the whiteness of the haole aside—after all, most people are part-white, just like most people are part-black, and many of the people I love are what we could mistakenly call white—I suspect the real point here is humor. Try this on: the farther you are from a nourishing source of your identity, the more of your humor that is lost. Humor, in other words, is like the size of Peter Pan's shadow, inversely proportional to its distance from the source of identity—the closer you are, the bigger the shadow of your humor. There is a story about a buffalo boy who gets his power from one pool of spring water. The farther he gets from it, the thirstier he gets, until he drinks from other pools and loses all his power. Humor is like that. The farther you get from it, the more certain it becomes that you will never get it back.

Or try this: if Eco is right that Americans seek the real and thus create the fake, then we could say that the faker you are the more serious you become, because you are hell-bent on making the fake real. When a student comes up to me and says, "I'm part Cherokee," my possible responses are, "So?" or "Which part?" Being part Cherokee is not a solution to being white any more than being white is necessarily something we would call bad.

The only solution to our colors is to know them and yet to refuse them. This is not the same as resisting them—changing the words or pretending that we don't sometimes fall prey to them; it is a refusal that comes from humor and cross-cultural understanding. The humor comes first, and it must not be lost.

In terms of laughter, the kind of humor we need to keep alive is perhaps ironical, but definitely satirical. Not burlesque. Burlesque, while often funny, usually laughs at someone's foibles or curious habits. Insofar as it is not cruel, burlesque is okay (burlesquing a retarded person, for example, or *Saturday Night Live*'s burlesques of Janet Reno are cruel; burlesquing O. J. Simpson or Richard Nixon is not, if only because satire is not available in regard to acquitted or pardoned felons like Simpson or Nixon). But when you laugh *at* (this is rather obvious) you don't laugh *with*; when you laugh *at*, you are laughing at how the object is different from you. Satire, on the other hand, pokes fun at something in such a way that we recognize our connection to it, see in an instant of self-awareness that "somethingness" in ourselves; and in laughing as a group, we are laughing at ourselves and a community of selves in a way that can even evoke change or induce understanding of the satirized behavior. Satire forms community, and it is this community that helps people endure and survive.

Chippewa man who performs for school children at the Nokomis Center: "You kids name some Native American Indian tribes?"

An eight-year-old boy gets his hand in the air first, metaphorically slamming his hand down on his jeopardized game buzzer.

"You."

156

"What is a Chippewa, Alex?"

"Chippewa. There's no such thing as Chippewa. Chippewa is a word that comes from white people slurring 'Ojibwa.' O-jib-wa. Oji-bwa. Ji-bwa. Chip-wa. Chip-e-wa. Chippewa. So don't call us Chippewa. We don't like Chippewa. We're Ojibwa. People of the Three Fires. O-da-wa. O-ji-bwa. Potawatomi. Got that?"

Silence. Gee, thanks, Alex.

"You white kids know any others? How 'bout you?" he says, pointing to Rachel Antonia Penn.

"Nez Perce?" Rachel offers, her face bright with an embarrassed red from being singled out.

"See? You see what colonization has done? It's 'Nez Pur-say,' not Nez Purse. Nez Pur-say. It's a French name. The French gave that name to the 'Nez Pur-say.' "

Didn't the French give the Ojibwa the name Chippewa? Rachel asked me later. An eight-year-old plumbs the depth of the Chippewa man's single-minded ability to be stupefied by politics and a sense of identity that is rice-paper thin.

"Did you tell him that you are Nez Perce [pronounced 'purse']?" I asked as we walked toward school the next morning.

"No."

I didn't ask why not. She was only eight, after all.

"He was mean, Daddy."

"I'll bet he was serious, though." I shook my head and laughed. "All of us," I said.

"What, Daddy?"

"Nokomis means 'all of us.' " I look down at her, more interested in selecting a ball of ice for us to soccer-kick to school, passing it back and forth in a silent communication. I grinned. "Guess we better leave it all of them, huh?"

She smiled as the ice ball skidded three feet down the road in perfect position for me to slide it back to her without losing a step. She knew full well that I was wondering where the all of us had gone with Indians like this pendejo.

"The old guy was there, though," she said three or four kicks later. And in so saying, she told me she knew where all of us were, because that elder had helped her and her friend Margaret make small drums one Saturday, without caring about whether Margaret was transparent or opaque. Rather than perform a burlesque of himself, he gently teased the kids, joking with them, demonstrated his ability to laugh at the world as well as at himself. Such an ability to laugh at yourself or to join in laughter with others, to be humorous, implies an attitude of refusal, recognition, and knowing that the community will survive (in part because you can see around you that it has survived). While resistance tends to be negatively defined and dependent on isolated anecdote seriously examined, refusal tends to be more balanced, with an equal or greater measure of positive attitude or feeling.

That elder has what I would call humor. The younger guy has what I would call a resistant strain of terminal *pendejismo*, and I've got some potholes in my pur-say to sell him for his road of life.

Daniel Reveles on the relation between borderland Mexico and borderland United States:

> "Buenos días. . . . How are things on the Other Side?"
> "Getting better every day. How are things in Mexico?"
> "We are making steady progress in our effort to emulate everything you do up there. We admire your efficiency. We only have two intersections with traffic lights, but the municipality has just installed left-turn-only arrows."
> "Why, that's marvelous, you'll see a big difference."
> "We already do. You see we don't have left turn lanes."[2]

Or, later in the same tale,

> "Did you buy the microwave?"
> "Sí, I went to one of your large department stores and met with one of your recycled people with a dormant soul, a woman with the look of defeat on her lifeless face. We conducted the entire transaction without exchanging a single word. So, just to see if she might be human, I said, 'The microwave is for my bedridden grandmother.' And do you know what she replied?"
> "I can't imagine."
> " 'Bedding is on the second floor, have a nice day.' I suspect she operates on two C-type batteries and a diet of microchip cookies."[3]

Without this balance, no narrative is trustworthy. When you say that Foucault says that all sexual desire is founded in incest, you have to say, "Well, *chinga su padre?*" and realize that even though you think Foucault is as nuts as hands waving with LSD, it might be you who is wrong.

On the simplest level, the balance is satirical commentary on Mexico, balanced by satirical comment on the Other Side, though even here the humor is much more complicated. And though Reveles makes us laugh time and again, he also is quite serious even when not making us laugh, but with a similarly complex balance in which he does not too much love one side or other of the border.

This complex balance is also what many Indian stories tell us to learn and maintain: without balance, we run the risk of loving frog songs too much. In the Menominee story, it is okay to enjoy the songs of frogs but quite another to love frog songs so much that you waste (and lose) your life and perspective listening to them. In a Mashpee story, it's okay to want a pot of gold that will allow you to feed and clothe your children, but not if it means loving the gold more than your children.[4]

What tradition(s) is this? Oral. And the oral in writing is narrative.

When I say that, however, I must clarify it: one cannot often refuse to be dominated by superior military force or political power or the money of ownership, as represented by the Catholic Church or Bill Gates; the Western Hemisphere "comes" as though Christianity and Windows 98 were preinstalled at the making of it. Yet even if those two dominations come preinstalled, and even if one uses Windows, one can refuse to be oppressed. How? By maintaining a sense of humor, by not participating in the attitudes and presumptions that come like Internet Explorers installed with Windows, by refusing to adopt the language and the attitudes that go with it, one can survive the temporary overlays of dominance.

How? By narrative and by the understanding that "temporary" may be a lifetime.

Let me first dispel some of the fears about "narrative." It is a word that has been used by non-Indios and Indios alike to establish the seriousness and reality of lies. Usually the criticism of narrative includes potshots at post-modernist "relativity" by judges such as Richard Posner, as well as by admirable people such as the brilliant and herein oft-quoted Stephen Jay Gould, as though they themselves were not exhibiting their own life of post-modern cultural paranoia (or what I alternately call the Chicken Licken or the George Will complex) by adopting such a small "scale" of perception and context that from the inside of their fragmented and frightened moment, they see only fragmentation and "relativity."[5] This is especially highlighted by Stephen Jay Gould, whose offhanded comment about post-modern relativity appears in an article in which Gould discusses "one of the most illuminating issues of intellectual life and nature's construction: the theme of scaling, or strikingly different ways of viewing the world—with no single way either universally 'normal' or 'better' than any other—from *disparate vantage points of an observer's size or life span.*"[6]

What Gould and Posner, along with George F. Will, my favorite and easiest target (the man is simply a Goldwater of attitudes, even ones with which I sometimes agree), may be saying is twofold: they may be arguing against seeing the world on a different scale of time and size, against seeing the world from a point of view different from their own; or they may think they are arguing against the use of contextual relativity to create a narrative that excuses a view of the world in which the social fabric is torn, first to quilting patches, and finally to individual threads, where each thread forms its narrative around the false and easy binary of "us" against "them."

Again, we are made to take up the question of intention. Using our imaginations and using language that eschews obfuscation (one of my father's oldest jokes), we have to adopt a temporally and spatially broader view (I recommend seven generations forward and backward) and ask what the intentions of any narrative are. In the broadest critical view, is it intended to delineate (and even fantasize or romanticize) "difference?" Or is it intended to find and describe "similarity," while noting small, though perhaps significant (and even nonnegotiable or unchangeable) differences along the way? The latter is what I call *semejanza,* using Spanish in a mild effort to remove it from the incredibly pervasive and powerful assumptions of eastness to westness, lowerness to higherness. *Semejanza* was in the Western Hemisphere ten thousand years ago; *semejanza* remains alive and well beneath the cemented fixity of the mainstream; *semejanza* allows *mestizaje,* or resistance, while focusing on the positive aspects of survival and endurance.

In narrative, *semejanza* reveals itself, first and foremost, in the revealed intentions of the expressed author (a more accurate description of Wayne Booth's "implied" author). It is not limited or marked out by race or background, although there can be something a little wearying about non-Indios jumping on the bandwagon without first apprenticing themselves to the band and maybe learning a little of the music.[7] It is, like the indigenous culture from which I take the word, "slow," but not slow of mind or slow of perception; rather, it is slow by contrast, because it always takes into account the fact that "civilization" is an artifice that must be made every day within a contextual scale of fifty thousand days, that human "progress" is mostly a commercial lie, and that change, if it occurs, is slow and indeed must not be hurried, in absolute contrast to the rush to appropriate, dominate, steal and use up that preoccupies the "fast" cultures bound by their sense that the here and now is large in time and meaning. It is "slow" because it brakes for human beings and human things (such as food, ritual or communal celebration, love, connection, etc.). The "fast" cultures do not brake, they accelerate; they do not connect, they divide; their brains are all awhirr with little, and their ears can't even hear themselves listening to themselves listening while paying no attention whatsoever to the voice, the speaker, the expressed authors of other scales and other ways of perceiving. Like those driver education films in which Mr. Centrifugal Force pushes the car outward from the radial center of a curve and makes the car crash into an oak tree, fragmenting car and driver alike, the hurry of the "fast" cultures causes them to spin out of control and fragment into smaller and smaller particles. They are the quarks of culture, and what they quark about is "civilization." They are disconnected from their generational backgrounds and the futures of the great-great-great-grandchildren, from the short history of their country, from any community (unless it's their Sunday Morning pretend communities, where they justify smiting non-Christians with everything from rods to MX missiles), from their families, from themselves. The intentions of the *semejanza* writer, then, are an expressed awareness of human connection as well as the connections of humans with all things living—and in many of the refusing and surviving cultures, all things that are not manufactured are believed to be alive, and thus the relation of human being to thing is a vital and respectful one.

If everything is connected and not separated the way many post-modernists seem to think ("subject" from group, author from book, one fragment of identity from all other fragments of it, this decade from the last, World War II from World War I, the "Indian Wars" from the greed for minerals and land and the need to prove that the truth is what lie you make it), then in order to express this connection, the *semejanza* writer must fully use his imagination to understand the fullness of the truth he wants to convey, a truth that when expressed may well be a conflation of facts.

It is not unlike the image of destiny in *One Hundred Years of Solitude* (*Cien Años de Soledad*):

> Trying to overcome his [Aureliano's] disturbance, he grasped at the voice that he was losing, the life that was leaving him, the memory that was turning into a petrified polyp, and he spoke to her [Amaranta Úrsula] about the priestly destiny of Sanskrit, the scientific possibility of seeing the future showing through in time as one sees what is written on the back of a sheet of paper through the light, the necessity of deciphering the predictions so that they would not defeat themselves, and the Centuries of Nostradamus.[8]

Although it is predicted, Aureliano grasps at the wrong thing: at the disturbing presence of his aunt with whom he will produce a child with the tail of a pig who is eaten by all the ants in the world. Nonetheless, despite its prediction (which is based on the first or original sin of his forebears, José Arcadio Buendía and Úrsula, who are related by birth), it gives us an image of how the survival of the non-European people in the Western Hemisphere is coming to pass. The European attitudes, so violent and so willing to dominate, are losing their voice. Losing their listeners, they have been shouting for some time now, and they are not just growing hoarse, they are growing voiceless. Having lost touch with the foundations of their own oral traditions and thus having lost touch with the truths of their histories that lie in narrative context, they are grasping—but often at the wrong things. And they are disturbed by the presence of people who still remember how to dance a quiet dance, a dance for the sake of the life of the dancing, and not the jerky electronic dance of the information highway. What is showing through the back of the paper is the very fact that, despite all their ownership and their nostalgias for a fundamental past that was an invention of their textbooks based on a willingness to ignore the truth, simple demographics is going to make them strangers in the land they stole. Strangeness can lead to solitude can lead to solipsism, and solipsism can give birth to ideas that are nothing more than bags of afterbirth with the tail of a pig.

My own image of seeing what is written on the backside of the paper goes like this: Christian Europeans colonized much of the world in a tide of violent self-righteousness; and in the short term of five hundred years, the colonization seemed successful. Indeed, much of it still seems successful because many of the colonized people who have achieved positions of prominence if not power are still running around like Chicken Licken, using the colonizer's language to declare their difference, and in their difference, their victimhood. But someone who sees him- or herself as victim, sees himself as acted upon and acted against and not as someone who has control over the results of his destiny as well as responsibility for that control. He or she submits to the typification that the arrogant of history have imposed upon people, typifications that are the result of false "difference." For instance, European colonialists typified Los Indios of North America as brutal and savage, a typification that first established the declarative false difference that Indian people were less civilized by destroying Indian civilizations purposefully (purposefully!), committing outrages against them and their ways of being in the world, and then focused on any defensive actions by the Indians as though they were first brutal retaliations and finally brutal and unprovoked aggressions. For instance, European colonialists typified Los Indios of Latin and South America as bloody and cruel by proclaiming a false difference between the blood sacrifice and weekly reenactments of cannibalism that they called transubstantiation and what the Toltecas, Aztecas, or Mayas enacted with various annual rituals of sacrifice and blood purification. These colonialists even got it wrong, confusing Huitzilopochtli with Quetzalcoatl, who was "as gentle and life giving as Jesus or Buddha" and who is "credited with the creation of a calendar, a measure of time more precise than the Julian calendar, the cultivation of corn, agriculture, the ethics and philosophy of Mesoamerican culture."⁹ Or, for example, the Euramerican colonists, who still grasp at their colonial attitudes like a memory that is "turning into a petrified polyp," turn the false difference of attitudes toward the pace and importance of life into the typification that Los Indios of the entire hemisphere are lazy, greasy, slow, backward, and unproductive. Or worse, mystical. But even the word *unproductive* implies that productivity is to be worshiped, as long as it is the Euramerican definition of Productivity, which sometimes seems all hurry to do nothing. Indeed, without sinking into the endless mire of nonproductivity labeled by false difference as "productivity," we can use the U.S. Congress as an example of the fakeries of productivity that produce nothing. Indeed, many of us are right to fear the day when Congress actually does produce something. Instinctively, many of us vote for stasis, picking Democratic presidents and Republican congresses (or the reverse). The danger arises when the president and the House majority are all of the same party. Heaven forbid that those in-group bureaucrats actually do something—it would probably result in all our children being born with the tails of pigs, and in us as parents and good people who deny all truths referring to our piggy-kids as "posteriorly challenged" or some such.

I, just out of simple skeptical perversity, refuse to play that game. People of color is just three words with the grammatical meaning of two, "colored people," and since I believe that people come in all colors ("are differently colored"?) but that the colors have little to do with anything important, when I play that game, I play it to make fun of it and call colored people "WEPOCS" or "We People of Color" and Indian people "PORCS" or "people of reddish color." I hope to be asking just how far we are willing to go to bureaucratize language into a meaninglessness that allows us to avoid the truth, which is that "race" is a false difference but that in talking about those false differences we can avoid talking about what is very real, which is racism or the attitudes that we ourselves perpetuate, even propagate, when we use fake language derived from false distinctions and used in sentences without active agency.

In other words, I am calling for people to begin to refuse to play the bureaucratic game or participate in it according to rules that are given. There is no beating them at their own game. And if you try, all you will succumb to is a sense of your own victimization by using those very methods of false typification. I, for one, will try not to homogenize myself (which in the language of victims is "be homogenized" by dominant other) and accept anything less than my own place in the caucus race.

In terms of storytelling or literature, a large part of this is a refusal to give in to the mainly British-American typification of non-British-acceptable-American literature. But part of it is the valuation of the literatures that refuse in a comparative and at least somewhat open process that looks to the oral roots, which means looks to the connections and similarities in those literatures. Thus, where José Saldívar sees *One Hundred Years of Solitude* as a political novel, I see it as a novel that, in encompassing the entire history of human beings, in imaginatively presenting both the creation and the revelatory destruction of the world, is political only in the sense that everything that has to do with human beings is "political." Saldívar is not entirely wrong in his assessment of the politics, but rather than focus on the one aspect of Banana Company politics in Macondo, if we look at the connections (some of them, here, since there are so many) we can see that to emphasize the politics may be to lift one segment out of its context, out of its relation to the other parts of the novel, and thus—if José will forgive me—to falsify it or falsely typify it. For *One Hundred Years of Solitude* is not a political novel—if it were, it would be tract or agenda (and one would wonder too often, as one does anyway, how the author of this book could maintain his friendship with Fidel Castro, whose attempts to declaratively rewrite history equal the behemoth falsifier to the north in scope until Fidel reduces his friend Che Guevara to an absurd resemblance to Princess Diana of England). The political portions of *One Hundred Years* do not just come inevitably, they come at a particular and particularly contextualized moment in the history of human beings in Macondo.

II

All this is fine and dandy. Repeatedly, I have made both arguments and outrageous statements (which, as William F. Buckley knows, are just too much fun and too irresistible), all of them hung like ornaments from a tree called the oral traditions. It seems time to bring some of the ideas together and even try to show how they work.

*

In the late 1970s I sat in a creative writing seminar that heard John Cheever, that wonderful short story writer and not-so-wonderful novelist (in fact, brilliant in the short story and pretty dull in the novel), offer a then-living example of WASP prejudices by asserting that *One Hundred Years of Solitude* was a mish-mash of clever images and metaphors in an uncontrolled structure in which one section could be interchanged with any other without any loss to the novel. Mary Cheever, who had up to that point sat quietly at the back of George P. Elliott's seminar-sized office, stopped any flow of easy agreement by accusing John of envy, hardly an insightful accusation but a necessary one, given her husband's articulate and clever ability to quash any argument from a bunch of twenty-to-thirty-somethings. Although I had taught García Márquez's novel several times—to my own classes and three times to George Elliott's graduate seminars in world literature—and even though George tried to give me the opportunity, in person I was no match for John Cheever. I knew it. In person I was, and I remain, everyone's favorite opponent because what I usually manage to say can be easily disregarded. So even though I disagreed with John Cheever and recognized how right Mary Cheever was (I had recently finished John Cheever's sometimes entertaining but unsubstantial novel that steals the plot of its cleverness from Alexandre Dumas, the title of which I can no longer remember, but the cover of which was blue), my defense of the structure of *One Hundred Years of Solitude* was weak, inarticulate, and ineffectual. Besides, Cheever had just called one of my short stories "brilliant," so I was pretty anxious to trust his judgment.

But I couldn't. Not about novels, anyway, and it didn't take much effort going back through *One Hundred Years of Solitude* to see plainly how that intricate stew of truth and mirages withstands Cheever's accusation that any one section could be lifted from its relative position and exchanged with any other. Where most contemporary (and often as dull as brass) novels provide relation with the tics of plodding chronology, this novel reveals, from the opening chapter, "provisions which serve purely to express the *relation* between the particular elements, and which articulate and graduate this relation in a number of ways."[10]

Using an omniscient author-narrator, the "solemn respect and gossipy irreverence" (368) is meticulously structured in the shape of a heliciform (spirally wound, like a watchspring) circling an irremedi-able axis. Viewed from the side, it would be the shape of two funnels placed mouth to mouth; and in the seam the watchspring twists once, so that as it spirals inward to a final point, things—character traits and the events propagated or participated in by those characters—are reversed. This structural image can be derived directly from the novel itself—from the provisions of its rhetoric—and it proves that our sense of repetitiveness is a sense García Márquez wants us to feel, while simultaneously it proves that one section cannot be exchanged with any other section in the novel any more than one section of DNA could be exchanged with another. Anyone can take a look at this novel and recognize that it is a parody of the chronicle form, see the controlled relations within and among the chapters themselves.

However, *One Hundred Years* is no ordinary chronicle, no ordinary history of the Buendía family. Rather, it begins the outward or expand-ing spiral of its "Genesis" with the phrase, "Many years later . . . ," followed by the rapid begatting of the Buendía family in a rapid succession of vernal equinoctial Marches. The expressed, rhetoric-controlling author directly defines the image he wants us to have:

> At that time Macondo was a village of twenty adobe houses, built on the bank of a river of clear water that ran along a bed of polished stones, which were white and enormous, like prehistoric eggs. The world was so recent that many things lacked names, and in order to indicate them it was necessary to point. (*11*; my emphasis)

Time is recent in Macondo, the city of mirrors, mirages (or both), so recent that it is a time "going back to before original sin" (22), a time without names—and naming is one of Adam's and Eve's Edenic tasks. It is a time without the belonging to a place that comes only after there is "someone dead under the ground" (22).

The mood of the opening as well as the closing scenes is very nearly biblical. Unlike the creations of the Bible, the rhetoric of this mood is apparently mocking, increasing the reader's distance from the metaphoric intensity of the language long enough to let him chuckle irreverently over José Arcadio Buendía's touching the gypsies' block of ice a second time and, "*as if* giving testimony on the holy scriptures," exclaiming, "This is the great invention of our time" (23). Even then there remains an undertone of solemnity in Aureliano, the future colonel of multiple revolutionary wars, saying that the ice is "boiling"—an undertone that García Márquez graduates into one of the most obvious metaphors of the novel: the frantic searching solitude of the frozen heart. Adding to this irreverent solemnity is Melquiades. On one hand, he is a gypsy who returns with each vernal equinox to display inventions and toys that amuse the youthfulness of the people of Macondo. On the other hand, besides the historic-religious echo of his name, Melquiades is an honest man,[11] prophetic and involved with the "darkest reaches of the imagination":

> That prodigious creature, said to possess the keys of Nostradamus, was a gloomy man, enveloped in a sad aura, with an Asiatic look that seemed to know what there was on the other side of things. He wore a large black hat that looked like a raven with widespread wings, and a velvet vest across which the patina of the centuries had skated. But in spite of his immense wisdom and his mysterious breadth, he had a human burden, an earthly condition that kept him involved in the small problems of daily life. (15)

In the second half of the novel, on the other side of things, we will discover that Melquiades's burden is one of solitude, the solitude of death that makes him return to Macondo.

Finally, there is the original sin. Given the background of Úrsula Buendía's family and its original flight from the sea as though Sir Francis Drake's attack on Riohacha were a necessary link in the causal chain, José Arcadio Buendía and Úrsula consummate an incestuous marriage "predicted from the time they had come into the world" (and it is not impossible to see that the Judeo-Christian Eve is very much a part of her husband Adam's genetic family). After José Arcadio murders Prudencio Aguilar, he leads the people who will found Macondo with him on an "absurd journey" away from the time (and place) before original sin toward "the land no one promised them"—toward the un-promised land.

Were One Hundred Years of Solitude simply a linear chronicling of the Buendías's wages of sin, John Cheever would be right. It would be a tedious display of extravagant imagery and repetitive metaphor, running in circles with each generation repeating the names and the characteristics that accompany the names (José Arcadios are different from the solitary Aurelianos) in a reductive progression toward death—either a journey laden with mulish solemnity and the

168

infantile irreverence of a weak novelist's love for his clever language, or a clever, puzzle-like deciphering of an ancient text of revelatory prophecies (a deciphering that Aureliano Babilonia is completing at the novel's end). But right in the middle of the book, a sudden twist occurs in the traits and names of the descendants of José Arcadio and Úrsula, a twist that confuses and in essence reverses the genetic make-up of our spiral, like parallel strands of DNA twisted one time. Úrsula, the most reliable narrator inside the novel, within whose planetary system the majority of characters revolve, cannot

conceal a vague feeling of doubt. Throughout the long history of the family the insistent repetition of names had made her draw some conclusions that seemed to be certain. While the Aurelianos were withdrawn, with lucid minds, the José Arcadios were impulsive and enterprising, but they were marked by a tragic sign. The only cases that were impossible to classify were those of José Arcadio Segundo and Aureliano Segundo. They were so much alike and so mischievous during childhood that not even Santa Sofía de la Piedad could tell them apart. On the day of their christening Amaranta put bracelets on them with their respective names and dressed them in different colored clothing marked with each one's initials, but when they began to go to school they decided to exchange clothing and bracelets and call each other by opposite names. The teacher, Melchor Escalona, used to knowing José Arcadio Segundo by his green shirt, went out of his mind when he discovered that the latter was wearing Aureliano Segundo's bracelet and that the other one said, nevertheless, that his name was Aureliano Segundo in spite of the fact that he was wearing the white shirt and the bracelet with José Arcadio Segundo's name. From then on he was never sure who was who. Even when they grew up and life made them different, Úrsula still wondered if they themselves might not have made a mistake in some moment of their intricate game of confusion and had become changed forever. (174–75; my emphasis).

Later, when José Arcadio Segundo reappears at the house, his character "linear, solemn . . . [with] a pensive air and the sadness of a Saracen," Úrsula reexamines her old memories and confirms "the belief that at some moment in childhood he had changed places with his twin brother, because it was he and not the other one who should have been called Aureliano" (244–45). Besides the echoing of the colonel's wife, who dies with crossed twins in her womb (89), along with the accidental uncrossing of the Segundo twins by their confused pallbearers during their simultaneous burial (327), we have Úrsula's dependability as a narrator—at this point—to give credibility to the belief that the twins exchanged names in their youth.

Perhaps this alone would be sufficient to prove the twisting (and reversal) of the strands of our heliciform spiral. Yet García Márquez does much more to articulate the importance, the Cassirer-defined *relation* of this middle chapter to the structural whole of *One Hundred Years*. Chapter 10—or, more precisely, the tenth chapter, since chapters purposely go unnumbered—opens with "Years later on his deathbed Aureliano Segundo would remember the rainy afternoon in *June* when he went into the bedroom to meet his first son" (174; my emphasis), a clear reminiscence of the opening of the first chapter, "Many years later, as he faced the firing squad, Colonel Aureliano Buendía was to remember that distant afternoon when his father took him to discover ice" (11). The colonel remembers a day in March, the month of the vernal equinox. Aureliano Segundo remembers a day from the month of the summer solstice. And in case we missed those clues, we are pointed to them by "the insistent hammering on the word *equinox, equinox, equinox,*" which Colonel Aureliano isolated from Melquíades's manuscript, at the time of Melquíades's death (75; author's emphasis).

To confirm this echo in the tenth chapter, Aureliano Segundo at the age of twelve pesters Úrsula about what is in the locked room (once Melquíades's study and sabbatical sanctuary) so that she gives him the keys:

No one had gone into the room again since they had taken Melquíades' body out and had put on the door a padlock whose parts had become fused together with rust. But when Aureliano Segundo opened the windows a familiar light entered that seemed accustomed to lighting the room every day and there was not the slightest trace of dust or cobwebs, with everything swept and clean, better swept and cleaner than on the day of the burial, and the ink had not dried up in the inkwell nor had oxidation diminished the shine of the metals nor had the embers gone out under the water pipe where José Arcadio Buendía had vaporized mercury. On the shelves were books bound in a cardboard-like material, pale, like tanned human skin, and the manuscripts were intact. In spite of the room's having been shut up for many years, the air seemed fresher than in the rest of the house. Everything was so recent that several weeks later, when Úrsula went into the room with a pail of water and a brush to wash the floor, there was nothing for her to do. (175–76)

In this room, Melquiades reappears. He is "under forty years of age" and is wearing the same hat and clothing he wore when, as children, Aureliano and José Arcadio first saw him. Aureliano Segundo recognizes him at once.

Here, on the other side of things, at the beginning of the heliciform's inward spiral that will end in the point of a pig's tail as the winds of destruction begin to blow, is the same Melquiades. This is not timelessness, as even my old friend and mentor, George P. Elliott calls it in his marginalia.[12] It is not a timeless static permanence. Rather, it is an insistence by our author on what the Nez Perce have called "Dreaming": if the context is appropriate (and one makes the context by "Dreaming"), then such events as the reappearance of Melquiades can occur; if the context is exactly the same, then the events are exactly the same. Here, the context is close to exact, except for at least one fact—that Aureliano Segundo is, in fact, by character and personality, actually a José Arcadio.

When in the same chapter Úrsula shouts, "I know all of this by heart. . . . It's as if time had turned around and we were back at the beginning" (185), she is almost exactly right. They are back and they are not. Except now, it is not a true beginning, but a beginning of the end.

Thus, the eleventh chapter spirals back on the end of the tenth chapter, picking up Fernanda del Carpio's background summarily, mimicking the relation the second chapter has to the first, where we are given Úrsula's background. But things have changed. The route across the mountains to the east and an outlet to the sea which José Arcadio searched for fruitlessly and which Úrsula discovers accidentally at the end of the second chapter was originally traversed by men and women "like them" (43). Now the same route is traversed by the "kitchen dragging a village behind it," the "innocent yellow train that was to bring so many ambiguities and uncertainties, so many pleasant and unpleasant moments, so many changes, calamities, and feelings of nostalgia to Macondo" (210). It will bring in the Banana Company employees and administrators who are in league with the government bureaucrats, but this will not be an indictment of Capitalism or so-called Democracy. Rather, it seems more like an indictment of technology overrunning humanity without consideration for the true quality of life; equally, it seems an indictment, not of U.S.-style Democracy, but of governmental bureaucracy and greed, and the willingness of military dictatorships or military-led governments (whether reputedly Marxist or Democratically Reformist) to slaughter thousands of people while controlling history to such an extent that the slaughter never officially happens. It is the broken promises of this dogmatic bureaucracy in government not an "ism" or pretense of any political-social agenda that, combined with the changes brought by technology and administrators of production and profit, that, before reaching their nadir, will cause Colonel Aureliano to believe "that it had been a mistake not to have continued the war to its final conclusion" (224).

Echoes of the first half of the novel abound in the second half, where the characters and events become humble replications of those in the first. On one side of the inversion, Úrsula sighs, "What did you expect? . . . Time passes," and Aureliano admits, "That's how it goes, . . . but not so much" (123). On the latter side, José Arcadio Segundo murmurs, "What did you expect? . . . Time Passes," and Úrsula says, "That's how it goes, . . . but not so much" (310). The gypsy band, the purveyor of amusement and wonder, is replaced by the herald of progress, the decadent yellow train that brings the Banana Company and the "ambulatory acrobats of commerce" (212). The Nostradamatic figure of Melquíades is echoed by the chubby and smiling American, Mr. Herbert, whose magic is performed with a scalpel, a pharmacist's scale, and a gunsmith's calipers. Mr. Herbert is quantitative, analytical, linear; the gringos' "magic" is overreaching beyond wisdom and wonder toward ultimate (final) wealth and power, self-endowed with "the means that had been reserved for divine Providence in former times" (214). Their whores are Babylonish and their wives are languid, unlike either whore Pilar Ternera or Úrsula. In the reversions of this world, it is José Arcadio Segundo, not Aureliano Segundo, who carries "the homeopathic pills of subversion in his pocket." And Úrsula once again confirms the inversion that this signifies, saying that José Arcadio is just "like Aureliano. . . . It's as if the world were repeating itself" (276).

Thus, the relation of events to the context in which they occur is subtly altered and inverted. All of the metaphors and images and character traits replicated and reflected in the novel's second half are reduced, humbled in magnitude of action or effect (and by extrapolation, lessened in purpose). Even in the passionateness of each interior narrator's rhetoric, the words are vitiated or opposite. Whereas the colonel's pride was described in nearly Christ-like imagery in the jail scene in the first half (120–28), José Arcadio's pride at the novel's end is priggish and decadent, and he is reduced to a dandified mime of the once well-endowed José Arcadios (see 336–44). Amaranta Úrsula, who was once just like Úrsula and who had the "lively eyes that Úrsula had at her age" and "the same strength of character" (326), returns to Macondo with "the Angels of December" (the winter solstice). The reader can easily predict the failure of her courage and character in restoring the House of Buendía in her description:

> She took charge of a crew of carpenters, locksmiths, and masons . . . so that three months after her arrival one breathed once more the atmosphere of youth and festivity that had existed in the days of the pianola. No one in the house had ever been in a better mood at all hours and under any circumstances, nor had anyone ever been readier to sing and dance and toss all items and customs from the past into the trash. With a sweep of her broom she did away with the funeral mementos and piles of useless trash and articles of superstition that had been piling up in the corners. . . . She was so spontaneous, so emancipated, with such a free and modern spirit, that Aureliano did not know what to do with his body when he saw her arrive. . . . Active, small and indomitable like Úrsula, and almost as pretty and provocative as Remedios the Beauty, she was endowed with a rare instinct for anticipating fashion. (347–48).

Tossing all customs from the past into the trash is equivalent to the Banana Company's tossing all humanity into the trash for profit, and either can create nostalgia. A good or happy mood in all circumstances indicates shallow thoughtlessness; where Mr. Herbert measures all things and thinks he knows them, she measures nothing and does not think at all. She is fully part of the race condemned to solitude (remember Bjork's "me learning about me") and solipsism, in a context where pride is measured by self-esteem without accomplishment or endurance, without anything estimable.

Melquiades's manuscripts reach one hundred years of age, at which point they can finish being deciphered (329), and the only person who can predict anything is this flighty, happy woman, who does not predict but anticipates, not human events, but the appearances of the Here and Now of fashion. Literature, once so joined with and informed by the past has become the "best plaything that had ever been invented to make fun of people" (357). Literature has become burlesque, not satire; and where making fun had its origins in the wise Catalonian bookseller's example, it is now without moral, ethical, or even ridiculously useful connections. How serious is this change? As the Catalonian bookseller, who came at the time the Banana Company came, says on his departure for his native Catalan village, "The world must be all fucked up . . . when men travel first class and literature goes as freight" (368).

The world—and the world García Márquez creates for us—is all fucked up. Dates have become confused, periods mislaid, and one day seems so much like another that one cannot feel them pass (334). Yet in spite of the disordered lives of Aureliano Babilonia and his companions, the four arguers, the Catalonian urges them to try to do something permanent.

Of course what they do—in a brilliant commentary on literary theory—is downright absurd. They try to find the thirty-seventh dramatic situation. Nonetheless, nostalgia is not the answer. The Catalonian feels nostalgia for Catalan, and so he returns. But the farther he gets from the trivial happenings of the recent past, the sadder his memory grows:

> [U]pset by two nostalgias facing each other like two mirrors, he lost his marvelous sense of unreality and he ended up recommending to all of them that they leave Macondo, . . . that they shit on Horace, and . . . [that] they always remember the past was a lie, that memory has no return, . . . and that the wildest and most tenacious love was an ephemeral truth in the end. (370)

The wise Catalonian, having once left his home for Macondo, and now leaving his new home for Catalan, ends up having two nostalgias facing each other like Augustinian mirrors, and their endless regressivity, like the endless regressions of post-modern post-structural literary theory, destroys his sense of unreality, his imagination. Aureliano Babilonia, the Catalonian's opposite, is the person with no nostalgia, no place, no real belonging, who, like the post-modern literary theorist no longer rooted in literature, has lost all sense of reality. And the only way for either to survive is to create a balance, to live with a gossipy irreverence with undertones of solemnity, to live in an intricate stew of truth (literature) and mirages (what we say about literature, using our imaginations).

Earlier, I said that George P. Elliott's marginal comment that certain aspects of *One Hundred Years of Solitude* exhibited or characterized "timelessness" was incorrect. For a moment I want to return to the ideas of time and timelessness, since it is in the sense of time that I find the greatest difficulty and the greatest difference between contemporarily oral cultures and the currently waning Euramerican culture (Jewish culture, if it isn't obvious, is one I associate with the former and not the latter). The greatest difficulty is twofold: it is difficult to explain to people who, like Aureliano Babilonia, seem to lack all sense of belonging, to lack any real nostalgia (though they are willing to steal or invent and adopt multicultural nostalgias without hesitation, according to the whimsy of fashion); and it is difficult to explain the difference, which is one of the barriers of understanding, not of Euramerican culture by oral cultures, but the other way around.

Part of the problem is that "time" is both a context and a movement within context in a complicated relationship not unlike general and specific theories of relativity or Heisenbergian principles of uncertainty in the context of cultural certainty. Time is something that, in the proper context or proper sense of Time, reveals truth and meaning; time does not heal any wounds at all, but entry into a proper sense of time, the proper context of time, allows the wound to be healed in a generational sense (it need not be handed down to children as an event they need to feel).

It is this sense of time within the context of Time in *One Hundred Years* that lends itself to the use of the word *timelessness*. For it is that gradual spiral outward to its middle and then slow but irremediable spiral inward along an axle of barely changing contexts that gives the reader the sense that the novel's progression or movement is slight or even nonexistent. And it is this that might cause the jealous reader like John Cheever (quintessentially Euramerican as he was) to assert, if not believe, that one section could easily replace another.

The most obvious device García Márquez uses is the "Many years later" and "Years later" sentences that begin each "half" of the novel. Within these halves, within the chapters themselves while existing in the generational Time, we are carried backward and forward in time by means of the use of these phrases, as well as phrases beginning with "he (or she) remembered" or predictive phrases of the immediate or near-future, like "Somebody is coming" (46). Narrators more concerned with the day-to-day time, who lose the broader sense of context, retard our sense of time's passage or claim that time is not passing at all, as when José Arcadio Buendía says, "but suddenly I realized that it's Monday, like yesterday," or "The time machine has broken" (80–81). But to give proper context to these words and events (time does pass, but not in the way we think), to help us sense the coming future through the lens of memory (and with imagination, with a sense of unreality, one can remember forward in time as well as backward), there are narrators who connect us to all time, narrators like Úrsula, the concubines—Pilar Ternera, Petra Cotes, and Nigromanta—and the manuscripts of Melquiades. Or there are the constant summaries of family history and recapitulations of events.

In addition to those technical attempts to interrelate and clarify Time and time, García Márquez provides an abundance of metaphors. The equinoctia and solstices graduate into conflict with direct horological metaphors such as José Arcadio Buendía's harmonious musical clocks, which, in the second half of the novel, become the grating, technical timepieces of the gringos, who toy with Divine Providence. The result of this conflict is a breakdown of the proper relational senses of time; and thus the narrative allows less recapitulation by the normative narrators (Úrsula, sane; the Colonel, serene; the concubines) and more by narrators who are reduced to, and examples of, madness or absurdity. In spite of Fernanda del Carpio's rigid adherence to the forms of the past, she is reduced to sing-song summary of the Buendía family history; and the dying Aureliano Segundo is driven to burning his wife's pessaries and burying live chickens while trying to raise money to send Amaranta Úrsula to Brussels by means of the Divine Providence Raffle, hawking tickets with such pathetic fervor that his community finally loses respect for him, makes fun of him, and in his last months no longer calls him Don Aureliano but Mr. Divine Providence "right to his face" (323–24). Formerly reliable narrators such as Úrsula become more unreliable as her lucidity becomes scattered like her connection to Time, allowing her to give us dependable interior narrations only in the brief moments when her lucidity coheres. And after Úrsula dies, we turn more frequently to the old, decrepit, but lucidly remembering concubine, Pilar Ternera, as one of the last narrators connected by direct experience to the generational Time of the past. Or we depend on the author-narrator's intrusions (never graceless) to tell us "That was how everything went after the deluge" and giving us a summary of Macondo (318ff.).

So the reader feels as though he drifts with the narrative, spiraling back on what he knows (remembers), drifts with the characters as García Márquez clearly intended, getting the feeling that time passes but not so much, drifts in an intricate stew of truth (generational Time) and mirages (Here and Now time). What I am calling generational Time is the reflected light that grows stronger through the sense of the here and now time's repetition as the epical, autochthonous past grows more distant. The reader is left, like Aureliano Babilonia as he deciphers Melquíades's manuscripts, with the "possibility of seeing the future showing through in time as one sees what is written on the back of a sheet of paper through the light" (360). As here and now time ends, or rather is fully contextualized in the full metaphorical relationship with generational Time, the light shines brightest. We skip to the end of Melquíades's manuscripts along with Aureliano Babilonia, and the spiral of character and event is compressed into one eternal moment—the moment Sir Francis Drake attacks Riohacha and the moment Aureliano Babilonia and Macondo are annihilated—and we discover the cause of the problem John Cheever had with the novel in the final justification of the novel's complicated structure: Melquíades's final protection of not putting events in the order of man's (and I would say, Euramerican man's and woman's) conventional time, but concentrating a century of daily episodes (the here and now) in such a way that they coexist in one instant (382). It is the recurrence of perceiving this instant that causes wise people like George P. Elliott to write "timelessness" in the margins of a novel and to mean something more complicated than that. It is seeing the future through the backside of an illuminated sheet of manuscript that causes people connected to the orality of their cultures to say that Progress is an illusion, that things do not change, and to mean something more complicated than that too—technology changes, but the users of technology haven't changed anything more than their clothes.

III

Whether it is Time and time in *One Hundred Years of Solitude* or in Eliud Martinez's *Voice-Haunted Journey*, in which Miguel's whole life gets told both by the voices of his family and by the voices of the subject of a biography he is working on, and all during one Pacific Southwest Airlines flight (generational Time collapsed into Aureliano Babilonia's momentary time by the very structure of the orally founded novel), oral stories demand structural metaphors, imagined and metaphorical language that connects the Here and Now to something much larger and much closer to apparent Timelessness, and images that flesh out, make, or support those connections.[13]

The same may be said of the narrative essay. It is not simply an essay that narrates ideas or feelings, especially not the limited feelings of the solipsistic "I"; and it is not simply an essay that uses various elements of imaginative writing (dialogue, description, authorial intrusion, poetry, various points-of-view, whatever). It must be an essay (or perhaps a collection of essays) that provides connection, giving context to ideas, and by giving context, creating a metaphorical relationship between the idea and the broader context. This metaphorical relationship, in turn, guides our interpretation. But that initial intentional process of telling the truth (as best we know it) by providing context in an interesting and broadly connecting way is one of the primary aspects of the oral rhetorical position.

In the Garden of the Gods

I

28 April 1994: Chipeta Elementary, Colorado Springs. The second graders sing patriotic songs.

And there is Scott, the child of my cousin (from the side of my family which, like Bartleby the Scrivener, I refuse), the eight-year-old kid who has sung, instead of "Glory Hallelujah," Alan Sherman's "Harry Louis," a song in which Harry Louis works for Ivan Roth and is cleaning out the warehouse where the drapes of Roth are stored—making Jews, Pocono vacationers, and anyone else who thinks Hal A. Lujah is more gory than glory laugh to the core of their worldview and belief—sung it aloud to his second-grade class. Scott is Jewish, the son of a Jew and my cousin, his mother, who converted.

It's a bit difficult to determine whether it was Harry Louis or Scott's Jewish laughter that pissed off the capacious woman in floral blue who plays the piano and cues the little darlings in and out of the songs, but it did. So Scott is relegated to the chorus to play backup to the little red-headed kids who hold hands with ebony children whose parents have bought a house large enough to make them less Black and more—if the new car lot out front of the school is any indication of identity—Honorary Members of the Order of Van-Americans, Non-conversion Chapter. Ward Cleaver must have driven a station wagon (I don't remember, at least in part because my father couldn't afford, and then refused to own, a television, so watching Ward and the Beave depended on the confluence of time and place in, I would say now, and given what I think of television, the wrong place and—as I always was—the wrong time, by which I mean not some nostalgic appeal to trendy traditionalism that is being cast as the mother of all pearls by television, movies, and books, but a sense of personal responsibility and circularity that argued against the fragmented, dulled imaginations of my friends who lived in Black and White and later became Persons of Interactive Color, eventually surrounded by sound as though the falsified emotions of *Chicago Hope* are more "authentic" in stereo). Ward Cleaver has come a long ways, baby, and with a lot more baggage to haul around with him, he's gone from wagons to vans in a revelation of the monologic diversity among the middle class.

It is a monologue, from what I can tell, an "authentic" diversity that—from the way Scott slips back from the marshaled line of second-grade singers, letting the line close on him so he becomes a head of serious hair behind the closed ranks of open mouths, barely visible to his mother, who is too short to overlook the kids in front of her boy—slips its hold on cousin Scotty's person every time its grip tries to catch on the slick of his faith and the solid of his being. Scott knows—unlike his little sister, named Elizabeth after my dead Anglo mother—they ain't ever gonna quite be comfortable with Jews in this town in which fundamental values act like condoms to keep them protected and not quite feeling the slip and slide of the truth that's all around them, values that tell them that Jews have money, and this makes them a little less hated than Indians who, as everyone knows, don't (and even if they did, they'd gamble it away in a peyote haze or under the influence of a most significant Anglo contribution to this continent—whiskey, scotch, or the variation bourbon, distilled from indigenous corn by the great American heroes, Jonathan "Jack" Daniels, his cousin James Beam or, in a sign of their respect for elders, Old Grandad).

So I am there with my cousin and her husband and their daughter, but not because I would ever go hear a performance of "patriotic" songs, even under the influence of Old Grandad. Frankly, I'd rather marry Lorena Bobbitt, except for the fact that Scott is family and I am a family man—when the family will have me (and Scotty's mother is one from that side of the family who will). Just as I'd protest but go to hear my daughter or son sing songs, patriotic or otherwise (and knowing now that I'll teach them both "Harry Louis," as well as "This Land Was My Land"), I have promised Scott that I'll come, a request he's made as though his somewhat removed cousin might protect him from the harpy who's waving her arms at the kids and nodding as though she has not merely made but invented these kids like god, and who hates Scotty.

The feeling is strange. My heart is estranged. I listen, trying to imagine who these tykes are, up on the risers with Scott, and worse (I look around, overwhelmed by) who their gene pools are, these van-driving descendants of the very gene pools that invented Geronimo and Joseph, Seattle, and Sitting Bull and who are now watching their kids sing out "This land is my land, this land is your land," half of which strikes half of my urban mixblood heart as real true. These happy parents and grandparents are completely unaware of the simple fact that their world is changing. Their children's world is already as changed as Old Joseph knew his was when he told Hinmot Tooyoolaktekht, his son, that he saw a day when the whites would take the Wallowa Valley from the Nez Perce. All you have to do is look at these people to know what Old Joseph knew: that if they can't quite forget how and why they took the land, they'll make up patriotic songs as a veneer to the truth and sing them out with the passion of holy rollers over and over and over again until in the song, they believe. They will give themselves "splendid memories and star-spangled amnesia."[1] They will tell themselves what Robert Weeks de Forest told the huddled homogenizing masses at the opening of the Metropolitan Museum of Art in 1924: "We are honoring our fathers and mothers, our grandfathers and grandmothers, that their art may live long in the land which the Lord hath given us."[2] Or, "in an instance of manifest manners and the literature of dominance," they will write that the massacre of women, old men, and children—many of them babies—at Wounded Knee was the "last major battle of the Indian Wars."[3]

Strange how much I disbelieve these songs the children are singing. It surprises me how the words that would make their feelings static become metaphor in the drum of my hearing. It is like hearing or seeing an anti-ceremony in which the skin is flayed from the corpse of the Van-driving world, in which the song and dance reveal the absolute fake to which Umberto Eco refers when he says that the American imagination demands the real and to attain it invents the absolute fake. Here, in this song and dance of these human units, is the American Reality, and I am surprised, not at the vision, but at the vision's virulence: as an urban mixblood writer, as a preserver and transmitter and not merely an ego (I hope, truly), I had thought I'd become sort of conservative (in the preserving sense) and staid (in the calm, habitual sense—the boring life of the writer who sits down every day and writes). But suddenly I want to shout out a sound that must be at least five generations old and take a stick to their coups of commerce, self-aware enough to know that were I to do that, I'd cause even more problems for my (Jewish) relatives, particularly Scotty, who is only a child. All I can do is lean over to my cousin and whisper and laugh—quietly—knowing that as an up-and-coming ethnomusicologist she believes no more in the message of these songs than in the baby Jesus, and that, as a Jew, she must have learned what I have always known in my dreaming heart: how quickly this generous fellow feeling behind these singers and songs can turn to murderous annihilation. First they see you as "an antithesis to themselves . . . [with] civilization and Indianness *as they defined them* . . . forever . . . opposites . . . as a threat to life and morals when alive," and then they regard you "with nostalgia upon . . . [your] demise—or when that threat is safely past."[4]

I try to smile with generosity and wisdom, with pity for these people whose most sexual experience is like Coyote behind the velutinous wheel of their Caravans and Villagers and "Grand" Cherokees and Astros (God! the names they pick, as though their vans could fly them like Carter Revard's songs up to the stars! It's too much; their vans—let alone their mechanical souls—are too heavy to do more than fart and die). I try to smile, and yet all I can hear is Jimmie Durham speaking, "I hate America. . . . I hate the culture of America . . ." and adding that he hates Indians too, the writers and intellectuals who are money-grubbing opportunists, and (sometimes hating myself, thus wondering if I am, or Jimmie Durham is, one of those latter and hoping to the stars that I'm not) I think, "That's it, isn't it? I hate America. I really do (at least when you aren't making me admit that I'm grateful for the life I do have) hate America."

I have always hated America, even from the time as a little lost kid I took up writing a journal as the only way I knew to speak the unspeakable (unspeakable, because my little friends, except maybe Bernie Schneider, would have laughed uproariously at me and turned it into another painful tease, enough of which already existed). And night after night I'd sit and pour out my hatred in words, English words, fast and unpunctuated but most always grammatical—having learned grammar's strengths and weaknesses better than my giggling peers—always feeling the anachronisms: women in curlers who would point the index of their fundamental values at me and sneer with distaste or men whose souls made them seem fat crows without feet or wings, blackened lumps of consumption: and always hiding the journals away, feeling guilty about the total, almost physical hatred I felt, exacerbated by the hurt, the hurt, always the hurt because when they laughed at me, they laughed at Father and Grandfather.

The same guilt I feel now. My wife may hate this essay. A mixblood herself, though with no indigenous American blood in the mixture, she sometimes wonders what is happening, here, with all this Indian stuff. She knows that over time I have gone from a voice that said I am a writer first, and a Native American writer second, to someone who now says, I am a Native American writer first, foremost, and only, because unlike Jim Barnes, who says there is no such thing as Native American Writing but only writing by Native Americans—a position I honor and respect—because unless you say that, "I am a Native American writer," it becomes all too easy for someone to say, "Forgive me for saying so, but Indians don't really make much difference these days."

So though my wife is proud and pleased and all those good things, she must sometimes wonder—as do I, as I sit here at Chipeta Elementary listening to the kids slide into a pressboard and glue composite of patriotism and conquest and possession and trivialization—"What happened? My husband has gone from a mixblood Indian kid to a token man, a boy who once sang the patriotic songs (I am a citizen first, a Native American citizen second), to someone else." I myself fear becoming a someone who will have (as I will tonight, by the historical-autobiographical way) diarrhea whenever he hears the strains of patriotism and possession, or a person who, in trying to debunk some of the myths and images and misconceptions, so enjoys the slurp of public approval for his debunking that he oversteps and becomes a jerk-kneed monologue of political correctness.

I fear it partly because I'd like to drive a minivan.

In other words, I don't always hate America, just its commercialism and exploitation and hegemonic attitudes and the flames of its self-righteous Christianity. Because I love my wife, I hope that she can accept this manner of revelation in me with as much understanding and belief as she accepts my cousin's becoming a Jew. I fear it because I have children, and they—as my grandfather allowed me—must come to their identities with pride and not with their hands out. And while I may guide, I have to let them be whatever they in their hearts know they are—and what if they decide they are not "Native American" but "Italian"—which is what I imagine my wife to be, given the way she can raise her voice and wave her arms about with passion and a certainty that vanishes when the argument's over?

I am determined to let them come to their identities like Scott, who asks, as we drive home, "Are you Jewish?"

We pass a country club formulated by one of the (is it vegetable or mineral?) Hunt family and propagated by the exclusive, patronizing (is it animal?) attitudes of the possessive rich (who would you trust if it was your brain? to which I answer, You trust teachers with the bumper-sticker brains of your children every day). I like to imagine that it's in an attempt to bond with me that Scotty's dad comments on it being a place that wouldn't let them or me join, so Scotty completes the logical circle and asks the one question his fledgling identity knows how to ask, "Are you Jewish?"

"No," I laugh. "No. I'm Indian." I laugh, happy in the words, adding, so Scott doesn't think I am laughing at him, "But my grandfather used to say that hating Jews is just three letters away from hating Indians."

"So you can't join the club?" Scotty asks.

"No."

Scott looks distressed.

"But look at it this way. Who would want to? Would you want to join a club that wouldn't want you as a member?"

Scott considers.

II

The problem is that I don't really hate America.

What I hate is this feeling of being strange. I hate the fact that what I want America to do is like me, appreciate me, my presence, my act- and inactivity. I want America to have its own, as well as to reward my sense of fairness and self-responsibility by valuing my presence. But America can't. Besides the fact that capitalism admits of fairness only when it profits, America wants me to be dead. When the president's commissions count up Native Americans in this country, it refuses to count me because I grew up in the cities and not on a reservation, so I feel insecure. It's a mungy feeling that has in the past taken more deadly aspects (the usual yawn of drugs and alcohol in this chemical civilization) but that now that I have a family remains in check—except that I get hurt and angry, sometimes, because of my insecurity. Nonetheless, I go on because, whether by dance or dream, singing or saying, I am compelled to try to make a place in the world for my children, as well as for the children, the same way D'Arcy McNickle tried to make a place for us children.

The way I chose to make this place—the way I chose from the very beginning, furiously writing, writing, writing, even as a lonely discarded child, immature diatribes against what I saw as *America Around Me*, and formalizing the process around age twenty when one of my two elder sisters gave me a blank five-hundred-page book bound with a bright upholstered orange cover for my birthday—was through stories. I filled that book with stories, and it was in my stories that I was strange and through stories that my strange became a comfort, acknowledged a place for myself, a place solitary, though not foolish enough to reach solipsistic, a place silent yet wanting to be spoken.

Stories like "Dwarfheart"—do I need to list the puns, make sure you get them all, the way my poet friends do?—in which the narrator is an illustrator for his best friend Little Hamm, a black kid from the neighborhood who mimes beautiful mimes. As Hamm's mimes grow stranger, as the sad audience of daily livers ignore his silent telling more and more, the narrator becomes less imaginative, more linear, less illustrative and more documentary (with logical consequences and the cancers of editorial pens of indelible red) and tries to record as sadness the humorous tragic end of Hamm as he disrupts the logical timing of a new subway system and, painting sexual organs on the fronts of the two trains that will mate as violently as most Americans in front of some foreign dignitaries visiting the "city," jumps between the trains in a final mime of Hamm.

Stories like "Pandora's Chinese Box," in which the narrator is in the second person, the voice detached—a story that opens, "The only problem, then, is there is no problem." A story in which the people are movie extras on a beach where a chess match is being played and where a "boy" learns awfully that you do not ever reach out and risk disrupting the game. A story in which in response to the disintegration and random separations around them, people invent Nature's nature. A story that twenty years ago envisioned yuppy's puppies taking to the new and improved fakes of natural foods and painful exercise in an attempt to extend the veneer of their lives while forgetting about the substance.

Stories I still have, like "nocket," written in part as a response to those business cards Born-Agains handed out all over town with bleeding stigmata and the boldfaced lie, "Jesus Loves You So Much It Hurts," and in part as a response to my friend Steve Curry's mistress lamenting to me after Steve had returned to his wife and my goddaughters. Steve is Stanley in the story, and Stanley is a serious fellow who gets confused in the narrator's mind with Jesus Christ.

Perhaps none of these stories is particularly good? Certainly, aspects of "nocket" seem immature. I have affection for them, however; and looking back at them now for the first time in decades, I fill with wonder at what I seem to have known then but forgot between "then" and "now" — now representing the last, oh, say six or seven years, and "then" embodying the potential that in my feeling strange while wanting to belong I might forget it all once more. I remember the years in Syracuse University's creative writing program; with the kindness and encouragement of my wonderful teacher and beloved friend George P. Elliott, I tried to make my stories (and myself) more acceptable, more "realistic," more palatable (less strange), but I couldn't quite. Though the surface changed, became in some people's opinions more mature, below the surface of those stories is the same estranged voice:

The solitary narrator who does not judge but wonders at being judged in "Tarantulas." A postal worker who has taken cards and letters home and recopied them and made them his own, he sits in jail and writes down what he will tell the judge and jury, ending:

> The oak stands against the winter, budless. It stands there like a dancer, arms arcing up, the fingers nearly touching high above the trunk. Its roots go far beneath the ground as if the earth has risen like dough around it and me, half sunk in the ground myself, and I can see the beginnings of a crack in the wall where the roots have tried to enter my cell. Yet, if I move my cot, the image of the tree against the white moon shifts, and if I rock my head, I can make the still dancer dance.

As I look out the window and wonder how guilty I am, and of what, really, I can see against the far-away sky the dark lines which tell me that what they call my crime is delicate and dark and can only be judged—truly judged in detail—against a yellow New Mexico moon.

I did not learn much at Syracuse—but then I guess no one was supposed to, really. One thing I did learn was that my stories were inevitably different. When someone seriously used a mechanical process to represent a human event and the rest of the class approved, I realized that in some sense "their" stories had gone all confused and that in the soft suck of emptiness any comparison may be made. It's not that to them machines seem almost alive—the way I have felt whenever one of them cheats me, stalls, or refuses to dish up what I have paid for. It's the reverse: to them, life is mechanical, or at least life is confused with the mechanical or the objective—that which may be turned on and off, used up, exploited, and sold.

For a long time I imagined that their stories were becoming so confused as to produce television, until I realized that the most narrative and the most imaginative elements on television were often found in the commercials, not in the vacuous cans of laughter and tears produced by the jovial one-liners of sitcoms and PBS. Commercials are their stories, and all the static images produced by PBS and the refuse of sitcoms are only filler to keep you coming back to the auction of commerce.

III

I feel close to D'Arcy McNickle, not because I imagine that I'll ever be as important or do as many good things as he, but because I imagine. I value that activity too much to let anyone restrict or limit it. It is one of the true, great things about America: the freedom and the energy available to our imaginations and our ability to envision as well as try to shape the visions.

I feel close to D'Arcy McNickle because in picking up his posthumously collected and published short stories, *The Hawk is Hungry,*[5] I recognize an urban mixblood writer whose "Indianness" is not shown by the writer's speaking from the soapbox of content but by the way in which the writer says, speaks, tells his stories—of which, at McNickle's best, there are none better. The way is a way that I have told stories; there are mixblood Indian things in the how and way of the stories, but there is little turquoise and fewer bright colors, only a question here and there and some Haida prints on the wall.

His novels are more apparently "Indian" in subject and event; his stories are American, and to recognize the "Indian" (not that the two are mutually exclusive except in our racialist fantasies) you have to pay attention to, for example, the way in which the point of his stories is neither plot—the end results of the events are often apparent from the first paragraph in combination at times with the title—nor message, but process, the how it is told and the sense, reinforced by the oral repetitions in, say, "Debt of Gratitude" or "Meat for God," that it may be told again and again. There are the elements that get called "post-modern," even though many of those elements are and have been for Indians always available—the jump-cuts, the departures from the strict lines of development, the embellishments and supplementations (or augmentations). There are the quiet understatement, the humor—always the humor ("Smiley" in "Debt" doesn't smile)—and the humane sympathies, especially for characters caught between two worlds ("Man's Work"), and the sense, around Henry Jim, of "history before there was history."

I don't want, here, to get too involved with the discussions about how there is no such thing as "Indian," only Osage, Choctaw, Nez Perce, Miwok, Lakota, Blackfoot, and so on; any more than I want to say "European" and get into how there is no such thing, only Germans, and French, Spaniards, and Italians (or Geats or Celts or Moors), and so on. I do want to offer the idea that there may be a couple of ways "Indians" look similar enough to be grouped: one way that is important is storytelling—not only the respect most of us have for it, but also the ways in which we tend to do it.

Our stories are told the only way they can be told. In a sense, they are from grandfather or grandmother and they get told as they have always been told. When people criticize the lack of plot, the minimal "character development," the "digressiveness," or the sense of conclusive inconclusion, most of us do not know how to reply.

Plot to us is as nothing: stories about Coyote or Snowbird or Bear are known, retold, and changed only in the details or fullness or language according to the age and experience of the participatory audience. Unless we write mystery novels, plot, a logically connected

188

sequence of events, is only a coat hanger on which to button and zip the clothes—which are the important parts—and now, given the falsity of logical sequence in a human and humane world, is a flat-out lie, a fake coat hanger on which only the emperor's clothes may be hung. The interest of life—and storytelling describes life—was in the twists and turns, the digressions and jump-cuts, the strange and strangely connected apparent dislocations and disparities. They are what connects one human being to another.

As for the accusation that the characters do not develop, or only minimally, well, characters don't develop. As stories in progress, or real people, we inherit the probabilities and characteristics of our grandfathers and mothers; and a uniqueness that can develop independent of those inheritances is a lie other people speak, not Indians. In stories, situations change, and the reader-listener gets to hear how the character responds to those changes. Bartell D'Arcy, Kurtz, and Tayo don't change; they perhaps reveal the characters they began with and will end with, whether happily or not.

Fighting against America's monologue did not make D'Arcy Mc-Nickle monologic. It did not kill his sense of humor by separating him from what is vital, the same way many of my colleagues have separated themselves from storytelling and become . . . what?

IV

In the week following the pageant of patriotic songs at Chipeta Elementary, I took some Colorado College students up to see the Cliff Dwellings Museum (Manitou Springs) in the Garden of the Gods.

"Hey, look at this," I laughed. "The Anasazi used cement."

A young woman frowned. "You mean this isn't real?" she asked. She was plenty worried by the notion that the construction of an "authentic" imitation of Anasazi cliff dwellings had no warning signs, no direct indication that these were not "restored" dwellings, but inventions.

"It's okay," I told her. "They're as real as any real thing. Even restored dwellings would be an invention." She didn't get it. But as we climbed through the "replica," I continued to point out the handrails of iron and the "logs" made of concrete and textured by machine.

In the gift shop—where we went to escape two school-bus loads of kids who arrived to learn about "Indians" (but who were really just there to give their teachers a break from the day-to-day training of squirrels and monkeys)—were pots and feathered mirrors and paintings and keychains and an endless assortment of wooden figures and cheap silver plate and embedded turquoise. Every item had a sticker with the authenticating name of the "Indian" artist who had made that crap, and before we left the gift shop and the rather cynical little "museum" with dioramas of Anasazi life and the conclusions drawn by deaf anthropologists ("They must have . . . ," "They believed . . . ," etc.), the metaphor had made itself plain.

We sat outside on some benches, and I asked my students who they considered worse, the man who appropriates cliff dwellings and builds a replica to make money in a location where the Anasazi never lived, or an artist who can prove quanta of blood and appropriates the image of himself that the anthropologists invented to make replicas in clay or words?

Whether it's the veneer of patriotic songs or the priceless veneer of an editorial call to "citizenship" (which means going along with the editor's hegemonies), it is all static, fixed, and lost between the sleeping and the waking. It is the result of cowardice. Fear. That's why they make up Betsy Ross or appropriate the "pagan" Eastre. That's why they call Wounded Knee the last battle of the Indian Wars.

Here in the Garden of the Gods we are heirs to two thousand years of cowardice. Here we meet men and women driven from among the laughing into seriousness. Here we meet up with ourselves, them as mostly non-Native in the fakery of Anasazi Cliff Dwellings, me as the re-membered Native in the fakery of "authentic" Indian art, all of us wanting a minivan.

But here too, we can learn how to dance the dance of skepticism, the dance of laughter, and we can see the truth that everything connects to everything else. The world is metaphorical, not logical; circular, not linear.

Here we can learn how and not the fake of what, process and not plot, if we'll stop singing patriot songs and listen.

Just listen.

Feathering Custer

I

The "inveterate xenophobe" General Pleasanton, who "built his career on intrigue" and "wanted to surround himself with senior subordinates who owed their advancement, and hence their loyalty, to him," made George Armstrong Custer a brigadier general at the age of twenty-three. The irony of his name aside, Pleasanton evidently believed sincerely that Custer was "the best cavalry general in the world."[1]

Custer's troopers agreed. One trooper among many wrote in 1863 that Custer was "a glorious fellow, full of energy, quick to plan and bold to execute, and with us he has never failed in any attempt he has yet made."[2] From numerous personal and historical accounts, letters, diaries, and after-the-fact tributes, a proper image of our younger Custer is of a bold and courageous leader who never lagged behind his men in the bloody charges of the Civil War. Time and again he outwitted and outflanked opponents; time and again he rode at the front of his troop charges, fighting, urging and encouraging, leading. It didn't take too long for him to be mythologized. But it was a real mythology in the sense that like the spherical accumulations of a pearl, at its center was the provocating grain of sand. Custer, the poor boy whose family was of the wrong party (Democrat) and "came from the wrong side of the tracks,"[3] changed from the playfully defiant, careless, disregardful, dead-last bottom of his class at West Point; made himself agreeable to the people in power; and then proved his mettle. In the best sense of the word, Custer assimilated himself into the higher ranks of the Union Army and the society that went with it.

Assimilation in large part means a loss of defiance and a sudden regard for authority. And yet there resides inside every boy who tries to be agreeable another one, a ghost, the spirit of the former boy who secretly resents being agreeable. It is a resentment that is easily hidden as long as he is well-treated. And as long as he can say he is well-treated, justly treated (which may, to someone who has sucked up to so much power, mean treated at least a little bit better than anyone else), insults or apparent slights can be overlooked. But once he perceives himself as ignored or mistreated, all the insults that he has overlooked show up like an avalanche at the door of his thinking.

As the Civil War progressed, Armstrong Custer seemed to forget where he came from, exhibiting signs of a similar boyish pettiness. Even as the real mythology surrounding him accumulated, Custer "conveniently" forgot "the role that partiality had played in his own rise," denouncing Brigadier General James A. Wilson—who received a command Custer wanted for himself—as " 'this Court favorite,' an 'imbecile and upstart' who 'had never even commanded a company of men' . . . [and who] 'has made himself ridiculous by the ignorance he displays in regard to cavalry.' "[4] Custer was already given to needing the admiration of his public, a need he demonstrates so clearly in his attacks on the men he perceives as his competition.

It is easy to imagine how needy he felt when the Civil War ended and all he had was the desk on which the peace was signed and a rank that was less than the one he had on the field.[5] He was Custer. The Custer. But he was not happy. He was not a general, not even an interim general. Custer determined to regain and hold the power and position he believed should be his by becoming an Indian fighter, much to the regret of Black Kettle's band, the peaceful Indians who had survived Chivington's massacre at Sand Creek and who were camped at the Washita River on the morning of 27 November 1868. Perhaps it was this determination that led Custer to reconstruct his identity as Custer, rather than to remember his inner identity, his upbringing as a poor Democrat. In his reconstruction, he no longer exhibited a playful or careless disregard of authority, but rather he misled himself into becoming Authority itself.

So determined was he to regain his position and make himself into the authority others could not disregard, that he became incensed by desertions from the dull, flat life of the cavalry in the West. When he was himself tried in a court-martial for being AWOL and for conduct prejudicial to good military discipline, he was additionally charged with ordering a group of men "making off in broad daylight to be ridden down and shot" and making a "public display of denying them medical aid."[6] Whereas absolute power may corrupt absolutely, partial power corrodes the understanding; and Custer's taste of partial power and vain-glory corrupted any awareness he may have had that good is unobtrusive and sometimes hardly noticed, while evil forces our recognition, which may be why so many evil people become famous in history. Partial power corrodes—look at Congress or Coyote, though remember that Coyote, unlike Congress, is a creative force and does much good—and at first what it corroded in the temporarily forgotten Armstrong Custer was his awareness of humanity, causing a complete loss of humility.

The arrogant can be charming in society by feigning humility in their overconfidence, but they reveal themselves at the office where the hierarchical lines are preestablished—there they become autocratic, inhumane, and sniffy. The poor democrat forgets who he is and becomes the Custer who, as historical narrative tells us,

> was not an easy man to deal with. Charming and ingratiating in his social relations, he managed to alienate civilians who encountered him in an official capacity. Joseph La Barge, the master of a steamboat contracted to ferry the Seventh [cavalry] across the Missouri in 1873, remembered Custer's imperious "Stand aside, sir," when La Barge had insisted on loading his own vessel, and the postmistress at Bismarck clashed with Custer over his assumption that mail destined for Fort Abraham Lincoln had priority. A squabble over the government key and a mailbag slit in a fit of pique were evidence of a petty streak and an overbearing manner. "Custer seemed to me to be generally unpopular, that is I rarely heard him well spoken of," La Barge remarked. Certainly his officers did their share of complaining. Custer was high-handed, demanding, unreasonable, and unfair.[7]

"Not an easy man" is not the part that bothers me. Easy men and women, it seems to me, are oftentimes stupefied by thoughtlessness, by a lack of passionate interest in things, living in Michigan, or television. There is nothing so sad to me as to ask "What is he like?" and have someone reply without enthusiasm, "He's nice." I beg my students to either hate me or like me but never to say in that flat, Midwestern, expressionless, mildly Christian, extruded way, "He's okay." I prefer my friends and acquaintances to be in a state of unease, to be quirky or thorny, motivated by an impassioned skepticism and curiosity. But I also like my quirky friends to be moved by humanity and involved in the human condition with love and imagination — and, as you might well imagine, I don't always measure up to my own standards.

So it is not in Custer's not being an easy man that I find his faults. It is in the words "to deal with." There he reveals his loss of humanity and humor, his forgetting of who he was and where he came from. As a former democrat who knows what it means to be at the bottom of economic society, he, of all colonels, should have remembered how to "deal with" a steamboat's master as well as its crew. He, of all officers, should have been grateful to the postmistress for the services she rendered, not the ones she could not in fairness do just for him. He should have been able to maintain military discipline with his officers out of their respect for him and his character; and he should not have become a pusillanimous, pugnacious administrator, alienating them with his high-handed unfairness. But, like low-level bureaucrats in general, with few enough particular exceptions to prove the rule, Custer had failed in his chosen career. And failure makes people high-handed and, like General Pleasanton, self-serving. Custer, forgetting his background, did not intuit the fact that power does not stand alone in a vacuum but that it occurs in relation and that there are generally two kinds of power: one internal that commands respect, and the other external that demands the enactment of the appearances of respect.[8]

If failure should teach us, so should success. Certainly a poor boy, if no one else, should have learned to handle success with some humility. But Custer's early success, though in large part deserved, taught him to forget who he was and where he came from. Otherwise, his later failure — in his mind, dropping out of the public's admiration was a failure — would have reminded him of his roots as a poor democrat in a republican world. The result is his obsession with the appearances of privilege and respect: Custer can choose to be AWOL himself, but let a trooper try it and he will be ridden down and shot. The sandy seed of Custer's reputation as an Indian fighter, it turns out, is more like T. S. Eliot's famous shred of platinum — in the chemical reaction, it has disappeared. There is nothing left but the administration of it. The bold bravery of his pre-dawn massacre of

194

innocent men, women, and children on the Washita puts him back in the public's eye; and he is so enthused by his resurrected and reconstructed reputation that he begins to think that the Washita was not a massacre but a battle.

Implicit in this transformation is what causes him to begin to tempt fate. When you have massacred the helpless, exercised power on the powerless, and then you revise the vision of what you have done to make it seem as though you have battled an equal enemy and won, or that your power has been given meaning by contesting with a nearly equal power and winning, you begin to think you are your old self, the brave Civil War Brigadier General. In the Civil War, you seemed almost invincible, protected by the spirit of your bravery, guarded by the passionate intensity of your leadership. You fantasize that in the so-called Indian Wars you can be and have all that again.

On 4 August 1876, Custer reconnoitered "on his own in the face of a concealed enemy and was almost cut off by the charging Sioux as he dashed for safety." And he ignored his scouts' warning that the Indians "were massing for a dawn attack" so that their morning ambush seven days later "came near being a surprise to Custer." He begins to "have trouble taking the Sioux seriously."[9]

The federal government has already decided to steal the Black Hills from the Sioux for gold and minerals. It wants to contrive a war against the Sioux in order to shroud the theft in righteousness. Just as Pleasanton sought out and promoted and used young men who would serve his interests, administrators of the "Indian Wars" look around for a petty patsy willing to be used. They find him in the arrogant and high-handed Custer, cut off from his origins and thus so weakened in his judgments that he is easily fooled by their public praise and his own ability to romanticize himself into a "hero" of Washita (not unlike the way John Wayne, the draft dodger, made himself into an icon of military service).[10] He confuses his selection, which is by default and not competitive choice, with a vote of confidence in him. They encourage him to incur on sacred Indian lands, escorting surveyors and settlers into the Black Hills to provoke some of the Sioux into fighting back. Some. And some are enough to create a pretext that all Indians were committing terrible outrages against peaceful whites. Even as the revitalized icon of George Armstrong Custer allowed miners and surveyors to trespass on the sacred land and the rush to gold in them there hills began, the Indian agents continued to insist that the "outrages [were] committed by the hostile Indians and renegade whites posing as Indians."[11]

In the sense that Custer was a failure at Washita—higher administrators must have heard the reports and known that a massacre of innocent and peaceful women, children, and elders at Washita was a "success" only insofar as the journalists reported half-truths and statistics, hard data of the numbers of "hostiles" dead—he continually reconstructs himself as a successful Indian fighter. The reconstructed Custer is the patsy who commits the necessary outrages. He becomes a "wétiko," a Cree term for one who characteristically consumes other human beings for profit. There are few moments more satisfying to a poor Indian boy's democratic mind than the historical "Oooopppss!" of the fate-tempting, arrogant little peacock as hundreds and hundreds of warriors ride out at him through the splash of the Little Big Horn River.

Think of it, George! Your only value is to die and have the circumstances of your death hidden in the reproduction of a sentimental and false image to sell beer. A powerful image, indeed, since Otto Becker's "Custer's Last Fight," which Anheuser-Busch reproduced by the hundreds of thousands and distributed to bars and saloons across North America, became and remains the painterly lens through which most Americans saw and continue to see their favorite image of your men's heroic sacrifice. Some heroism:

> I saw a soldier shoot himself by holding his revolver to his head. Then another one did the same, and another. Right away, all of them began shooting themselves or shooting each other. . . . For a short time the Indians just stayed where they were and looked. Then they rushed forward. But not many of them got to strike coup blows on living enemies. Before they could get to them, all of the white men were dead."[12]

If your death by arrogance has any other meaning, it is as a mobilizing nostalgia, like the Alamo or the bait of Pearl Harbor, turning uninformed public sentiment against romanticized Indians, the way the Alamo and Pearl Harbor did against Mexicans and Japanese. Either way, there you are, standing alone in your arrogance and blinded by a lack of humility, realizing that the only people who are afraid of you are a handful of white soldiers who kneel close to you, soiling their pants before they turn their pistols on themselves. You must feel lucky that beer and fantasy still create the nostalgias that most Americans take to be true, and that it takes larger and larger lies to get them up from their inebriated complacency, to stir them into support for the action the upper administrators in the government want their reconstructed patsies to undertake (and even have the patsy sons and daughters die for). Otherwise, you would fade from the public fantasy altogether, to you a fate worse than death.

On the other side of the Little Big Horn River sits another icon of the nostalgias Americans call history, Sitting Bull, a man of superior powers whose internal authority commands respect and honor. Success does not spoil him, and the image of him as a visionary will outlast the sheer joy of the Little Big Horn victory, despite the subtly vindictive pictures we get of him from a soldier who was at the battle:

> "Sitting Bull," a Huncpapa Sioux Indian, was the chief of the hostile camp; he had about sixty lodges of followers on whom he could at all times depend. . . . All visitors paid tribute to him, so he gave liberally to the most influential, the chiefs, i.e., he "put it where it would do the most good." In this way he became known as the chief of the hostile camp, and the camp was generally known as "Sitting Bull's camp" or "outfit." . . . He was the autocrat of the camp—chiefly because he was the host. In council his views had great weight, because he was known as a great medicine man. He was a chief, but not a warrior chief. . . . A short time previous to the battle he had "made medicine" and had predicted that the soldiers would attack them and that the soldiers would all be killed. He took no active part in the battle, but, as was his custom in time of danger, remained in the village "making medicine." Personally, he was regarded by the Agency Indians as a great coward and a very great liar, "a man with a big head and a little heart."[13]

Agency Indians? Who are "agency Indians"? To someone like me, raised on the belief that no one—not another Indian, and especially not a bunch of white folks in the U.S. government—can tell you who or how you are (or are not), an agency Indian is someone who has rolled over to the power of the conqueror and has, whatever his inner feelings, become a sort of Native Step-and-Fetch-It. It is very difficult for a Wallowa Nez Perce to forget the rollover, suck-up Indians like

Lawyer, who heartlessly sold out Chief Joseph and the Wallowa Valley and then felt powerful and protected enough by the whites guarding the reservation to publicly criticize Joseph to his face for resisting. So I would not trust, necessarily, agency Indians' opinions of Sitting Bull.

Moreover, there is Godfrey's causal "so," which implies that because visitors paid tribute to Sitting Bull, "he gave liberally to the most influential, the chiefs." The perception of "putting it where it would do the most good" is the perception of a person who may be one of the last people afraid of Custer and who wants to denigrate Sitting Bull. Yet Godfrey comes from a cultural background in which "chiefs" got together in mead halls to pay tribute to each other, giving gifts to the most influential (those without influence are not recorded by the *Beowulf* poet) and putting "it" where it would do the most good as happily as CEOs buying each other dinner. From a cultural background in which Christmas bonuses, soft money for bribing politicians, and tax-deductible business gifts are common, Godfrey sees fit to characterize what may have been a tribal or generally Indian value. Ten thousand years ago (or so), Clovis (so named for the New Mexican archaeological site), along with his relative Folsom Man (also a New Mexican site discovered by a Black cowboy and former slave), was dedicated to reciprocity: sharing food and resources, for Clovis, meant protection from short-term set-backs. Great honor was accorded to those who provided best and shared most willingly; hoarding resources was both a public and a criminal transgression, punishable by the community.

Godfrey seems to think that giving to "chiefs" is simply oiling the heads of tribes. But for Sitting Bull, giving to "chiefs" probably was a form of honoring and even accepting the most respected leaders of their bands, leaders who were chosen, not by inheritance, but by performance, and who, as heads, were most likely the heads of what may be seen as extended families. By giving to them, Sitting Bull honors them, and they in turn give to the people in their bands. Unlike the culture from which Godfrey comes, where hoarding seems to be equal in value to the mead hall distributions of expensive trinkets, if the "chiefs" do not share, they run the risk of losing their position, of being run out of office, so to speak.

Moreover, it is the Sitting Bull of the historical big "Ooooops!" at the Little Big Horn who, meeting the Nez Perce leader White Bird and his band who flee north into Canada while Chief Joseph surrenders, dismounts from his horse and leads his warriors in "wailing and crying when told what happened to the Nez Perce resistance."[14] A man of real internal power is able to humble himself, to show both humility and strong emotion, and to lead his followers or admirers to it.

And the Sitting Bull that Godfrey wants to criticize treats the ragged and starving Nez Perce with generosity, sharing the resources of the Sioux Buffalo hunts—which, though efficient, are not sufficient to feed all the Sioux and Nez Perce well—and leaves his own people hungry, though not starving. The people who starve are the Assiniboine south of the border because so few buffalo get past the Sioux—the Assiniboine, or "Big Bellies," who murdered Tipyahlahnah Kapskaps, White Bird's stepson, and six other Nez Perce who sought refuge with them.

The stories that tell why the Nez Perce, safe in Canada though hungry much of the time, returned south across the border vary. Some say that they wanted to try to return to the Wallowa Valley with the hope they'd be left in peace; others, like my grandfather, put the cause on Sitting Bull, suggesting that his generosity and desire to treat the Nez Perce refugees well eventually waned. Possibly both are true, and the fact that it is Sitting Bull himself who gets blamed proves in reverse how wrong are Godfrey's perceptions of Sitting Bull's honor: just as honor requires a man like Sitting Bull to dispense gifts, so honor attracts blame to itself; and while it may have been unnamed individuals whose generosity and treatment failed, it is their leader who takes onto himself the historical of storied blame. Sitting Bull, his people murdered, starved, helped to alcohol while ripped from their place—which is life to many Indian people—with nowhere to turn, may have had no choice but to begin to hold back from the Nez Perce. Certainly, he had few choices, in any existential sense.

So despite some stories told of him by some Nez Perce, perhaps Sitting Bull, a great leader with powerful medicine and able visions, found himself trapped and embittered—and bitterness can lead one to a loss of understanding, a tendency to withdraw from the generosity of dispensing gifts or to seem exclusive. Unlike Custer, though, he never seems to lose his sense of who he is, never loses his internal power, the feeling people get when they come into his presence, even after he allows himself to be reconstructed into a role in Cody's Wild

West shows in which he pretends to take an active warrior's part in the battle of the Little Big Horn. Perhaps in this reconstruction we have something closer to the truth, and though I imagine it was a painful choice, a difficult role to play, I also have a sense that it is his strength of character that allows him to play it. We get in the image a picture of a man who was a visionary, who once dispensed the gifts of approval, now driven, out of impoverished despair or hopelessness, to participate in a tableau that was a fantasy of lies in which he is buffaloed and billed as someone—a fighting warrior—into a historical moment in which he was not as billed, but something else. And yet behind the fantasy is not a man trying to maintain his notoriety, his public image, but a man who needs to stay alive, who privately understands he has to do this to survive.

The fantasy of Cody's shows begins to destruct in contextual concert with the Indian accounts of Custer's soldiers shooting themselves or their comrades, committing suicide and murder in their fear, rather than the Anheuser-Busch image of them fighting bravely to the last man. And it is a fantasy that must make us all wonder what fantasies we are allowing to be reinvented or are reconstructing ourselves into, and which ones we are playing roles in, especially given that most of us lack both the wisdom and the power and the sheer character of a man like Sitting Bull, especially given that most of us who would be known or recognized are probably a lot more like Custer.

Sitting Bull, like Custer, came from somewhere: Custer from the poor family that belonged to the Democratic Party in a Republican-controlled period; Sitting Bull from the long heritage of his people and their experiential contact with white European fantasies. One actively creates and recreates the foundation of his response to the world (which is what I mean by "identity" or "who you are") in order to construct and reconstruct a foundationless public image that in turn is misconstrued to be his identity. The other more passively allows it to happen out of despair. In the one, it causes not only arrogance but incredible risk taking, even to the extent that Custer hires Crow scouts and then ignores their repeated expressions of great worry over the sheer number of hoof prints they have seen near the Little Big Horn site. In the other, possibly, it allows him to play a role for money by painfully setting aside the real pride and power of his medicine and to act the warrior for a public willing to pay for their pornographic fantasies of belonging to an adventurous rugged individualism of a West they've never touched. In this one, it is probable that his power and identity were so secure, so firm, that play-acting did not affect or change them at all. It is hard to know. Either way, to have Sitting Bull only sitting in the Wild West shows, to have him quietly portray the great visionary that he was, predicting the defeat of the white soldiers and taking a leader's role but not taking an active warrior's part in that defeat, would not make Elizabeth Custer want to see the show the eighteen or so times she saw it, and then she would not call it—as in her loving nostalgia for her husband she did—a great and true representation of history.

II

Now that the Indian Wars take place on different grounds, mostly in the academies, where the spirit is separated from life and called committees, entire careers rest upon the invention of fantasies as people jockey for snippets of emasculant power, which in our beery age is "fame" and which so corrupts humility and understanding, whether of success or failure. What if, we have to ask, the power jockeys, in some sense, don't begin with a core identity, a background? What if they don't come from anywhere, or from an anywhere that can be clearly felt as a presence and not an absence, as in having a grandfather or father who taught them, or as in not being adopted or not adopting a tribal family? Or what if, culturally, they begin their conscious public lives overlooked, like Indians, and yet the humidity of contemporary politics expressly says the opposite, that they should be noticed and even honored, not for merit but for background, and while they claim the blood, they lack that background? What if they just plain want to be other than they are, like a New Age feeler who collects the stuff, the appurtenances and appearances, of being an Other and then insists on the reality and truth of those appearances? What, in other words, happens on either side of the little Little Big Horn if those who would claim power are not remembered in their identity but constructed or re-constructed in it, especially in the late twentieth century when few Americans come from extended families, from geographies in which have lived generations of those who make them?

The reconstruction may, in some ways, be a piecing together out of whole cloth. Like old professors who were hired in the 1960s when there was a shortage of them, you can become like Custer, who is the only person available who is crazy enough to do the administration's bidding, while all the while thinking you are doing something important. You can become like the reductive image of George Custer jockeying for power and position, become an authority in name only and hold "position" out of fear, not respect or admiration. Or you can become a Head Indian on campus who, in defending yourself against all the Custers, ends up skirmishing over turf with other Indians rather than dispensing the gifts of honor and respect.

Let's imagine. Having been involved with a national circle of Native writers and storytellers for some time, I have heard many stories, so what we'll imagine is not actual. It's a compilation, but it's very real.

First, let's imagine a modern reconstructed Indian in situ on a bend in the road, his offices and the offices of his allies hidden among the trees or cactuses that line the river or canyon or defile that divides the campus. It is a small river or canyon or defile, and the offices, though small, are many; combined, they make up a "studies" program, an "institute," or a major emphasis. It does not have departmental status; if it does, then it becomes equal in funding, status, and activity to all other departments in the college, something few universities ever accept (the first of which, by the way, was the University of California at Davis). As an unequal, as its own ghetto in progress, without the ability to hire or fire but only to draw in faculty already in departments, this program is given moderate amounts of money to dispense, money which the Indian in charge protects as though it is the lifeblood of his or her great-grandchildren.

This is not to denigrate what universities have often accomplished in the way of diversity. Well-intentioned universities began to hire minorities to satisfy their own individual visions of diversity decades ago, when the number of available Indians with advanced academic degrees was finite and small. The Head Indian, we have to imagine, was hired without real competition. He (and most often, it was a "he") does not begin by earning the power and wisdom of Sitting Bull. He is granted it by a bureaucracy on the claims he lays to bloodlines; in other words, he comes already fully enrolled in the Wild West show of the new age university. In comparison to a historical wise man like Sitting Bull, he arrives like new underwear, preshrunk in both purpose and stature. He begins small and reconstructs himself as someone who has the power to hand out gifts, among which is the gift of his approval. In all likelihood, he reconstructs himself as a "Native American," and the Good Housekeeping Seal of (his) Approval depends greatly on whether or not you are willing to accept that reconstruction without question.

He has many names, some of them good. Here, however, we'll call him Uncle Gyro. The university is a confusing place, with unwritten codes along with written rules that sometimes get followed. Universities, after all, have an inertia, a life of rest and motion all their own, almost despite the applied efforts of administrators and faculty; and Uncle Gyro, for good and for ill, depending, maybe just for survival, becomes a spinning mass, able to maintain his angle of attitude and action with respect to the inertial coordinates of the university. For years he's the only sandwich on the menu, and what is at first a kind of loneliness and separation becomes a way of thinking and evaluating.

When another Indian shows up in Gyro's university, Gyro greets him. He wants to make sure the Newind knows who he is; and besides, as the Head Indian, he can afford to seem friendly. Like Sitting Bull welcomed the Nez Perce, he can share his goods; and he feels, doing this, good and wise and deserving of verbal tribute, if nothing else.

"So how are you liking it here?" he asks at the first college meeting.

It must seem, somehow, inappropriate there in the midst of a college meeting to tell the details of how his wife arrived in town and burst into tears, which were like the tears of a great grief—capable of appearing at any moment as though the sadness were stored in the sponge of her eyes. Nor does it seem wise to tell how their first visit to the twenty-four-hour superstore of food, lawn mowers, film developing, and dress shoes had frightened her with the look of its basic customer as though warehouse food produced a strain of mutant shopper, pale-faced with searching Jell-O eyes beneath a fluorescent indoor moon. So, being Indian, he makes a joke about how nice everyone was.

Now if he comes, as half of us do, from a city like Los Angeles, Chicago, or like me, New York ("New York isn't going to tell us what to do or not to do," the supervisor of campus security yelled at me when I tried to explain how the New York transit plates on my new car are supposed to be good for 60 days even in the swamp of Michigan; all I wanted was a temporary parking permit to unload books in my office before I spent the money to buy Michigan plates, money I would not have until I got my first paycheck), not yet having lost his energetic sense of humor to the overcast flat of the Great Midwest (which, in attitudes, extends from the Poconos to the Sierras), he may go on too long—which, in the part of the Midwest I live in, means to go on at all. (Hell, in New York, you can stand at the market's check-out counter while the Dominican checker purposely ignores you, making it a point to finish her conversation about mascara and the printless plumage of orange lip gloss before deigning to lift your jug of milk and pass it over a scanner that beeps from curd on its screen. The surprise in Michigan of having the check-out person ask after the health of your firstborn and give you tips on removing stains from bathroom tile while happily passing your purchases over a spotless scanner that generates money-saving coupons for your next "visit" is both pleasant and not a little surreal to a New Yorker [which to the campus security supervisor, his brass belt buckle polished by the lap of his belly, his white hood hidden in his Ku Klux Kloset in Howell, means not a place but a race, and that race is "Jews"]).

"Everything is so nice, here," he concludes. "Sometimes I worry that I'll get niced to death." (Ho ho. In my case, the very day we moved into our house the nice neighbor across the street nicely invited us over for nice dinner to be eaten outdoors because it was such a nice night. My wife, raised in New York City, met me in distress on one of my U-Haul trips from the storage garages, saying, "Something awful's happened. I'm so sorry. I just didn't know what to do." Turned out that the woman across the street invited, nay, insisted we come to dinner, and my wife didn't know how to get out of it. "It's okay," I tried to calm her by laughing, "That's probably how it is here." My wife thought the woman was pushy, much pushier than the conventional stereotype of New Yorkers who, we had yet to learn, are much, much friendlier than Midwesterners. I, of course, with the same naive lippitude with which I had told her that my new department chair really wanted me and not just a statistic, held my wife, hugged her against the sheet-lightning shock of suburbia Midwestern-style, and told her that our new neighbor was probably just being friendly in the only way she knew how. Another story to be imagined at another time.)

We can easily imagine our Newind being cut short by a colleague who is concerned to make him feel welcome and right at home. "If it bothers you so much, why don't you just go back where you came from?" she inquires acidly.

Newind will sigh. Relief. He isn't sure. But he detects a certain directness and honesty that he appreciates. (If he's from the cities, he may think he hears in her dulcet voice the reminiscent timbre of the New York traffic cop, pestered by an aging British tourist for directions, who says, "Lady, I ain't a fucking road map.")

"Thanks for making me feel at home," he says, laughing.

Uncle Gyro will smile dimly at this exchange. Having learned how to get along with colleagues, he will not laugh out loud. Gyro knows that everything isn't so nice here, and if he or Newind had foresight, they'd see why *Blue Velvet* was true, an accurate portrayal of the Midwest. But they don't have foresight. Gyro because, well, he's busy spinning and turning and trying with the thick weight of his head compounded by his years of being the one true source of advice and counsel, to stay upright. Newind because, well, he's just plain stupid, stupefied by his sudden entry into the Ivory Tower with all its hidden chambers and invisible devices, lacking only Henry VIII to make full use of it.

This meeting, this greeting is often the first and last meeting of Gyro and Newind. Phylogeny recapitulates ontogeny as Newind himself begins to spin, to twist and turn as he tries to find his own moral and intellectual compass in a world he never imagined. Gyro will return to his offices across the river (or canyon or defile) to the ghetto of his entertainments at the institute. Gyro never calls him. Busy making small mistake after small mistake, Newind will assume that's the way Gyro wants it. Besides being busy, Newind may be a shy sort of person or a person from a completely different sort of tribe, and, busied by his own duties, he may never call Gyro either. He (and these days, she) works on getting settled, fitting in, contributing where he can, and teaching as well as possible, even though his department chair counsels him to spend less time teaching and more on doing his own work of writing books. Maybe, like me, he has a new baby whom he swaddles and cradles in the crook of his left arm as he works, and he learns to type fairly well with his right hand.

Regardless, years pass.

One day, Newind's imitation of a department chair calls him in to warn him that Gyro has written the provost in favor of denying him tenure. (Walter Adams, my neighbor and a former president of my own university once asked, "So you like your department chair?" "Yes, very much," I replied. "Well enjoy him," Walter snarled, " 'cause the next one will be an ass.")

Being very new or from a very different tribe in which, perhaps, telling the truth counts for something, he goes straight to his office and calls Gyro.

Being from a completely different background, Gyro will, of course, assure him or her that he likes him or her fine, that he has not written the provost or composed the letter. But, honesty not completely gone from his heart, he will add a vague sort of threat. "I have to tell you," Gyro may add, "there are a lot of complaints about your lack of scholarship." This vague threat will keep coming up in this conversation like salmonella chicken.

To Newind, it will seem almost like a joke. In many instances, the Head Indians have gotten little or no real work done in the way of publishing. Indeed, at my own university, it is an oft-told story that Gyro himself has never published anything but a little monograph-sized book that he co- co-authored with two men who afterwards accused him of doing none of the work and taking all of the credit. Whether true or not, I haven't bothered to find out. At other colleges I have heard of Head Indians who, in search of promotion or advancement, always in search of money, have argued that grant applications—applications, mind you—be considered as "publication" in the triadic research, teaching, and service of large research universities.

To Newinds, who are slightly corroded and sometimes as dull as brass because they are not so new anymore, involved in their own processes of fitting in, Uncle Gyro seems to have become someone whose public sense of himself, his power, and his place is high-handedly disproportionate. The smart Newind, however, will not be interested in getting into a battle with Gyro. All that does—and we have many current examples—is damage the students and hurt the cause of Native American studies. ("See," my head of campus security would say, "They can't even get along with each other.") Newind should do what the grandmothers and grandfathers teach us to do, keep a firm grip on one's own identity and balance, and let the remainder go.

Perhaps Newind does not understand Gyro. Certainly, young and naive, I didn't. It is a failure of my own and any other Newind's imagination that he does not see the Head Indian as hurt and embittered by our lack of tributary attention; and though we are right, it is way too narrow only to wonder such things as why it is that people who claim to be most "Indian" often act least Indian, and if the people who essentialize most are not people hiding their own doubts and falsehoods behind the smokescreen of the essentialism.

Gyro, hurt and angry, will start to do things to try to injure Newind's career. He may even go so far as he did in one case I heard about and start telephoning presses, using the indirect power of rumor and innuendo to tell the editors that Newind is, Gyro suspects, not even "Indian" and to try to stop the publication of Newind's book or essay. Again, when this happens, other Newinds will do what my friend did and wish simply for Gyro to stop doing these things. Intrigues of this or any other kind won't attract him or her because intrigues require constant vigilance and behind-the-scenes consideration and activity; to participate in intrigue, you have to become nasty, and not only does your heart shrink, but the amount of time free to spend with your family or on your work shrinks right along with it. Instead of bringing lawsuits or becoming obsessed with Gyro, all Newind should do, I think, is want Gyro to go his way in peace and leave him to his or her way.

Unfortunately, it is not so easy. It is all too easy to forget that real enemies must have stature if they are going to be fought, and this stature must be earned the way Sitting Bull's was, not simply given the way most of us get it within environments like universities. It is all too easy to see oneself as a victim, and once one manages that trick of the light, once one pities oneself too much for events that are not going easily one's way, our solipsistic age demands that one seek redress. Then the fun really begins. Gyro sees himself as injured. Newind sees him- or herself as injured. Each sees himself as at the center of all things, and all things that occur relate directly to him. It is a limited and limiting fantasy—and boy can it spin out of control!

But don't universities have rules? you may ask.

Sure they do. But the first rule of any big bureaucracy—think of government, the police force, or any large corporation, which is what a university is—is not to be seen in its underwear without its hair gel and makeup on. My old teacher and one of the wisest people I ever knew, George P. Elliott, taught me that one thing universities do not like is to be "embarrassed." And he was right, although the severity of what might cause embarrassment seems to rise incrementally with each instance when a university gets caught with its pants down.

So universities depend on lower-level bureaucrats to keep things in check. In essence, one of the most important jobs of a department chair these days is to keep the lid on, keep the higher administrators from having to deal with angry minorities, women, or people of power.

For the time being, then, we need to pause in our story of Gyro and Newind to invent Chairperson Three Pee, Gyro's very real enemy on this side of the Little Big Horn River (or canyon or defile). He knows Gyro, has known him since his hiring, which he opposed, using some arguments about meritocracy to circumvent his very real disbelief at affirmative action. Though Three Pee comes from privilege, has had a privileged education that gave him the privilege of the connections that generate privileged jobs for graduates, he does not see what that has to do with anything. The best are simply the best. Gyro (it's true) may well have less than the best education. Moreover, being Indian, he may not see education as the same thing Three Pee does. He may see it as a process that connects and not a process that develops an end product—the educated man—and instead of majoring in a "discipline," he may have taken a degree in a "Studies" program—say, American Studies, where there is room for the less-intelligent or less-disciplined as well as room to study things beyond the limitations of the canon of worthy literature Three Pee believes in. A lot of fifth-rate people come out of "Studies" programs; a number of first-rate people do too.

Every Native person has encountered a figure such as this: the bureaucrat whose career, like Custer's, started on a successful note—he achieved a modest reputation and showed every promise of becoming a generally important scholar—but either the world of intellectual fashion has changed or he has, and his career seems to languish, his reputation having somehow fallen out of the sparrow's eye of academic repute. He himself feels the notes of his success evaporating around him like humidity from a hot tub, so he turns to bureaucracy and administration in order to get salary raises, chosen by the dean, not because he is a good administrator who manages not to be high-handed with the barge pilots and postal mistresses, but because there is no one else even adequate to the task who is as willing as Custer to make rules and bring order. Order, in many respects, is good, and bring it he does. But like our Head Indian, in order to reconstruct himself fully as the head bureaucrat, he has to forget who he once thought he was. Like Gyro, he remembers what he had to go through to get "this" far, and therefore everyone else should have to go through similar trials and disappointments. Where once he may have been somewhat generous and knowledgeable about the ways of the world, he becomes cheap, a quibbler over rules and procedures, a pettifogger. Because the higher administration does what it does, keep the pressure on him to bring them the statistics they need to prove their own worth, he becomes increasingly quarrelsome and pugnacious. He begins to manipulate the people in his department to force the trains to run on time while carrying ever-increasing loads of students. He is increasingly conservative, using his pettifoggery to find obscure rules and regulations to follow, while finding extremely clever ways to circumvent rules that are in his way (the very nature of departments comprising twenty-five to fifty would-be individualists is to be procedurally conservative). He will present a bold front, but deep down inside he is afraid not to do the job he thinks the university wants him to do. (You want dead Indians? Then just let me go get a peaceful band and slaughter them. Not, of course, that the university wants dead Indians.)

We are all cowards. Indeed, in the arts and humanities, because we lack almost all power and are subject to public disdain for trying, as Santayana said, to teach the utility of useless knowledge, we are always afraid of not being able to justify the ways of literature to man, and so we move farther and farther away from literature into sociology, psychology, or some errant forms of "activism," or we move farther and farther into the protective cells of our monastic hiding, our offices, from which we try not to disturb anyone. Eventually, we don't even disturb students' complacent minds because we get into trouble if we try. If a parent complains (and cowards themselves, they do so anonymously), the cowardly administrator calls the cowardly director, who calls the cowardly professor, who assures the cowardly director that they can be brave, that there is no substance to the complaint, especially not the anonymous complaint; and the director, a lion having gotten courage in Oz, phones Dorothy in the administration to say what he or she should have said all along—there is never any substance to anonymous complaints, and we have known that since we realized that student evaluations were professionally meaningless, in part because they go unsigned. In a world in which you are presumed guilty even after you prove yourself innocent, we all become cowards, even the courageous professor, even if he or she can successfully reassure the director. He or she may not know it yet; over time, he or she will become weary of these silly, unsubstantial complaints and do what all professors end up doing, give undeservedly high grades. Who cares? Certainly, students don't. Parents don't. The few who do will make themselves known, and with them the professor can bravely venture all the way back to Socrates and maybe even teach them something.

So we are all cowards. Our imagined chairperson is only more cowardly. He is not alone in cowardice, and it makes him feel brave, which, in such a powerless world, means he becomes pusillanimous. Pettifogging, pusillanimous, yet pugnacious. Three Pee.

Rules are rules. And even minority faculty cannot behave the way Gyro has. Like the head of campus security, our chairperson is a beleaguered white person who is not to blame for racism in America, and secretly she or he resents someone who seems like a seagull, a protected species who gets paid more than he thinks they're worth because there are so few of them with Ph.D.s. Any Native person surely has met the chairperson who reasonably explains how he is not qualified to teach Shakespeare, not even in London, England, with the help of the Globe Theatre staff, but who—sometimes in the same conversation—makes it clear that he thinks anyone, especially any Native faculty, can teach a course in indigenous oral traditions. Every Native professor has met the colleague who is happy to have him teach Native literature with the unstated assumption that the moment it interferes with other literature it will be understood that Native literature, while important, is not as important as X. (In many cases, it's not; the American Popular almost unerringly celebrates the second- or third-rate of any minority literature with few, but of course important, exceptions; nonetheless, there is plenty of first-rate Native writing out there in print to be read and taught). These colleagues, sometimes faced with the proliferation of courses in minority literature—a proliferation that may serve student wishes but may not serve educational needs—may begin to look for ways to reduce the measure of importance of nonwhite literature and faculty, even if only to reach what to them is a level playing field. These colleagues may become chairs. And these chairs, once they become pusillanimous or pettifogging or pugnacious will do what the self-glorifying Custer did, gather their forces and send out scouts in search of more easy victories or massacres.

Meanwhile, back at his office, Gyro, equally pusillanimous, trying to maintain his own position of power as Head Indian, continues breaking the rules. He needs to set back Newind if he can, so he is telephoning, telephoning, telephoning, gathering his own forces. Now we all know, Indian and non-Indian alike, that using modern tools like the telephone is, for an Indian, a difficult technological task. He is forced to read the instruction manual each time he tries to dial off-campus, and when he dials on-campus, he keeps getting Campus Security when he wants Philosophy. Gyro, however, has learned to close his eyes and, in an act of faith, use the automatic dialer buttons. As a reconstruction, he has become fairly versed in the use of modern tools, and he can happily use them to interfere with Newind's tenure review.

So here we have the situation, a modern face-off on the dried up Little Big Horn River, with two cowards facing off for battle. Three Pee thinks he gets his power and authority from the university. His right to use it comes from his sense of privilege. But Gyro is only an Indian. One has to wonder where he gets any of his sense.

In some cases, it's an enrollment card. At least two of the Gyros I know wheedled enrollment cards out of small and very newly federally recognized tribes, and in both cases, tribes where the elders are rumored to be angry over the uses they are putting the cards to. But what does a card matter, anyway? Where (or how) I grew up, you either were or you weren't. A card was not going to make you any more Indian than dressing the part for the Wild West shows. Perhaps as a reconstruction uncertain of who he is, Gyro tends to think of an enrollment card not just as a meal ticket but also as a coup stick he can use against those whom, in his notional jealousy, he fears and whom he begins to fantasize are not "Indian" or "Indian enough." With such jealous limitations, perhaps he fails to imagine the possibility that other people are, and they are not afraid of who they are. Perhaps he cannot imagine that they even have proof of who they are that they refuse to show just everyone because they morally object to having to show anyone (Scots, after all, don't have to "prove" they are Scottish any more than Blacks that they are African, Caribbean, or Latin American).

Sometimes Gyros think their association with other Head Indians gives them power and privilege. They imagine they get power from their own (General) Pleasanton, perhaps from one of the original masters of intrigue and innuendo who has played word warrior in the Wild West shows of the New Age for many years. Or they imagine they get protection from their friendship with angry Head Indians who wear aviator glasses and offer false truths of history to counter false truths of history (e.g., the Aztecs did not sacrifice human beings as a falsehood meant to counter the falsity that indigenous peoples are more savage than the invaders). Or maybe it is money, or association with money and the momentary fashions that give out fame—literary, dramatic, filmic, federally consulting fame—that makes Gyro feel so special, even though he himself has done little more, in his constructed fantasy of self as the most important Indian on campus, than feather himself while trying to tar other Indians and use acronyms like NAGPRA liberally to show his currency, all the while whining to the provost.

In the case mentioned above, where Gyro tried to stop the publication of my friend's book, Uncle Gyro actually telephoned a Native American series editor to "wonder" if my friend was "Indian" at all. Although both the series editor and the press deny that such happened, the Moccasin Telegraph—which may be counted on to be sometimes reliable—says that it did. Certainly, after the phone call(s), the press's editor "released" the book manuscript it had accepted, sending Newind the bad news while he was out of the country and could do nothing about it. In this instance, my friend could not prove that it happened; and even if he could, why would he waste his time and energy? "I am who I am," he told me, though like everyone else, he sometimes gets confused and has to spend time alone remembering just who that who is. He does what he does. "My grandfather and grandmother wouldn't let the Feds tell them who they were; why would I let Uncle Gyro tell me who I am supposed to be or not be in the context of the university?"

Gyro must have felt as powerful as the reconstructed Custer sneaking up on a Native encampment of old people, women, and children in a pre-dawn massacre. In Custer's case, the newspapers made it out to be a great and heroic success. Likewise to Custer, Gyro must have been, in his way of thinking, really happy, as happy as he could feel, preventing another Indian from passing him by in rank. For that, we would learn, was the subtext. I can only imagine his disappointment to hear that another press accepted my friend's book, a disappointment that must have doubled when, after hardcover publication and good reviews, the original Native series decided maybe it had been wrong and bought the paperback rights.

Here's where it gets weirder than the three sisters opening *Macbeth*. You would think Custer would recognize the falsity of the newspaper reports—after all, he was physically there—and exercise caution, try to keep the truth from being found out, rather than tempt fate. You would think that Gyro would see that sneaky actions often misfire and would let things go and use his energy to do more good things for needy Native students.

Unfortunately, it is not the end of Gyro's reconstructed love of the appearances of authority. Like a feathered Custer, he begins to take unnecessary risks. When my friend comes up for promotion again because he is about to publish a second book, Gyro, who evidently is a little thick-headed and slow to knowledge, tempts fate and makes another one of his bold, pre-dawn attacks by telephone. The call begins with innuendo and devolves to slander. His first mistake is in ignoring his scouts: this editor is not in the grip of other Head Indians but is, rather, a professional; he records the contents of the call and reproduces it in writing. At first Gyro lies and swears that he did not make the call. Though guileful, Gyro, who is no Coyote, who thought he was protected by the medicine of behind-the-scene innuendo and false rumor that had always worked before, who deluded himself into thinking he was protected by the umbrella of Wily Word Warrior's favor, has made the call from his office at the university where all the times, dates, places of origin, and long-distance numbers called are recorded on a central computer. When Gyro realizes that he has made a serious miscalculation (a slow, tedious process that for this dishonorable man takes months), he changes his tack to a frontal attack. The fact that his honor is gone for good because he has sworn one thing only to admit another when cornered doesn't seem to faze him, even though to be called a liar, a person who is not true to his words is, to most of my Indian friends, anathema. Gyro admits to making the call, while insisting that he, Gyro, The Uncle Gyro, does not have to abide by the rules of decency and professional collegiality that the university requires of its faculty.

It is a high-handedness worthy of Custer himself.

Talk about role reversal and confusion. In this case, as with many others, the university's response is to keep things out of the public eye (for good reason—the public cares little for education and is given to unfairly criticizing universities at the slightest provocation). It chooses simply to remove Uncle Gyro to another department or studies program, separating my friend from Gyro by assigning them to different and distant acres on the university's intricate reservation system. As with the first book, the first promotion, and the first set of phone calls, that was enough for my friend. At the insistence of his department chair, he did ask for a letter of retraction and apology and the promise that Gyro would never question his purpose or his identity again.

"He will, of course," my friend told me.

"Will what?"

"Try to hurt me where he can."

"So why don't you take him down, now?" I asked.

"I just can't get up the energy to care. My department chair wants me to. But every time I start to think of what I might do, I just start yawning. Sort of like watching television, you know? I mean, who cares? Why do I need to make Gyro suffer? Revenge isn't mine to have. Vengeance takes its toll on the vengeful; and opponents who are cowards and liars—and remember, I know he is a liar and he knows I know it—do not measure up to being an enemy, someone who is worth battling, whom you can respect. I just care that I know the truth and that the truth is there for anyone smart enough to see it. Besides, every time he attacks me, I get promoted along with a good-sized raise. Sometimes I think I should call him and get him to launch another one of his little attacks."

I have to admit that I felt ashamed, because I had initially felt like my friend's department chair. But my friend is right: vindictiveness is for the Custers, the heads of campus security, the bureaucrats of the small heart. Initial success followed by apparent failure (even if it is not really failure at all) creates a dangerous enemy for whom all that remains is administrative vindictiveness, and if there is proof of failure, it is in the very attempts at vindictiveness. For vindictiveness is not for the truly successful. Success breeds generosity and grace. Vindictiveness is the cauldron in which proto-failures, who want you to fail with them, find themselves flailing about without any help from you. You don't get to put them there or dance about the boiling fire unless you want to become like General Sherman, whose uncompromising policy was to treat surrendering Indians ruthlessly (to Sherman is attributed the origination of the phrase, "The only good Indian is a dead Indian," and he was recorded in 1867 as saying, "The more [Indians] we can kill this year, the less will have to be killed the next war").[15]

My friend clearly understood how the eyes of false or little power can become beady and how, if that power becomes one's obsession or meaning, the heart can shrink to the size and hardness of a nut. He had sympathy for the Gyros of the Native academic world who began with something important and, trying only to survive, twisted and turned so many ways and times that eventually they took a wrong turn. The farther one gets from the original importance, the less meaning one's actions or life has. Suspecting this in an inarticulate and unarticulated way, the way one builds a dike against the sea-surge of this realization has these days become, more and more, to attack, deny, or denigrate—for the most part—other Indians. Not non-Indians. Other Indians. One cannot admit to feeling threatened. One certainly can't say that his attack is based on honest, well-spoken disagreement; one is, after all, as the First and only Head Indian for so long, unused to disagreement. And one can't admit that all this gyrating has kept one so busy that one has accomplished so very very little, little more than the repetitions of a circular dance, doing the same things in different guises or jackets over and over again until one is trapped in the cul-de-sac of banality without even knowing it. Unable to admit any of these things—and who could, really?—he attacks the New Indians on campus for the one thing no one can prove (or should want to), their blood quantum. For the suspicions that have caused his attacks, he already suffers terribly, if only because people know who he is. As a full-fledged liar, he cannot trust anyone, even if (or when) he claims to be their friend.

So maybe bureaucrats believe in the kind of revenge that the federal government took on the "renegade" Indians by slaughtering the innocent and helpless Indians at Washita. For Uncle Gyro is little more than that. Though not peaceful, fooled by his own sense of derived power and reconstructed insistency, Gyro has no positive power, and no power at all other than the tidbits the university feeds him when they need him to dress up and act the wild Indian. Gyro is, essentially, as helpless as an old woman in the frozen dawn.

Uncle Gyro barely exists (although he barely exists all over at several major universities). This is mainly imagined. But it is not all fantasy. It happens. When it happens to you, perhaps like my friend you will be a little sympathetic toward the Gyros and Three Pees and remain content to do nothing more to them (or the head of campus security) than ask that you meet no more again this or any other year.

The problem with imagined stories is that they don't end easily. Nevertheless, Gyro and Three Pee are just extremes, made up or invented out of the experiences of friends as a way to raise questions. As inventions, they must make us wonder if we really want the power to injure others. If I ever have power, I hope (and I am as, if not more, fallible than most) I use it to promote and not to demote, to help younger or newer people find their way and not to make them join mine. It's what I hope to offer here: not what non-Indians might call revenge but what young Indians might see as hope—the hope of avoiding the nasty jealous politics just waiting in the world to cause them to lose themselves fighting enemies who don't exist in an attempt to maintain an appearance of power that is not worth having. But I know this: I am as able to fool myself as Custer, and I can be as small as Gyro or Three Pee. It often gives me, as they say, pause.

III

George Armstrong Custer and Sitting Bull are iconographic myths not unlike the powerful, double-barreled mythologies of Frederick Jackson Turner's and Buffalo Bill Cody's versions of the "Frontier." In their contemporary bureaucratic forms, they are once removed from the "Real Thing" that Coca-Cola lays claim to, but they are nonetheless similar in the reconstructions of their mythographies.

As someone who likes to think of himself as just being, like a frog in a stream, I do know that there are things about me that make people angry, that annoy them. In some cases, it's as simple as size; and I have five decades of experience of small males picking fights with me, wanting to prove themselves. Big men get all sorts of little men sticking their noses into their personal space in bars, in class, at jobs, in meetings, and essentially saying, "Oh, yeah? Yeah? You want to fight about it?" (I asked a big colleague if he'd experienced that. He thought a minute and said, "You know, I have. All my life. I'd never really realized it though.").

I realized it because I changed schools so often, and I still remember Pete Wright and Dan O'Something, the thugs of my sixth grade school to which I was new, picking a fight and making me wrestle them to the ground and sit on their chests with my fist raised as though I would strike, making them say "uncle." (Pete? Dan? You probably don't read, but if you do, you could have won those tests by refusing to cry uncle, because I don't think I am capable of hitting someone so helpless.)

And then there was the added lesson of Vicki O'Dell. Playing on the beach in Ventura, California, Vicki and I tossed sand at each other in play, and a grain got in Vicki's eye. My loving mother spent the next several hours, as we drove Vicki to the emergency room and waited anxiously for the sand to be removed, telling me that she could end up blind in that eye, that if Vicki never saw again out of that eye, it would be my fault entirely. I don't know if I was given to boyish violence before that incident. I do know that as that eight-year-old boy waited for the bandage to come off Vicki's eye to learn that her sight was not damaged, whatever desire he had to physically hurt someone vanished or buried itself so deep that you would have to threaten my children and wife before I'd strike out. So maybe Mom did me a favor.

Nonetheless, I can be stubborn and aggressive for things I believe to be fair, just, or good. I have a Nez Perce way of speaking what I believe is the truth, and I have a Nez Perce willingness to have that truth corroborated or disagreed with. Maybe in a world of reconstructed people forming committees to give them a sense of life and importance, it is an attempt at directness coming from so unlikely a source (a poor nobody boy from a democratic, relocated family)—is this what annoys?

Ultimately, I come down to my sense of identity, my sense of self that comes both from my background and also (perhaps) from growing up with the knowledge that at birth I was never supposed to have lived. The two are hard to separate. But whatever the reasons, this froggy desire to stay in contact with my own moral sense of things seems to drive some folks just plain paddleless.

Like the name of any particular university, it isn't the Gyros or Three Pees who are important here, any more than the real reconstructed historical fake of Custer. Their places in this life and the afterworld are assuredly not the same as ours; they have to be who they are (or aren't), and we need to try to wish them no further ill. The important point is that they are examples of people who seem to lack a sense of Being, of being Who they are without the crutches of public acclaim or reputation, reconstructing themselves with such thoroughness and lack of humor or self-awareness that they begin to confuse reality with appearance, authority with the outward shows of authoritarianism, and they begin to think they have the power to decide on peoples' fates or destinies. What they—and others like them—don't seem to understand is that people of intrigue like General Pleasanton and Wily Word Warrior protect you or remain loyal to you only insofar as it advances them and not you. Fashion, similarly, changes. Meanwhile, you have to go on being you—a depressing thought, I should think for some—without a moral compass.

A person of intrigue lacks what Wayne Booth calls the "moral sense" when he writes: "works [of literature] are marred by an impression that the author has weighed his characters on dishonest scales," not because "he explicitly passes judgment," but because "the judgment he passes" does not seem "defensible in the light of dramatized facts."[16] Earlier, quoting Henry James, he suggests that:

the "moral sense of a work of art" depends completely "on the amount of felt life concerned in producing it." Though he [Henry James] qualifies this statement by including the "kind" and the "quality" of "felt life," he is still unmistakably clear that the morality of the work—that which gives the "enveloping air or the artist's humanity"—comes from the "quality and capacity" of the artist's "prime sensibility."[17]

I have written elsewhere that, as a Dreamer, I believe only in story-telling. Stories provide context and even analysis of human experi-ence, and stories make or create the world and let us learn how we are to live in it and survive. Literature, to me, is storytelling. And much Native American storytelling involves the problem of identity. Stories, even implicitly, in the shadow of the implied or expressed author, remember who we are and more importantly *how* that who is. It is not a matter of "fiction" versus "nonfiction." It is all fiction, and much of it may be called true fiction, true storytelling, when the writer/teller demonstrates that "moral sense" and creates, along with the world of the story, our trust in his or her ability to tell that world accurately on a human or "felt" level.

When the rememberer or creator of a story has his thumb in the pan of the balance scales because he is involved in the reconstruction and maintenance of public reputation, he—like Custer—loses all proportion in the perceptions and judgments of his continuously recontextualized (storied) life.[18] If he is involved in intrigue and innuendo rather than straightforward attempts to "tell" the world, he soon achieves a kind of delusional madness that makes him take stupid risks because he believes himself to be invulnerable or unassailable or just entirely and completely in the right. He loses all proportion in his life and his judgments.

We, then, can work backward to discover the intriguer—the way all readers of stories work backward to discover the implied author—whose life or whose perceptual framework lacks that simile to moral sense, lacks what I might call Foundational Being.

The fake.

No matter how many feathers he wears, he will always be *playing* Indian, and until he reaches the furthest extreme—which Gertrude Bonnin, in her claims of relationship to Sitting Bull, never quite reached—he will always suspect himself of playing Indian, a fantasy he will try to hide by attacking other Indians—other Indians!—for being "not Indian enough."[19] No matter how many memos Custer sends, it is not merely history but example that he teaches us. We can pity him, but we must not overlook the truth of what he is. He is, in the late twentieth century, the end product of committees, using up precious energy to separate the spirit from life and then recycling the forms of life. The lives of these reconstructed or reconstituted people become all data and dullness.

It is madness.

And remembering the Little Big Horn, for me the results aren't really in need of imagining at all.

Critical Arts

When Dadaism actively opposed making a "religion" of art, it failed. It failed in part because Dadaists like Duchamp needed the priestly voices of "experts" to mediate between what the artist "found" ready-made and called "art" and what the public perceived as artistic. The clever perceptual challenges that a urinal labeled "Fountain" might offer was cleverness only. With an elite corps of critics, however, who were willing to declare cretinous anyone who saw "Fountain" as less than "art," a reputation can not only be made but made expensive. The origins of the word *Dada* itself contain the same seeds of non-art requiring the high priest to declare it mysterious and above rational inquiry: if—indeed, if—the name Dada ("hobbyhorse") was chosen at random from a French dictionary, it says much about luck but little about art, which is not random and which is neither hobby nor horse. And, at the extreme, "found" art can become shit—human excreta—dropped on the polyurethaned wooden floors of Soho galleries.

In a commercial, confused world, in which the unknowable mysteries of art are not merely explained but are also promoted to increase the monetary value, the high priests of art and those who sell the mysteries, the owners of galleries, tend to fuse, to become one and the same, mediating between the increasingly isolated artiste and the *pendejo* public who simply cannot understand the complicated, subtle ways of the artiste.

Just as institutional food requires that you gradually do away with the consumer's taste, so art critics "problematize" taste in such a manner that, if it is not done away with entirely, makes claims of tastefulness suspect and even derided. How many times, I wonder, did Vincent Price get asked if what he called good painting wasn't just a function of his taste—as though taste is something floating in the air like a virus and could be acquired too easily by anyone? How many times must he have wanted to reply, "To take the notions of a fool as educated opinion would be to act like the fool himself

221

(or herself)?" Vincent Price knew, appreciated, and could articulate a good deal about the qualities of visual art in a way that few visual artists can. (Matisse, for example, should have provided a lesson to most painters, one that taught them to keep their mouths shut and let their paintings do the talking for them.) But Vincent Price was a rare critic, who must have instilled horror among the majority of art critics. The most cynical of us might claim that the critic does away with taste so that the masses will eat crap while he or she enjoys fine cuisine in secret, much the way Andy Warhol made a fortune off of "Pop" art, only to reveal after his death that in the inner rooms of his home he hung and enjoyed paintings by older, recognized masters.

Except for the fact that people still maintain a delusional belief in their abilities to read literature, whereas the modern painting-viewing public gets stereotyped by its ignorance ("I may not know anything about art, but I know what I like"), literary critics have evolved into something akin to gallery owners and art critics.[1] With God dead, the author becomes godlike in his creations. At first, the literary critic comes along to tell us the value of those creations. But eventually he comes back to tell us all that the author-god has died and that with him dead, it takes the critic to justify the ways of art to Man, it takes the critic to explain, to properly problematize and thematize and theorize. And so much depends on that red wheelbarrow "properly" that one can move whole molehills with it. In the so-called postmodern world, the critic can begin to imagine that he or she no longer needs the creating, ordering, structuring, guiding author, that, like "God" in the modernist world, the god-like author has died and all that is left is criticism, which—and I quote a theorist and friendly acquaintance—is an "art." The religion isn't even art in this scheme; the religion is art criticism.

There are at least two ways to look at the statement that criticism or theory can be an "art." One is laying claim to territory that the critic can inhabit only after he or she colonizes the territories of art and kills off the authors. The other is that the critic intends to begin a process similar to what medicine is beginning to go through with doctors who are good physicians but imperfect healers, not merely realizing but understanding that what a medicine man or woman does is cure the spirit or soul and not the physical framework for that soul in this world.[2] Real and unreal are two in one, Wallace Stevens told us, and to separate the two is to neuter the other. In this sense, the theory-as-art critic would mean to say that knowledge is never pure and that ideas abstracted from literature can—when the soul of literature and authorial intention (the spirits that inhabit books) is killed off—become literally absurd, a futile exercise that is nothing less than foolish. This "artistic" critic, then, understands narrative and understands how narrative demands that you let go of the linear argument, forget your preconceived agendas and conclusions, and follow ideas the way a novelist follows his characters, glad when they behave but wishing they would act more like friends than perverse iconoclasts. The novelist knows that if you try to force a character, a sentence, a structured book to say what you want it to say and not what it has to say, you will kill it. If you "position" yourself as a critic and have a point of view out of which you read and interpret, your "positionality" is already deadness, the fixity of Melville's leaden sea at the opening of "Benito Cereno."

If anything, then, the artist-theorist needs to be disinterested, to want the reciprocal involvement of his audience and not the elitist exclusion of it by obfuscation and pretentious absurdity, and to involve himself in the processes of rhetoric. His criticism can be, in part, about itself: most (if not all) literary novels are in part about the act of novel writing or storytelling, and they always include an aesthetic justification of themselves structurally and metaphorically. But it always must be about Other, about not-itself, about the real and unreal mixture of life, art, or literature; and it must have intention and the expression of an authorial presence that takes responsibility for its success or its failure. An artist critic cannot be a "pure" theorist or an extremely abstract theorist. He or she can leave that to the Frederick Winslow Taylors of the post-modern world, who want to describe minutely discrete individual tasks and then recombine those discrete elements into something that looks less like a novel or story with human spirit and more like Mr. Potato Head. An artist theorist should be an artist first, an author first, and a theorist or critic second. Art overcomes criticism in a true artist just as art overcomes and transcends politics.

An author's job is to be in some sense approachable. While his or her job is to make particular that which can be general, it is not to make particular to the point of banality, obvious patterning, or relative speciality in the form of allusions or jokes that only the "in" group can know and understand. The point of banality is reached, true, in *Less than Zero*, Brett Ellis's book that is so repetitious and uninformed that it is dull enough for all those who would fake an interest in reading to buy it and read it. *The Joy Luck Club* is so predetermined in its erector-set structure that each generation is interchangeable in language and meaning with another, as though the messiness of this novel was edited and the novel was reconstructed in a lifeless pattern (which is, I suspect, what happened).

But opposite to those rather easy, nonliterary targets, we could pick on Joyce and wonder if *Finnegan's Wake* does not demand that the reader join a club in which membership is limited, a club that cracks the code and then shares the joke privately with the other club members who are willing to be tyrannized by one man's joining together the obscure contributions and allusions of several helpers (*Wake* is, in its formation, one of the first "group" novels or books of the twentieth century). If we call *Finnegan's Wake* a "text," which participates in a modernist "discourse" of theory and criticism, couldn't we say the opposite: that from the multiple but very similar points of view of indigenous oral traditions, *Finnegan's Wake* is not a lot better than *Less Than Zero*? Only the in-group gets its jokes, and only a very small group bothers to read all of it.

Of course, when you kill off God or the Creator, then the author, and then make all things equal (In the beginning was the textuality and the textuality was good), you have made the distinctions of art questionable. To all but the artist. Like the maker of fine wines, the artist knows that even if you try to make the world "grape" and thus one "drinks" the world, there is still a difference between a good Cabernet and Mad Dog 20/20, no matter how theorized or problematized that difference becomes.

If the "artist" theorist wants to write about theory to make more theory, he or she needs to become increasingly abstract. But art is like Laura Esquivel's recipes, and the recipes of art are not there to make more recipes, but to let us eat cake. To let us drink the wine and, perhaps, enjoy its complexities more. Art is not solely self-referential, though theory seems often to be. Art is about something. The art of criticism should be about literary books; let sociology be about the multiple "texts" of the boring commercial world. Criticism, if film is what is being studied, should be about film and not movies. One should eat good food imaginatively prepared and participate in the completion of the process the cook begins with his recipe. One should not try to live on the holes of donuts.

Art is not separation—which the Marxisms and feminisms and post-this-isms and -that-isms require—separation each from the other, so that critics can talk about a "feminist" interpretation or a "Marxist" interpretation. Art is not the abstract overreaching of "The Legend of Godasiyo" or the "Tower of Babel," in which the result for each story is the inability of each to understand the language of the other, of each to sympathize with the story of the other.[3] Art is connection. It is not abstraction but specifics generalized to a primary level of consensus, to the first intersection of where many intelligent readers agree. It is not about itself but about what is human in all of us.

When theory becomes art and involves itself in the participatory process of the oral traditions, then it will use narrative to make connections. The critic will tell us who he is aesthetically or intellectually (but not personally or emotionally because we don't give a rat's farthing)—even indirectly or in his "as ifs." He'll tell us a story of an idea or a set of ideas that for however long takes dominion of our ideas and connects them, organizes them, gives them meaning, which then dissolves until the story is retold and reheard. Criticism will return to something that first puts the writer of criticism back into his or her work, admits his or her intentions (of which the lowest denominator is politicized agenda), and takes responsibility for what he or she tells or makes. Critics won't communicate it as though they are bureaucrats in hiding but will tell it in poetic (making) language and not language already made, the prefabricated language of critical "discourses" that lead to the conventional banalities of Modern Literature Conferences. They will use new words, clean up old ones, but not try to exhibit their intelligence by using language that simply drives the hearer-reader away. Maybe they will even learn to follow the suspicion or hint of ideas, like characters in a novel or a slip of paper in my study. They will try their hardest not to lose the reader-listener: to lose your reader is the one great sin of literary art.

For once, they will give up ideas of difference and begin to register, not the discrete unrelated particles of Euramerican science, but the human and connected similarities, the *juntar y relacionar* of Western

Hemispheric oral traditions. And in that way they will, for the first time in human history, be American—by which I mean Nuestra America—learning from the oral and critical traditions of people who have long been in resistance to the hegemonies of Euramerican fads.

European criticism is of some value—or it was. But possibly it has gone the way of contemporary "mainstream" or Euramerican poetry and become arcane, unrelated, uninteresting, solipsistic, about itself or its "pain" and nothing else. Like European art, it seems to have gone to the extreme tendencies of fragmentation, evidently a European urge that runs counter to the oral tradition and the foundations of oral cultures, even its temporally distant own. As it fragments and recedes, difference is being replaced by *como uno para otro*, the likeness of one thing to another, the connection and organic interrelatedness of all life—and stories, in oral cultures, are life.

Drawing only what remains useful from Euramerican theory, Nuestra American theory will be like the mixblood whose foundation is in the more lasting, surviving culture, but who can assimilate and use what is residually useful from the other parts of his own background or bloodlines. Nuestra American theory and criticism will find its identity in the oral storytelling traditions of the Western Hemisphere, though it may also use what remains of the mainstream or dominant theories as they fragment and recede. Curiously, what will remain may well be the volunteer, vestigial seeds of Euramerican literature and theory, the oral traditions that it has, for the most part, spent a thousand years covering over with quatrosyllabic words sprinkled with Zees. Then a theorist of authority may well become an author too. He or she will have to be an intellectual mixblood who does not lead with the roundhouse right of assumed and elitist superiority of European abstractions, who does not seek difference but similarity, does not end in discretion but in wholeness, "*Encontrar y recontrar y juntar. Relacionar esto con esto, eso con aquello, todo todo.*"[4] He or she will have to tell, and by telling, demonstrate his or her ability to wave at us in our trees and for the first time in Nuestra America make us want to wave back, perhaps, at times, with a solitary finger.

226

Notes

TONTO MEETS CHUANG TZU
1. Oscar Wilde, *The Importance of Being Earnest* (New York: Avon Books, 1965), 45.
2. After reading Donald Hoffman's essay, "Whose Home on the Range," in *Melus: Popular Literature and Film* 22, no.2 (summer 1997)—an excellent, well-written, and thoughtful essay on "Dances with Wolves," "Posse," and "The Ballad of Gregorio Cortez"—it seems possible to wonder if teaching and writing at less than the first rank of universities (Hoffman teaches at Northeastern Illinois University) does not allow a kind of intellectual and rhetorical freedom. Much of the best and most readable work seems to be coming out of places that are unburdened with the pretensions of importance.

PAVING WITH GOOD INTENTIONS
1. D. H. Lawrence, *Studies in Classic American Literature* (New York: Penguin Books, 1961), 8.
2. Salman Rushdie, *The Moor's Last Sigh* (New York: Vintage Books, 1977).
3. He is referring to Jean Franco's foreword to Rosario Ferré, *The Youngest Doll* (Lincoln: University of Nebraska Press, 1995), x. The one time we discussed this novel, he complained of Franco's introduction, asking, "Am I wrong to understand the logic of page x and xi to say clearly that dumping her husband and kids (both, evidently, part of the 'waste and inanity' of women's lives) allowed Ferré to 'write as a woman,' which, in the same paragraph, is to adopt a 'gossipy' 'vernacular' voice for the title story? Wouldn't the point of a rich and privileged writer adopting a vernacular voice be that it lifts her (or him, as long as he quit his

job, dumped his wife and kids and all that waste and inanity, and learned to write 'as a man') out of her normal, habitual ways of perceiving and expressing? And then don't we have to ask if the story is any good?" (It is, by the way.) I countered that Professor Franco deserves great respect and admiration for the work she has done to bring Latin American writers to the attention of North American readers, but that he was right, that to be grateful to her did not mean we have to accept her essentializing statements as reasonable. As an Indian who writes, he knows that one cannot write "like an Indian," and that one who would try is either an Indian who is very insecure with who or what he/she is or a New Age, mindless fool.

4. As I record our conversation, I cannot help but remember his anecdote of a Nez Perce and a Coeur d'Alene storyteller being observed by anthropologists. The storytellers claimed that they could "reproduce" each others' stories after hearing them just once. The anthropologists don't — can't because of their commitment to self-defeating, predeterminate attitudes — believe it. So to prove their point, the Nez Perce woman tells a creation story. When she finishes, the Coeur d'Alene man tells a creation story. Many of the elements and details and events are the same, but it is nowhere near the verbatim, word-for-word reproduction the anthropologists expect. When he finishes his story, the Nez Perce woman smiles, nods, turns to the anthropologists, and says, "You see?" But, being people whose lives are committed to "scientific" reproduction to the extent of absurdity, they of course don't.

5. See *Studies in Classic American Literature*, 34–35.

6. Wallace Stevens, *poems*, selected and edited by Samuel French Morse (New York: Vintage Books, 1959), 14.

7. I later learned that this was a direct reference to the end of Tomas Rivera's, *And the Earth Did Not Devour Him* (Houston TX: Arte Publico Press, 1993). I suppose it is an allusion that suggests that he liked and admired Rivera's novel a good deal. He would think of the reference as praise, not as intertextuality. I no longer know what I would call it.

8. Lately, with as much respect as I have for Wayne Booth (see *The Rhetoric of Fiction* [Chicago: University of Chicago Press, 1961] for a good discussion of what is usually meant by "the implied

author"), I have begun to wonder if "implied" needs to be altered to "expressed." Implication leaves it to us critics to find and even rescue the author; but the implied author is expressed by him- or herself in structure, language, syntax, rhythm, and chosen image, *if* he knows what he is doing as an artist. Even if we consider a writer who does not know what he is doing as an artist, an immature diarist, for example, we can find that as the immature diarist comes to meet his immature feelings or ideas and realizes that he doesn't want to be that for posterity, even if posterity is only himself, he will alter the details, words, and sentences to express an author who is more amenable to his posited audience. As you can see, what happened to him has affected my thinking.

9. I found the article he was talking about in Charles E. May, ed. *New Short Story Theories* (Athens: Ohio University Press, 1994). Frankly, I wish my articles were as good.

10. Though given what has occurred, I will, regretfully, probably never see him again, the paper was presented by Prof. Nicholas Smith, Department of Philosophy, Michigan State University, in the

spring of 1997. I've changed, I guess, and not necessarily for the better. I am sorry for that.

TRADITION AND THE INDIVIDUAL IMITATION

1. Michael Kammen, *Mystic Chords of Memory: The Transformation of Tradition in American Culture* (New York: Knopf, 1991).

2. Arnold Krupat, *The Turn to the Native* (Lincoln: University of Nebraska Press, 1996), 20.

3. See *Indian America: A Gift from the Past*, a film produced by Robin Cutler, Dave Warren, and Karen Thomas, and narrated by Wes Studi, Media Resource Associates, Inc. (Washington DC) 1994. This is an informative and thoughtful film about a Makah village, buried in a mudslide for hundreds of years, being revealed by the shift in tide and wind on the northwest coast. Recording Makah people talking about the recovery of their artifacts and tools, what they mean to them, and why they have built a museum to house them, the film documents an instance of ownership of the past that needs no debate, although it may inform the way in which the debate may be approached.

4. Kammen, *Mystic Chords of Memory*, 348.

5. Ibid., 349.

6. Ibid., 350.

7. See Gerald Vizenor, *Manifest Manners: Postindian Warriors of Survivance* (Hanover NH: University Press of New England, 1994), especially "Postindian Warriors of Survivance," for a description of the literature of dominance and the literature of survivance.

8. I am grateful to my colleague and friend, Professor John Coogan of the Department of History at Michigan State University for this and some of the following ideas.

9. Vizenor, *Manifest Manners*, 5.

10. Ibid.

11. Ibid.

12. These statements and implications are derived from a lecture Richard White gave on "The West" to an audience at Michigan State University in July of 1995.

13. See Evan S. Connell Jr., *Son of the Morning Star* (San Francisco CA: Northpoint Press, 1984), as well as James Welch, with Paul Stekler, *Killing Custer: The Battle of the Little Bighorn and the Fate of the Plains Indians* (New York: W. W. Norton, 1994), for views of Custer's psychology, his life, and his actions.

14. Angie Debo, *A History of the Indians of the United States* (Norman: University of Oklahoma Press, 1970), 194–95.

15. A young Ojibway woman came to my office to tell me how a professor from another department taught that Indians "asked for" what happened to them by trading with the French for guns and kettles. She also apologized for not really being Ojibway because, although her father was enrolled, she was "only one-eighth" Ojibway, and because, even though she'd grown up among her father's people, she was not allowed to enroll. This was obviously painful to her, and I am forced to wonder, was her pain less — only one-eighth — what her grandfather's pain would have been to hear the same professor say the same silly things? What will her father's tribe do when all the children have been denied? Where will the money — for that is what it's all about, isn't it? — go then?

16. See James R. Grossman, ed., *The Frontier in American Culture: Essays by Richard White and Patricia Nelson Limerick* (Berkeley: University of California Press, 1994).

17. Rodney Frey, *Stories That Make the World* (Norman: University of Oklahoma Press, 1995), 82.
18. Ibid., 91.
19. Ibid., 158.
20. Ibid., 177.
21. Kammen, *Mystic Chords of Memory*, 206.
22. Frey, *Stories That Make the World*, 153.
23. Samuel Hynes, *The Edwardian Turn of Mind* (Princeton NJ: Princeton University Press, 1969), 307.
24. Quoted in Vizenor, *Manifest Manners*, 25.

LEAVING THE PARLOR

1. José David Saldívar, "Texas Border Narratives as Cultural Critique," Working Paper Series No.19 (Stanford CA: Stanford Center for Chicano Research, April 1987), 2.
2. Ibid.
3. Note that the colonial plantations such as the Virginia Plantation were modeled on what the British saw as a successful model, the Plantation of Ulster, otherwise known as Northern Ireland.
4. Briefly, the story goes, the priest, after years trying to convert this one hesitant Lakota elder to Catholicism, finally succeeds by convincing the elder that the Catholic "God" and his ways are not much different than the Sioux Creator. So the elder grows weary of the priest's efforts and finally becomes a Catholic. But then one day during Lent, on a Friday, the elder's son brings him a gift of fresh deer meat, which the elder cannot resist making into venison stew and eating, despite all the priest's admonitions about not eating meat on Fridays. When the priest hears about the stew, he storms into the home of the elder to accuse him of eating meat. But the elder hears the priest coming, and just as the priest enters the room where a steaming big pot of venison stew is sitting on the table, the elder tosses water on the stew, makes the sign of a cross, and says, "I baptize thee fish."
5. The reference to "C-type batteries" is from Daniel Reveles's book, *Enchialdas, Rice, and Beans* (New York: Ballantine, 1994), 21.
6. *Njal's Saga*, translated from the Old Icelandic with an introduction and notes by Carl F. Bayerschmidt and Lee M. Hollander (New York: New York University Press, 1955), 159.

7. Tomas Rivera, . . . y no se lo tragó la tierra (And the Earth Did Not Devour Him), trans. Evangelina Vigil-Piñon (Houston TX: Arte Publico Press, 1992).

8. Consider the too-easy compliance by a thoroughly peaceful people like the Bahamian Taino, who were used for labor by the Spaniards and made extinct.

9. Note the respect for age that linguistically associates viejo with authority.

10. Rivera, Tierra, 151–52.

11. Ibid., 147.

12. W. S. Penn, Killing Time with Strangers (Tucson: University of Arizona Press, 2000).

DONNE TALKIN'

1. W. S. Penn. The Absence of Angels (Sag Harbor NY: Permanent Press, 1994), 49.

2. I continue to be obliged to apologize for the use of "white." It is caused by the lack of a better term and an unwillingness to say "person of the dominant assumptions that mostly derive from the commercial capitalist presumptions and historical arrogance of Britain, France, Germany, Spain, and perhaps Italy." "White" is easier, shorter, and metaphorically more colorful, being a colorless all color ("of atheism," Melville added, which is fine as long as you include among your atheists those Midwestern Presbyterians and Methodists whose unexamined beliefs are a form of not believing).

3. However you excuse Richard Nixon—the usual way is to credit him with significant foreign policy gains or with signing some good legislation for Native American people and reversing the annihilistic mood of legislative America toward Indians—he remains, as each newly released White House tape shows, a classically thorough anti-Semite. In the latest tape, it is not just Henry Kissinger but rich Jews he goes after—rich Jews who steal and cheat and are staunch donors to the Democratic Party. But then we know that Nixon was, as Watergate showed, anti-Democratic.

4. See W. S. Penn, ed., The Telling of the World: Native American Stories and Art (New York: Stuart, Tabori, and Chang, 1996), 85–87.

5. See Stephen Jay Gould, "The Dodo in the Caucus Race," *Natural History* 11 (1996): 22–33. All page references in this section are to this article.

6. Once again, I find myself thanking Professor John Coogan, Department of History, Michigan State University for his way of presenting the mind-set of the Spanish invaders and inventors of the New World.

7. Coronado, seeking one or more of the Seven Cities of Cibola, led his men by horseback all the way into the plains of what is now known as Nebraska. Interestingly, even here conquest and colonization are umbilically joined to religion by the Fray who, unwilling or afraid to return from the Pueblo territory with nothing more than the truth, invented the Seven Cities of Cibola, cities of gold that the friar embellished as freely as a nineteenth-century ethnographer. Ironically, the friar must have understood the power of invention and belief from his profession of an administrator of Christian rites.

8. Sorry. I can't resist this cute reference to "as long as the rivers run and the grass is green" of broken treaties.

9. At a 1998 conference on "Aesthetics and Difference" at U.C. Riverside, a pompous white male keynote speaker pretended to offer a hairless defense of Cultural Studies. In his snide dismissal of people who question their value, he offered everyone who was listening living proof of what is wrong with Cultural Studies. In the course of his presentation, he portrayed John Rollin Ridge's *Joaquin Murieta* as a necessary "text" at the top of his list of Native American novels. The onanism of his guilt was recognized, discussed, and joked about by the Chicanos, Native Americans, and one or two "white" critics who have done real work in the field. We recognized in Mr. P. C. someone who does not know what he's talking about when he's talking about us, but likes to welcome the corpses of our grandfathers and mothers into the Big House with sadness and regret while continuing to control the futures of our children. As one Chicano noted, Mr. P. C. loves Native American novels so much that he overlooks Native American novelists, even ones who are experts on Ridge's work. Were this fathead less infatuated and able to read Ridge, he might understand that *Murieta* is an interesting historical document, one

that shows John Ridge highly confused about his own attitudes toward Indian people, but that as a novel, it's awful.

10. "The Man Who Loved the Frog Songs," in Penn, *Telling of the World*, 82.

11. See George P. Elliott, *An Hour of Last Things and Other Stories* (New York: Harper & Row, 1951), 284.

12. And it is not dissimilar to the endless stream of queries about Indian legends or stories, as though every Indian is a walking compendium of Native lore.

13. Wallace Stevens's poem "Domination of Black" ends: "Out of the window, / I saw how the planets gathered / Like the leaves themselves / Turning in the wind / I saw how the night came, / Came striding like the color of the heavy hemlocks. / I felt afraid. / And I remembered the cry of the peacocks." See Stevens, *poems*, 11.

14. It occurs to me that not everyone will recognize this as an allusion—Jeez, I felt like T. S. Eliot footnoting "The Wasteland" there for a moment—to Wallace Stevens's wonderful poem "Anecdote of a Jar."

15. I refer to the new edition of the *Larousse Standard Spanish-English English-Spanish Dictionary* (El D.F., Mexico City: Ediciones Larousse S.A. de C.V., 1996).

16. *The Complete Poetry and Selected Prose of John Donne*, edited with an introduction by Charles M. Coffin (New York: Modern Library, 1994), 292; Donne's emphasis. All references to Donne's work are from this edition.

17. Robert H. Ruby and John A. Brown, *Dreamer-Prophets of the Columbia Plateau: Smoholla and Skolaskin* (Norman: University of Oklahoma Press, 1989), 73.

18. Charles E. May, ed., *New Short Story Theories* (Athens: Ohio Universtiy Press, 1994), 245–46.

19. See Carter Revard, *Ponca War Dancers* (Norman OK: Point Riders Press, 1980) or *Cowboys and Indians, Christmas Shopping* (Norman OK: Point Riders Press, 1992). See also *Family Matters, Tribal Affairs* (Tucson: University of Arizona Press, 1998).

KILLING OURSELVES WITH LANGUAGE AS SUCH

1. Gabriel García Márquez, *One Hundred Years of Solitude* trans. Gregory Rabassa (New York: Avon, 1971). All page references are to

this edition. I wish I could claim that I made this up, but I didn't. I actually had a student whose essay was content to define the Buendía family as "dysfunctional."

2. Toni Morrison, *Beloved* (New York: Penguin, 1988), 190.

3. This is an adapted application of Stephen Jay Gould, who, in discussing the "bushiness" of hominid evolution, says, "We shall be massively and seriously fooled if we extrapolate a current reality to a characteristic situation in the history of human evolution" (*Natural History* 106, no.3 [April 1997]: 22).

4. English does have advantages of flexibility and—if not co-opted by television or Microsoft "grammatiks"—inventiveness.

5. José David Saldívar, *The Dialectics of Our America: Genealogy, Cultural Critique, and Literary History* (Durham NC: Duke University Press, 1991), 44.

6. Walter Benjamin, *Reflections: Essays, Aphorisms, Autobiographical Writings*, trans. Edmund Jephcott, ed. Peter Demetz (New York: Harcourt, Brace, Jovanovich, 1978), 315.

7. See Herman Melville's story, "Bartleby the Scrivener."

8. See Roy Harvey Pearce, *Savagism and Civilization*, with an introduction by Arnold Krupat (Berkeley: University of California Press, 1988), 49.

9. Lately I have noticed in advanced fiction writing classes that what hip and ostensibly thoughtful students take for deep thinking is mainly the commercial bumper-sticker thinking given to them by their electronic babysitters as they grow up. It began with bumper-sticker psychology, the "plague" Freud said that he and Carl Jung brought to American shores. Characters were often boring case studies in neurosis or anxiety. But now it seems to pervade all aspects of character creation, making characters flat and empty vessels of cow-like thinking that only the unimaginative writer finds unusual or interesting.

10. Pearce, *Savagism and Civilization*, 63.

11. Ibid., 74.

12. The "parlor" is a reference to Kenneth Burke's parlor of genteel literary discussion and argument in *The Philosophy of Symbolic Form*. See "Leaving the Parlor" in this volume.

13. Judge Richard Posner, in his criticism of "critical race theory," associates critical race theorists with a lack of rational inquiry, say-

ing that the critical race theorists forswear "analysis for narrative. Rather than marshal logical arguments and empirical data, critical race theorists tell stories—fictional, science-fictional, quasifictional, autobiographical, anecdotal—designed to expose the pervasive and debilitating racism of America today" ("The Skin Trade," *New Republic*, 13 October 1997, 42). As one who is committed to narrative essays, the mistake Judge Posner seems to be making here is not reasoned: fiction is often true in its meaning; narrative does not simply equate with eschewed rational inquiry; and autobiography, if the "I" is fully a part of the "we" and thus is representative and not merely personal, can offer us true insights. Autobiography told from the limited and solipsistic sense of self and its victimhood is nothing more than a plea for the superiority of one's very limited and probably unimagined experience. Properly imagined fiction can tell us more about our world than the "factual" declarations of the EPA or the facts of history (that the eastern Cherokee were "relocated" in 1838–39 hardly gives us the "truth" of the story). And analysis without narrative is as false as narrative without analysis. As much as my friends want to deny the "intention" of the author of a literary or narrative work, it is this refusal of intention that Judge Posner wants to criticize. According to Posner, Richard Delgado wants whites not to enter the field(s) of civil rights. We are encouraged to conclude that Delgado wants to accomplish two things: keep the money for himself and protect his job, and circumscribe human imagination—both the imagination of whites and the imagination of non-whites. What we are not encouraged to consider is the ancient history of European anthropology and policy making in which the objects (Indians, Chicanos, Blacks, Asians) are never consulted about what might be best for them. From that point of view, Delgado might simply be asking for partial self-determination in political spheres (though in his letter of reply, he seems to imply that minorities have a vested and therefore superior interest in and ability in creating civil rights policy, which means Delgado is not considering the very real possibility that there are minorities who want, in the crudest sense, to keep the money for themselves).

14. I try to remember that only 25 percent of U.S. students think and write at a college level; thus, no more than 25 percent belong

at a university. On the other hand, as the "oppressor" knows, to expel incompetent or lazy students would swell the ranks of daycare programs for the still infantile and unemployment lines to a crisis level. Nonetheless, with the Daycare Generation (that's what put the "X" in "Generation X") entering college, raised on television and given self-esteem by the products of Schools of Education, students are having greater difficulty than ever before in learning to question and think. Their writing and language abilities seem no longer like unused muscles, but like muscles that have devolved out of existence, not unlike the Dodo's ability to fly.

15. Stephen Jay Gould, "This View of Life," *Natural History* 106, no.3 (April 1997): 23.

IN THE GAZEBO

1. Daniel Reveles, *Enchiladas, Rice, and Beans* (New York: Ballantine, 1994), 6–42. Antonio Burciaga, *Drink Cultura* (Santa Barbara CA: Joshua Odell Editions, 1993), 9–13.

2. Reveles, *Enchiladas, Rice, and Beans*, 14.

3. Ibid., 21.

4. See "The Man Who Loved Frog Songs" and "A Mashpee Ghost Story" in Penn, *Telling of the World*.

5. See Stephen Jay Gould, "The View of Life," *Natural History* 106, no.10 (November 1997): 22ff. See Richard Posner, "The Skin Trade," *New Republic*, 13 October 1997, 42. As for "cultural paranoia" as a phrase that allies the problem of temporality with schizophrenic fragmentation, I am indebted to Patrick O'Donnell, *Latent Destinies: Cultural Paranoia and Contemporary U.S. Narrative*
(Durham NC: Duke University Press, 2000).

6. Gould, "View of Life," 68; emphasis mine.

7. Gayle Ross, a powerful person of great character and a prominent Cherokee advocate for storytelling, reviewing my anthology *The Telling of the World*, wrote, "Also significant is the fact that, for the most part, the voices heard here are Indian voices. The few non-Indian writers, such as Richard Erdoes and Jarold Ramsey, *have spent so many years in the Indian community that they speak well*

from within the culture" ("Tales of Creation and Beyond," *Carnegie Magazine*, July/August 1997, 11; my emphasis).

8. García Marquez, *One Hundred Years of Solitude*, 397.
9. José Antonio Burciaga, *Spilling the Beans* (Santa Barbara CA: Joshua Odell Editions, 1993) 127.
10. Ernst Cassirer, *The Philosophy of Symbolic Forms*, vol. 1, *Language* (New Haven CT: Yale University Press, 1955), 304; emphasis his.
11. Melquiades was the Bishop of Rome from July 310 to January 314.
12. I am working from the copy that George P. Elliott, the writer and professor who directed my doctorate, used to teach the course in which I was first introduced to *One Hundred Years of Solitude*.
13. Eliud Martinez, *Voice-Haunted Journey* (Tempe AZ: Bilingual Press, 1990).

IN THE GARDEN OF THE GODS

1. Michael Kammen, *Mystic Chords of Memory: The Transformation of Tradition in American Culture* (New York: Knopf, 1991), 343.
2. Ibid., 349.
3. Vizenor, *Manifest Manners*, 50.
4. Robert F. Berkhofer Jr., *The White Man's Indian: Images of the American Indian from Columbus to the Present* (New York: Vintage Books, 1979), 29; my emphasis.
5. D'Arcy McNickle, *The Hawk Is Hungry*, ed. Birgit Hans (Tucson: University of Arizona Press, 1992).

FEATHERING CUSTER

1. Gregory J. W. Urwin, "Custer: The Civil War Years," in Paul Andrew Hutton, ed., *The Custer Reader* (Lincoln: University of Nebraska Press, 1992), 15.
2. Ibid., 17.
3. Ibid., 14.
4. Ibid., 20.
5. As a tribute to Custer's bravery and service, General Sheridan bought the desk on which he co-signed the peace and had it sent to Elizabeth Custer.
6. Brian W. Dippie, "Custer: The Indian Fighter," in Hutton, *Custer Reader*, 105.
7. Ibid., 108–9.

8. Originally I planned to quote Hans Jonas, who is recorded by Richard Wolins ("The Philosopher of Life," *New Republic*, 20 January 1997, 138) as having written: "Power meeting no resistance in its relatum is no power at all: power is exercised only in relation to something that itself has power." However attracted to the truth of this statement, when I recall that Jonas was, in part, responding to the Holocaust, I have trouble understanding how Richard Wolins can so easily approve of the words he quotes and not question them. A concentration camp guard beating a Jewish child to death seems to me power being exercised in relation to something that in itself has *no* power. Perhaps I am being too particular? That would be my failing, as one who sees theory unapplied as leading, in the extreme, to such distance from nature and humanity that it can produce the thinking that led Heidegger to German Nazism. And yet we have repeated instances of this kind of exercise of power in Chivington's massacre of Black Kettle's band at Sand Creek and Custer's re-massacre of the same band—what was left of it—at Washita, where Black Kettle's band had been "settled" by the local fort administration just so they would have someone to punish if the "renegade" and "hostile" Indians stirring up trouble couldn't be found, caught, or killed.

9. Dippie, "Custer: The Indian Fighter," 109–10.

10. John Wayne comes to mind not only because he avoided the draft only to become the icon of people who hated draft "dodgers" during the Vietnam War, but also because he is associated with the Custer myth by John Ford's *Fort Apache*. His coffee crystal romanticization of "the regiment" at the end of that movie is amusing, coming from someone who used movies to keep himself out of the regiment.

11. Edward S. Godfrey, "Custer's Last Battle," in Hutton, *Custer Reader*, 267.

12. Kate Bighead, as told to Thomas B. Marquis, "She watched Custer's Last Battle," in Hutton, *Custer Reader*, 369–70.

13. Godfrey, "Custer's Last Battle," 269.

14. L. V. McWhorter, *Hear Me, My Chiefs! Nez Perce History and Legend*, ed. Ruth Bordin (Caldwell ID: Caxton Press, 1992), 514.

15. Alvin M. Josephy Jr., *The Nez Perce Indians and the Opening of the Northwest* (Lincoln: University of Nebraska Press, 1979), 615.

16. Wayne C. Booth, *The Rhetoric of Fiction* (Chicago: University of Chicago Press, 1975), 79.

17. Ibid., 45.

18. The phrase "thumb in the pan" is one I remember from graduate school thirty years ago and is, if I'm not mistaken, D. H. Lawrence's way of describing what a writer cannot do with his or her characters.

19. I was reminded of Gertrude Bonnin's claims to relation with Sitting Bull by my dissertation student and friend David Medei.

CRITICAL ARTS

1. People grow up reading newspapers (though uncritically), web pages, and stop signs, so they think they are "literate," that they know how to read; whereas they rarely learn how to see, how to look, whether at the world around them or at paintings.

2. I owe this realization to Jennifer Penn, who made the suggestion when we were discussing the science of medicine.

3. For a version of "The Legend of Godasiyo," see Penn, *Telling of the World*, 150. The Tower of Babel is found in the Bible in Genesis 11.

4. Rivera, *Tierra*, 75.